Crime and Social Justice

Edited by

Tony Platt and Paul Takagi

M

First published 1981 by
THE MACMILLAN PRESS LTD
London and Basingstoke
Associated companies throughout the world

ISBN 0 333 28260 4 (hard cover)
ISBN 0 333 28261 2 (paper cover)

Printed in Hong Kong

Critical Criminology

Editorial Group

John Clarke, Mike Fitzgerald, Victoria Greenwood, Jock Young

Contributing Editors: Rosa del Olmo (University of Caracas), Tamar Pitch (University of Perugia), Herman Schwendinger (State University of New York), Annika Snare (University of Oslo), Boaventura de Sousa Santos (University of Coimbra, Portugal), Ian Taylor (University of Sheffield), Anthony Platt (Institute for the Study of Labour and Economic Crisis, San Francisco).

This new series aims to publish work within the radical criminology perspective. It is international in its scope, providing a rallying point for work in this rapidly growing field. The substantive areas covered are the sociology of crime, deviance, social problems, law and sexual deviance. It includes work in ethnography, historical criminology and the practice of social work and law as it relates to radical criminology. The series is two-tiered, publishing both monographs of interest to scholars in the field and more popular books suitable for students and practitioners. One of its aims is to publish the work of radical organisations in the area, particularly that of the National Deviancy Conference, the European Group for the Study of Deviance and Social Control, the Crime and Social Justice Collective and La Questione Criminale.

Titles in the Critical Criminology series

Published

Peter Archard: *Vagrancy, Alcoholism and Social Control*
Dario Melossi and Massimo Pavarini: *The Prison and the Factory*
National Deviancy Conference (ed.): *Permissiveness and Control*
Tony Platt and Paul Takagi (eds): *Crime and Social Justice*

Forthcoming

Steven Box: *The Medicalisation of Social Problems*
John Clarke: *Youth and the State*
Ian Taylor: *Crime at the End of the Welfare State*

Contents

Preface by Critical Criminology Editorial Board   vii

Introduction by Tony Platt and Paul Takagi   1

Part I   Criminology and the Definition of Crime

1. **'Street' Crime: a View from the Left**
   Tony Platt   13

2. **Intellectuals for Law and Order: a Critique of the New 'Realists'**
   Tony Platt and Paul Takagi   30

3. **Social Class and the Definition of Crime**
   Herman Schwendinger and Julia Schwendinger   59

Part II   Crime

4. **Karl Marx, The Theft of Wood and Working-class Composition**
   Peter Linebaugh   85

5. **Delinquency and the Collective Varieties of Youth**
   Herman Schwendinger and Julia Schwendinger   110

6. **Any Woman's Blues: a Critical Overview of Women, Crime and the Criminal Justice System**
   Dorie Klein and June Kress   152

Part III   The State and Criminal Justice

7. The Penal Question in *Capital*
Dario Melossi   187

8. A Garrison State in 'Democratic' Society
Paul Takagi   205

About the Authors   220

About 'Crime and Social Justice'   221

Preface

The journal *Crime and Social Justice* has been a major focus of debate for both American and European scholars. At a time when the majority of official criminology journals are largely left unread by students of criminology, this radical magazine is notable for its panache and relevance. There is scarcely a significant debate in the recent period to which *Crime and Social Justice* has not offered a substantial contribution, if not indeed initiated. But it has been difficult to obtain and the Critical Criminology series is issuing this reader, which is to be published simultaneously in North America and in Britain. The final decision on the selection was made jointly by ourselves and the Crime and Social Justice Collective.

JOHN CLARKE
MIKE FITZGERALD
VICTORIA GREENWOOD
JOCK YOUNG

Introduction

Several students and two faculty members of Berkeley's School of Criminology were responsible for publishing in 1974 the first issue of *Crime and Social Justice* (*CSJ*), 'a radical journal for a people's criminology'. The format for the earliest issues included articles by academic criminologists, reports on popular struggles for justice, course outlines, and review essays of books. The political roots of *CSJ* are to be found generally in the experiences of the New Left – especially the student, anti-war and women's movements – and particularly in the academic and state repression of progressive students and intellectuals at Berkeley and other universities.

Out of the School of Criminology came radical activists and theorists who participated in local anti-repression organizations, supported the prisoners' movement, turned the classroom into a place of debate and controversy (an unusual occurrence!), and challenged the hegemony of bourgeois criminology. Given the long history of systematic repression and exclusion of Marxism and critical thought in North American universities (Schwendinger and Schwendinger, 1974) it is not surprising that a price had to be paid for this rebellious insubordination. By the time the first issue of *CSJ* was published, Herman Schwendinger and Tony Platt had been denied tenure and the demise of the School of Criminology was imminent. Many progressive individuals have experienced academic repression in the United States but this was the first time that a criminology program was totally dismantled because a minority of its faculty and a majority of its students tested the *bourgeois* doctrine of 'freedom of speech'. After a protracted struggle led by thousands of students, in which thousands of individuals were politicized and many people's commitments were strengthened, the School of Criminology was closed in 1976. A detailed account of this experience has been chronicled and summed up elsewhere (Schauffler, 1974; Schauffler and Hannigan, 1974; CSJ Collective, 1976).

There were personal casualties as a result of our radical praxis: several students were harassed and intimidated by Berkeley's administration, and some had difficulty finding jobs; Herman Schwendinger was unable to get an academic job until his appointment in 1977 at the State University of New York, New Paltz campus; Tony Platt could not get a job in a criminology program; and Paul Takagi, who could not be fired because he had tenure, was academically ostracized on the Berkeley campus for over a year.

But overall the repression did not break us. Rather it confirmed our experience and analysis, as well as solidified our political commitments. In 1976 we wrote:

> While we suffered a set-back in Berkeley, we definitely scored a number of important victories and for the first time are building a progressive alternative to what is perhaps the most reactionary field in the social sciences. It is important that we learn from our struggle at Berkeley and use that experience to deepen our political consciousness and tactical capacity. (CSJ Collective, 1976)

Since 1976, the constituency of *CSJ* has grown to over 2000, primarily intellectuals, students, and libraries, but also community organizations and prisoners. Despite a resurgence in recent years of a decidedly rightward movement among intellectuals, our experience at professional conferences indicates a great deal of interest in Marxism among students and younger faculty and state functionaries. As Herman Schwendinger noted in the editorial to the first issue of *CSJ*:

> For three quarters of a century, political repression has successfully restricted the most highly developed radical perspective, Marxism, in virtually every discipline and professional school. One can hardly expect the scope of academic criminology to have been any less restrictive, considering its direct organic connections with the most coercive political institutions in our society. Indeed, in light of these connections, it is remarkable that the recent emergence of a radical criminology has occurred at all.

It is a testimony to the power of Marxism that radical criminology is growing despite the loss of an important base at Berkeley. Many individuals who were first politicized in the academy continue to be politically active in their new jobs and workplaces. Some of us who were active at Berkeley created the independent Center for Research on Criminal Justice (publisher of *The Iron Fist and The Velvet Glove*), later to become the Center for the Study of Crime and Social Justice, a component of the Institute for the Study of Labor and Economic Crisis in San Francisco.

In this book, we have selected a limited number of articles which have appeared in *CSJ* between 1974 and 1978. Admittedly, they reflect, in our judgment, the more mature theoretical materials that have appeared in the journal. They are by no means limited to the Berkeley 'school', they are not representative of *CSJ* in general, and they do not in any way discuss the practice of radical criminologists in the United States. A thorough critique of the Berkeley 'school' and a political evaluation of academic collectives remains an urgent task, though a modest self-criticism has been attempted in the journal *Synthesis* (Platt, 1977).

We will limit ourselves in this introduction to providing some background and textual comments to the selections in this anthology. For a deeper understanding, we suggest that you consult the journal in its entirety (see the back of this volume for information about subscriptions).

Perhaps the most important development in radical criminology in the United States was the publication of Herman and Julia Schwendinger's 'Defenders of Order or Guardians of Human Rights?' in *Issues in Criminology* in 1970. When the Schwendingers re-opened the debate on the definition of crime in this article, it was either misunderstood or deliberately misinterpreted by some criminologists. For example, Gilbert Geis, past president of the American Society of Criminology, viewed it as an indication of moralism–a 'tendency of critical criminologists to create their own categories of crime' (1978).

To develop a *scientific* definition of crime is a complex and difficult enterprise. It has a long history among Western criminologists, going back even further than the 30-year controversy initiated by Thorsten Sellin in 1938. In an earlier monograph, published in 1937, Sellin reviewed the literature on the relationship between economic conditions and crime, and recommended the construction of a more sensitive crime index as an alternative to measures which relied on official police statistics. As Sellin noted, this was not a new proposal: in 1895, Tarde had called for the study of unpunished crimes; in 1910,

Henri Joly had noted that it would be a grave error to assume that convictions accurately reflect the scope of criminality; and, in 1922, J. S. Roux had urged the necessity of studying what he called 'masked' criminality (see Sellin, 1937, p.72). Sellin did not construct an index until much later, but back in 1937 he apparently thought that it was futile to use criminal statistics for index or scientific purposes and consequently wrote his controversial 1938 monograph which rooted the explanation of crime in 'conduct norms' (Sellin, 1938).

What Herman and Julia Schwendinger have added to this debate is an alternative *scientific* and *moral* definition of crime, a *Marxist* alternative based on a proletarian class outlook. In 'Social Class and the Definition of Crime' they sum up their previous articles and further elaborate on their socialist definition of crime. It is a timely piece. As liberation struggles unfold all over the world, it is clear that people's movements cannot rely upon bourgeois legality to defend national independence and socialist construction.

Tony Platt's 'Street Crime: A View From the Left' (1978) is based in part on an editorial first published in *CSJ* in 1976. Both pieces represent a long overdue Marxist analysis of the high rate of criminal victimization within the U.S. metropolis. Prior to these essays, there was a tendency among radical criminologists to either romanticize street crime as a form of 'primitive rebellion' or to engage in one form or another of liberal apologetics. Defense of the prisoners' movement led many of us to celebrate the collective defiance of many convicts while denying the predatory behavior and individualism which accounted for their imprisonment. In the article published in this anthology, Platt discusses how street crime weakens and demoralizes the working class as a whole, while tracing its origins to both the labor market and social relations of production under capitalism.

The Schwendingers' 'Delinquency and the Collective Varieties of Youth' provides the necessary historical background for understanding contemporary criminality. This article takes criminality out of the usual liberal metaphysics about the inevitability of crime and grounds it in a thoroughly materialist conception of history. Examining the economics of marginalization and the political destruction of collective social relations – both inherent in the development of the capitalist mode of production – the Schwendingers lay the basis for repudiating psychological and cultural theories of delinquency. Some of the themes of this paper are elaborated upon by Takagi and Platt in their analysis of class, racism, and crime in San

Francisco's Chinatown. This article, 'Behind the Gilded Ghetto', does not appear in this anthology but can be found in the Spring–Summer 1978 issue of *CSJ*.

Peter Linebaugh's chapter, 'Karl Marx, the Theft of Wood and Working-class Composition', while specifically concerned with Marx's analysis of the criminal law and capitalist property relations in Germany during the 1840s, raises larger questions about the boundaries of criminology and class analysis of criminality.

'Intellectuals for Law and Order' (Chapter 2 in this anthology) was originally published as an editorial and was presented at the annual meetings of various criminology associations in the United States. We have received more requests for copies of this article than any other essay published in the journal.

While the law and order ideologues are in the ascendant, they are not without some opposition from liberals who continue, on the one hand, to defend correctional *treatment* by referring to scattered research findings which seem to demonstrate the effectiveness of rehabilitation (Palmer, 1975; Glaser, 1976), and, on the other hand, to do research which indicates that criminals are not deterred by punishment or its threat (Meier and Johnson, 1977; Van Dine *et al.*, 1977; Smith, 1977).

The intellectuals for law and order, who include many embittered and disillusioned liberals, dispense for the most part with theories of crime causation, considering such efforts futile. Their arguments on behalf of the death penalty, mandatory and longer penal sentences, and 'post-punishment incapacitation' are theoretically based on a utilitarian model of rewards and punishments. The parameters of this 'theory', as well as its underlying ideology, are fully discussed in the article.

But another increasingly popular strand of neo-conservatism (not discussed in 'Intellectuals for Law and Order') is sociobiology, with claims that this 'new synthesis' will eventually subsume all the social sciences (Wilson, 1975). Ray Jeffrey, president of the American Society of Criminology, is its foremost supporter among criminologists; and a recent planning session, attended by nationally prominent criminologists and chaired by Marvin Wolfgang, was devoted to the physiological and sociobiological aspects of criminality.

The relationship between class, crime, and male supremacy or sexism (as well as white supremacy or racism) continues to be neglected by the field and *CSJ*. This anthology contains one of the few systematic papers on this topic – 'Any Woman's Blues' by Dorie Klein and June Kress. Other contributions (not in this anthology) by the Berkeley 'school' include an important critique of the conventional literature (Klein, 1973) and a rejoinder to Freda Adler's *Sisters in Crime* (Weis, 1976). The Schwendingers' 'Rape Myths' (1974) and their review of the literature on rape (1976) provide a Marxist alternative to liberal victimology and bourgeois feminism, exemplified by Menachem Amir's *Patterns in Forcible Rape* and Susan Brownmiller's *Against Our Will*. Anne Peters's book reviews in the Fall–Winter 1977 and Spring–Summer 1978 issues of *CSJ* provide further ammunition against the Freda Adler thesis that women's liberation is responsible for the rise in female criminality.

In the final section of this anthology, we have included two essays which examine repression in a historical and political–economic context. Dario Melossi's 'The Penal Question in *Capital*' provides an important textual critique of Marx's writings on the origins of the prison. Drawing upon and adding to Rusche and Kirchheimer's pioneering monograph, *Punishment and Social Structure*, Melossi focuses on the modern prison as a peculiarly capitalist institution, whose origins are inextricably linked to the social relations of the capitalist factory.

Paul Takagi's essay, 'A Garrison State in "Democratic" Society', takes a contemporary and seemingly narrow issue – the death penalty – and develops it into a macroscopic analysis with far-reaching significance for theory and practice. Extracting capital punishment from its usual legalistic boundaries, Takagi examines police killings, which average about 400 a year in the United States, as a form of class justice, whose victims are primarily blacks, browns and other super-exploited sectors of the working class. This essay and another updated essay, 'The Management of Police Killings' (Harring *et al.*, 1977), have been widely distributed and used by many community organizations which are fighting against state repression and political surveillance.

CSJ has consistently tried to avoid becoming a local or sectarian journal. We have many readers and contributors from countries other than the United States. In addition to Dario Melossi's paper in this anthology, we have also published Falco Wekentin *et al.*, 'Criminology as Police Science: Or How Old is the New Criminology?', (*CSJ*, no.2); Thomas Mathiesen, 'The Prison Movement in Scandinavia', (no.1); Nguyen Khac Vien, 'With Survivors from Saigon Jails', (no.2); Yvon Dandurand, 'Radical

Criminology in Canada', (no.4); Rosa del Olmo, 'Limitations for the Prevention of Violence: the Latin American Reality and its Criminological Theory', (no.3); Gill Boehringer and Donna Giles, 'Criminology and Neocolonialism: The Case of Papua New Guinea', (no.8); and Ivan Jankovic, 'Labor Market and Imprisonment', (no.8).

CSJ has pursued this policy for two reasons: first, we attempt to publish the best theoretical materials written by Marxists and other progressive scholars; and secondly, the problems of crime and repression must be understood as part of the capitalist system as a whole and therefore not only as a phenomenon limited to nation states.

Berkeley, California   TONY PLATT AND PAUL TAKAGI
June 1979

References

Crime and Social Justice Collective (1976) 'Berkeley's School of Criminology, 1950–1976', *Crime and Social Justice*, 6 (Fall–Winter) 1–3.

Geis, Gilbert (1978) 'White Collar Crime', *Crime and Delinquency*, 24, 1 (January), 89–90.

Glaser, Daniel (1976) 'The Effectiveness of Correctional Treatment', *Journal of Research in Crime and Delinquency*, 12 (July) 179–82.

Harring, Sid, Tony Platt, Richard Speiglman and Paul Takagi (1977) 'The Management of Police Killings', *Crime and Social Justice*, 8 (Fall–Winter) 34–43.

Klein, Dorie (1973) 'The Etiology of Female Crime: A Review of the Literature', *Issues in Criminology*, 8, 2 (Fall) 3–30.

Klein, Dorie and June Kress (1976) 'Any Woman's Blues: A Critical Overview of Women, Crime, and the Criminal Justice System', *Crime and Social Justice*, 5 (Spring–Summer) 34–49.

Meier, Robert and Weldon Johnson (1977) 'Deterrence as Social Control: The Legal and Extralegal Production of Conformity', *American Sociological Review*, 42 (April) 292–304.

Melossi, Dario (1976) 'The Penal Question in *Capital*', *Crime and Social Justice*, 5 (Spring–Summer) 26–33.

Palmer, Ted (1975) 'Martinson Revisited', *Journal of Research in Crime and Delinquency*, 12 (July) 133–52.

Peters, Anne K. (1977) 'Freda Adler: Sisters in Crime', *Crime and Social Justice*, 8 (Fall–Winter) 74–9.
—— (1978) 'Carol Smart: Women, Crime and Criminology', *Crime and Social Justice*, 9 (Spring–Summer).
Platt, Tony (1977) 'The Petty Bourgeois Politics of Research Collectives', *Synthesis*, 2 (Summer–Fall) 48–56.
—— (1978) 'Street Crime: A View From the Left', *Crime and Social Justice*, 9 (Spring–Summer) 26–48.
Platt, Tony and Paul Takagi (1977) 'Intellectuals for Law and Order: A Critique of the New "Realists"', *Crime and Social Justice*, 8 (Fall–Winter) 1–16.
Schauffler, Richard (1974) 'Criminology at Berkeley: Resisting Academic Repression, Part I', *Crime and Social Justice*, 1 (Spring–Summer) 58–61.
Schauffler, Richard and Michael Hannigan (1974) 'Criminology at Berkeley: Resisting Academic Repression, Part II', *Crime and Social Justice*, 2 (Fall–Winter) 42–7.
Schwendinger, Herman and Julia R. Schwendinger (1970) 'Defenders of Order or Guardians of Human Rights?', *Issues in Criminology*, 5, 2 (Summer) 123–57.
—— (1974) *The Sociologists of the Chair: A Radical Analysis of the Formative Years of North American Sociology, 1883–1922* (New York: Basic Books).
—— (1976) 'Delinquency and the Collective Varieties of Youth', *Crime and Social Justice*, 5 (Spring–Summer) 7–25.
—— (1977) 'Social Class and the Definition of Crime', *Crime and Social Justice*, 7 (Spring–Summer) 4–13.
Schwendinger, Julia R. and Herman Schwendinger (1974) 'Rape Myths: In Legal, Theoretical and Everyday Practice', *Crime and Social Justice*, 1 (Spring–Summer) 18–26.
—— (1976) 'A Review of Rape Literature', *Crime and Social Justice*, 6 (Fall–Winter) 79–85.
Sellin, Thorsten (1937) 'Research Memorandum on Crime in the Depression' (New York: Social Science Research Council Bulletin, no. 27).
—— (1938) 'Culture Conflict and Crime' (New York: Social Science Research Council Bulletin, no. 41).
Smith, Gerald W. (1977) 'The Value of Life-Arguments Against the Death Penalty', *Crime and Delinquency*, 23 (July) 253–9.
Takagi, Paul (1974) 'A Garrison State in "Democratic" Society', *Crime and Social Justice*, 1 (Spring–Summer) 27–33.
Takagi, Paul and Tony Platt (1978) 'Behind the Gilded Ghetto: An Analysis of Race, Class and Crime in Chinatown', *Crime and Social Justice*, 9 (Spring–Summer) 2–25.
Van Dine, Stephen, Simon Dinitz, and John Conrad (1977) 'The Incapacitation of the Dangerous Offender: A Statistical Experiment', *Journal of Research in Crime and Delinquency*, 14 (January) 22–34.

Weis, Joseph G. (1976) 'Liberation and Crime: The Invention of the New Female Criminal', *Crime and Social Justice*, 6 (Fall–Winter) 17–27.

Wilson, E. O. (1975) *Sociobiology* (Cambridge, Mass.: Harvard University Press).

Part I
Criminology and the Definition of Crime

1

'Street' Crime

A View from the Left

Tony Platt

According to survey after survey, 'street' crime ranks as one of the most serious problems in working-class communities. In 1948, only 4 per cent of the population felt that crime was their community's *worst* problem. By 1972, according to a Gallup Poll, 21 per cent of the residents of metropolitan centers reported crime as their *major* concern.[1]

People not only *think* that they are threatened by crime; they are also taking action to defend themselves. Several years ago, Chicago citizens formed the South Shore Emergency Patrol, composed of some two hundred black and white residents, to patrol the streets at night and weekends; in Boston's Dorchester area, the community has begun crime patrols; in New York, Citizens Action for a Safer Harlem has organized block-watcher programs, street associations and escort services for the elderly, while an armed citizens' vigilance group patrols the streets of Brooklyn on the look-out for arson and burglaries; in San Francisco, a member of the Board of Supervisors recently urged the formation of citizen anti-crime patrols to curb muggings; and in the relative peace and quiet of a college town like Berkeley, the Committee Against Rape and several neighborhood associations are meeting to plan ways of stopping violent attacks against women.[2]

The phenomenon of 'street' crime has been largely ignored by the U.S. left. On the one hand, it is treated moralistically and attributed to the parasitical elements in capitalist society, mechanically follow-ing Marx and Engels's famous statement in the *Communist Manifesto* that the 'lumpenproletariat may, here and there, be swept into the movement by a proletarian revolution; its conditions of life, however, prepare it far more for the part of a bribed tool of reactionary intrigue'.[3] On the other hand, 'street' crime is either glossed over as an invention of the FBI to divert attention away from the crimes of the ruling class or romanticized as a form of primitive political rebellion. Whether it is a form of reactionary individualism, or a fiction promoted by the bourgeoisie to cause confusion and false consciousness, or another manifestation of class struggle, is not a matter of theoretical assertion and cannot be decided by dogmatic references to Marxist texts. What is first needed is a thorough investigation of the scope and nature of 'street' crime, concrete information about its varieties and rates and an appreciation of its specific historical context. This essay sets out to summarize and analyze the available information, thus providing a realistic basis for developing political strategy.

Reporting crime

In 1931, the International Association of Chiefs of Police developed the Uniform Crime Reports (UCR) system and selected seven felony offenses for index purposes, on the grounds that the victims, or someone representing them, would more likely report such crimes to the police. The seven offense groups include homicide, robbery, aggravated assault, forcible rape, burglary, larceny (grand theft) and auto theft. These are the crime statistics from which trends in the incidence of criminality are regularly reported in the media. When these reported crimes are converted into rates per 100,000 population and comparisons are made across time, for example 1968 to 1973, each of the index crimes, with the exception of auto theft, increased 25 to 50 per cent. In 1976, according to the UCR, nearly 11.5 million serious crimes were reported to the police, a 33 per cent increase from 1972, and a 76 per cent increase from 1967.[4]

Critics of the FBI's reporting system have pointed out that the dramatic increase in crime rates is exaggerated and misleading since it reflects higher rates of *reporting* crime, technological improvements in data processing, better record-keeping systems and political manipulation by the police, rather than a real increase in the level of crime. While there is no evidence to support sensational media announcements about *sudden crime waves*, crime is certainly not exaggerated by the FBI. On the contrary, it is grossly underestimated.

The most accurate information about the scope of 'street' crime is to be found in the federal government's Victimization Surveys. The Surveys, part of a statistical program called the National Crime Panel created by the Law Enforcement Assistance Administration (LEAA) in 1973, are an attempt to assess the extent and character of criminal victimization by means of a representative probability sampling of households, businesses and persons over the age of 12. The Surveys, which do *not* include homicide, kidnapping, so-called 'victimless' crimes (such as prostitution, pimping, sale of drugs, etc.) and business crimes (such as fraud, false advertising, tax evasion, etc.), are limited to personal (rape, assault and armed robbery) and property (theft, auto theft and burglary) crimes.

Most 'street' crime is not reported to the police. The Census Bureau recently concluded that there were nearly four times as many crimes committed in 1975 and 1976 as reported to the police.[5] A 1973 victimization study found that fewer than one in five persons report larceny to the police.[6] Some experts estimate that only 10 per cent of all rapes are reported; the reporting rate for wife-beating is even lower.[7] A 'self-report' study estimates that about one out of every thirty delinquent acts comes to the attention of the police.[8]

The primary reason for not reporting crimes is the belief that the police are either incapable of solving crimes or are likely to aggravate the situation by brutalizing or intimidating the victims. This distrust of the police is realistically based on the extensive experiences of working-class communities, especially racial and national minorities, with police brutality and ineffectiveness. According to a recent national public opinion survey, blacks think that the police are doing a poor job almost three times more than do whites.[9] (See Figure 1.1.)

FIGURE 1.1 *Evaluation of police performance (per cent responding 'good') by family income and race of respondent, eight impact cities: aggregate*

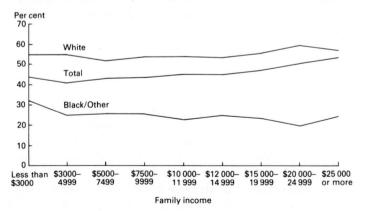

SOURCE: James Garofolo, *Public Opinion About Crime* (U.S. Dept. of Justice, LEAA, 1977).

According to a recent study by Paul Takagi, black males are killed by the police at a rate 13 times higher than for white males.[10] But police killings are only a small part of the total level of state brutality directed at the civilian population. It is not an exaggeration to say that millions of Americans now alive have been beaten by the police. Data cited by James Q. Wilson, a political scientist at Harvard, show that 5 per cent of all blacks (over one million people) and 2 per cent of all whites (over four million people) report themselves unjustifiably beaten by the police. And sociologist Albert Reiss, in a LEAA-financed study, found that the police used unnecessary force in 3 per cent of all police–citizen encounters, representing hundreds of thousands of cases of brutality per year. When these data are understood in the context of peer and family relationships, a very large proportion of the population on a day-to-day basis faces or fears the possibility of police violence.[11]

Additionally, the police have a very poor track record in solving and prosecuting serious 'street' crime. A two-year Rand study, released in 1976, reported that substantially more than 50 per cent of all serious crimes reported to the police receive no more than superficial investigation by detectives and investigators. Unless the patrolman on the scene makes an arrest or a patrol car accidentally stops a burglar for speeding, concludes Rand, there is little chance of a successful prosecution.[12]

The selective recruitment and militaristic training of the police, aggravated by institutionalized racism and sexism, encourage them to regard 'high crime' areas as either a combat zone requiring the dispassionate objectivity of a professional soldier or a 'subculture' of violence and depravity where victimization is culturally inevitable. Not surprisingly, policing the ghettos and barrios vacillates from extraordinary violence to cynical resignation.

This does not mean that all rank and file police operate in this way. There are many individual officers and a small number of progressive caucuses, such as the Afro-American Patrolmen's League in Chicago and Officers for Justice in San Francisco, who are genuinely concerned about protecting working-class communities from crime. But their efforts are easily frustrated, partly because the roots of 'street' crime are deeply embedded in social conditions over which they have no control, and partly because their efforts are continuously undermined and sabotaged by the political police and 'red squads', who make it their business to destroy community and political organizations which are trying to combat drug pushing, pimping, rape and other forms of parasitical criminality.

Scope of crime

According to a 1977 Gallup Poll and a survey of 70 countries, the U.S. has the highest crime rate of all capitalist and European countries. One of every five homes was victimized by crime; 15 per cent of working-class communities reported that they were afraid of being victimized by crime in their own homes, while 43 per cent thought that crime had increased in their neighborhood.[13]

During 1974, according to the Victimization Surveys, over 39.5 million persons over the age of 12 were victimized by selected, serious crimes, an increase of 7.5 per cent over 1973. In 1975, there was another 2 per cent increase to nearly 40.5 million estimated incidents of victimization.[14] And the latest Census Bureau study reports over 41 million for 1976.[15] This is almost four times higher than the FBI's UCR index. Moreover, it should be remembered that these estimates do *not* include homicide, 'victimless' crimes (illegal drugs and prostitution, for example) or the 'hidden' figures of 'white-collar' crime – price-fixing, health and safety violations, tax fraud, embezzlement, false advertising, etc. – which cause immense suffering and untold deprivation in working-class communities.

The Victimization Surveys have caused considerable embarrassment to the government, which had hoped to use them to demonstrate that LEAA's 'war on crime' was winning some major battles. The Surveys, however, have instead demonstrated that the rate of 'street' crime has gradually increased, despite the 55 per cent increase in criminal justice expenditures from $11 billion in 1971 to $17 billion in 1975; despite the fact that the number of police almost doubled in the decade between 1965 and 1975; despite a flourishing criminal justice-industrial complex which has upgraded the technological capacity of the police and introduced computers, weapons systems, data retrieval devices and modern communications equipment to a hitherto 'backward' bureaucracy; despite the advice and thousands of research studies conducted by the 'best and brightest' scholars from the most privileged universities and corporate think tanks.

Not surprisingly, the federal government recently called a halt to the Victimization Surveys, even though they were widely regarded as one of the very few worthwhile and reliable projects initiated by LEAA. The reasons for this action are quite obvious. Not only did the Surveys expose the bankruptcy and incredible waste of the government's 'war on crime'. They also supported the conclusion that 'street' crime is not simply a *by-product* of the capitalist mode of production, a logistics problem to be solved by technocrats trained in 'systems analysis'. Rather, it is shown to be a phenomenon *endemic* to capitalism at its highest stage of development.

Victims of street crime

'Street' crime is primarily an *intra-class* and *intra-racial* phenomenon, media stereotypes to the contrary.[16] White women are most likely to be raped by white men; young black men are most likely to be robbed by other young black men; and working-class families are most likely to have their homes vandalized or ripped off by strangers living only a few blocks away.

The victims of 'street' crime are overwhelmingly poor people, particularly blacks and Chicanos living in metropolitan areas. LEAA's 1973 Victimization Surveys found that, with the exception of theft, families with annual incomes under $3,000 were the most likely to be victimized by serious crimes of violence and property loss.[17] Another study, using the same indices, reported that the unemployed were more likely to be victims of crime in rates two to three times higher than those employed.[18]

Racial and national minorities, especially blacks, have the highest rate of victimization. A 1975 LEAA study in the five largest cities found that:

Blacks and Chicanos in Philadelphia and Los Angeles are most likely to be victimized by assault and robbery.

Blacks in Philadelphia and Chicago are the most victimized by theft.

Black family households in all five cities suffer the highest rates of burglary and auto theft.

In Philadelphia, blacks are twice as likely as whites to be burglarized.

In Chicago, blacks are twice as likely as whites to be victimized by auto theft.[19]

Follow-up nationwide studies, released in 1976, similarly found that the highest incidence of violent and property crime is among the poor and unemployed, specifically, the superexploited sectors of the working class, young men and single or separated women. Blacks have higher victimization rates than whites for rape, robbery and assault. Moreover, blacks over age 20 are robbed at two to three times the rate of their white counterparts.[20] (See Table 1.1.)

While crimes of violence account for less than 10 per cent of 'street' crimes, they are an important source of demoralization and victimization in working-class communities. Rape, assault, child- and wife-beating and homicide not only cause great personal suffering to the victims and their relatives and close friends, but also undermine collective solidarity.

TABLE 1.1

Type of victimization	Race of victim	
	White	Black and other races
Base	143 217 000	19 019 000
Rape and attempted rape	90	158
Robbery	599	1 388
Robbery and attempted robbery with injury	207	473
Serious assault	108	294
Minor assault	99	179
Robbery without injury	213	589
Attempted robbery without injury	179	326
Assault	2 554	2 929
Aggravated assault	954	1 656
With injury	301	599
Attempted assault with weapon	653	1 057
Simple assault	1 600	1 272
With injury	399	289
Attempted assault without weapon	1 201	983
Personal larceny with contact	267	678
Purse snatching	57	126
Attempted purse snatching	44	47
Pocket picking	166	504
Personal larceny without contact	9 209	7 671

SOURCE: Michael Hindelang et al., *Sourcebook of Criminal Justice Statistics: 1974* (U.S. Dept. of Justice, LEAA, 1975).

This is *not* a recent phenomenon. Family life under industrial capitalism, as Engels observed in *The Condition of the Working Class in England*, was 'almost impossible for the worker'. Impoverished living conditions, long hours of work and little time for recreation made family life a continuous round of problems and tensions. Wives and children, doubly exploited by economic dependency and male supremacist ideology, are regular targets of brutal assaults. 'Yet the working man', noted Engels in 1845, 'cannot escape from the family, must live in the family, and the consequence is a perpetual succession of family troubles, domestic quarrels, most demoralizing for parents and children alike'.[21]

Under monopoly capitalism, social and family life is particularly difficult in the superexploited sectors of the working class, where economic hardship, a chaotic labor market, uprooted community life ('urban renewal') and deteriorating social services provide a fertile environment for individualism and demoralization. A recent study, prepared for the W.E.B. DuBois Conference on Black Health in 1976, reveals for example that about 95 per cent of blacks victimized by homicide are killed by other blacks:

> In 1974, almost 11,000 of the 237,000 deaths of nonwhites in the United States, the overwhelming majority of whom were black, were from homicide. More than six per cent of the black males who died during this year were victims of homicide as were over two per cent of the black females. Among blacks *homicide* was the *fourth leading cause of death*, exceeded only by major cardiovascular diseases, malignant neoplasms, and accidents. All of the infectious diseases taken together took a lesser toll than did homicide.

White men are killed by homicide at a rate of 9.3 per 100,000 compared with a rate of 77.9 per 100,000 for black men of comparable age. To put it another way, 'the difference in life expectation between white and black males is seven years. Almost a fifth of that is due to homicide . . . More than twice as many blacks died from homicide in 1974 as from automobile accidents, and homicides accounted for about 40 per cent as many deaths as cancer'.[22]

While the Victimization Surveys and other studies show that minorities are responsible for a higher incidence of violent 'street' crimes, such as rape, robbery, assault and homicide, than whites, this does not mean that crime is simply a *racial* phenomenon.[23] Historically, 'street' crime has tended to be concentrated in the marginalized sectors of the labor force and in the demoralized layers of the working class, irrespective of skin color or ethnic origin.[24] Today, it is those families with annual incomes below the poverty line which fill the police stations, jails and hospital emergency rooms. Since blacks, Chicanos, Native Americans and Puerto Ricans are disproportionately concentrated in the superexploited sectors of the working class, they are also disproportionately represented in police records and as victims of crime.

The risk of victimization is closely tied to the material conditions of life. Black women suffer a higher rate of rape than white women because they are more exposed to the insecurities of public transportation and poorly policed streets; the elderly, living on fixed incomes in downtown rooming houses, are much more physically vulnerable than their counterparts in suburban 'leisure' communities; families that cannot afford to install burglar alarms or remodel their homes into fortresses are easier prey for rip-offs and thefts; small businesses, unable to buy the protection of private security agencies, are more likely to be burglarized; apartment buildings, guarded by rent-a-cops, doormen and security fences have a lower rate of burglary than public housing projects and tenements; and working parents, hustling low-paying jobs with erratic hours in order to pay the daily bills, cannot hire tutors, counselors and psychiatrists or turn to private schools when their children become 'delinquency' problems.

Crime and class

The current high level of crime and victimization within the marginalized sectors of the working class can be partly understood in the context of the capitalist labor market. The 'relative surplus population' is not an aberration or incidental by-product. Rather it is continuously reproduced as a necessary element of the capitalist mode of production and is, to quote Marx, the '*lever* of capitalist accumulation . . . It forms a disposable industrial reserve army that belongs to capital quite as absolutely as if the latter had bred it at its own cost. Independently of the limits of the actual increase of population, it creates, for the changing needs of the self-expansion of capital, a mass of human material always ready for exploitation'.[25]

For this population, the economic conditions of life are unusually desperate and degrading. The high level of property crime and petty hustles cannot be separated from the problems of survival.

Commenting on the process of primitive accumulation in fifteenth-
and sixteenth-century England, Marx observed that the rising
bourgeoisie destroyed the pre-existing modes of production through
the forcible expropriation of people's land and livelihood, thus
creating a 'free' proletariat which 'could not possibly be absorbed by
the nascent manufactures as fast as it was thrown upon the world'.
Thousands of peasants were 'turned *en masse* into beggars, robbers,
vagabonds . . . and "voluntary" criminals . . .'[26] For these victims
of capitalism, crime was both a means of survival and an effort to
resist the discipline and deadening routine of the workhouse and
factory.[27]

But crime was not only a manifestation of early capitalism, with its
unconcealed plunder, terrorism and unstable labor market. Crime
was endemic to both the rural and urban poor in eighteenth-century
England.[28] And at the peak of industrial capitalism in the mid-
nineteenth century, Engels vividly described the prevalence of theft,
prostitution and other types of widespread victimization in working-
class communities. 'The British nation', he concluded, 'has become
the most criminal in the world.'[29]

With at least 41 million persons annually victimized by serious
'street' crimes in the United States, it is clear that monopoly
capitalism has aggravated rather than reduced the incidence of crime.
Recent studies, prepared for the United Nations report on *Economic
Crises and Crime*, support the argument that the rate of criminal
victimization is not only correlated with crises and 'downturns' in the
capitalist economy, but also with the 'long-term effects of economic
growth', [30] thus giving support to Marx's 'absolute law of capitalist
accumulation – in proportion as capital accumulates, the lot of the
laborer, be his payment high or low, must grow worse'.[31] The
economic underpinnings of 'street' crime are underscored by the
findings of the Victimization Surveys that over 90 per cent of serious
offenses are property-related (theft, burglary, robbery, etc.).[32] Not
surprisingly, most 'street' crime is disproportionately concentrated in
the superexploited sectors of the working class where unemployment
rates of 50 per cent are not uncommon.

But 'street' crime is not only related to economic conditions; nor is
it solely restricted to working-class neighborhoods. A series of
national studies, conducted by Martin Gold and his colleagues,
found little difference in rates of juvenile delinquency between blacks
and whites or working-class and petty bourgeois families.[33] Their
latest study reports that 'white girls are no more nor less frequently or

seriously delinquent than black girls; and white boys, no more nor less *frequently* delinquent than black boys; but white boys are *less seriously* delinquent than black boys'. (See Figure 1.2.) Moreover, when delinquency is correlated with socioeconomic status, it is found that 'higher status' boys (i.e., the sons of the petty bourgeoisie for the most part) are more likely than working-class boys to commit thefts, steal cars and commit assaults.[34]

FIGURE 1.2   *Frequency and seriousness of delinquent behavior by race and sex*

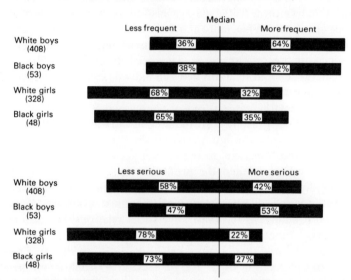

SOURCE: Jay Williams and Martin Gold, 'From Delinquent Behavior to Official Delinquency', *Social Problems*, 20, 2 (Fall, 1972).

'Street' crime, like white chauvinism and male supremacy, is most brutal in (although by no means limited to) the superexploited sectors of the working class. Monopoly capitalism emiserates increasingly larger portions of the working class and proletarianizes the lower strata of the petty bourgeoisie, degrades workers' skills and competency in the quest for higher productivity, and organizes family and community life on the basis of its most effective exploitability. It consequently makes antagonism rather than reciprocity the norm of social relationships.[35]

Under monopoly capitalism, family and peer relationships become even more brutal and attenuated. The family as an economic unit is totally separated, except as a consumer, from the productive processes of society. Adolescents are denied access to the labor market and forced to depend on their parents, who bear the costs of their subsistence and education. As a result, millions of youth, including many of the children of the petty bourgeoisie, 'become subject to an extraordinary variety of social problems that accompany the statuses of dependent able-bodied persons in our society'.[36]

'It is only in its era of monopoly', writes Harry Braverman in *Labor and Monopoly Capital*, 'that the capitalist mode of production takes over the totality of individual, family, and social needs and, in subordinating them to the market, also reshapes them to serve the needs of capital.' While more and more of the population 'is packed ever more closely together in the urban environment, the atomization of social life proceeds apace . . . The social structure, built upon the market, is such that relations between individuals and social groups do not take place directly, as cooperative human encounters, but through the market as relations of purchase and sale.'

As more family members are required to work and the pressures of urban life intensify, the family is required to 'strip for action in order to survive and "succeed" in the market society'. Thus, urban life, governed by capital and the profit motive, 'is both chaotic and profoundly hostile to all feelings of community'. The 'universal market', to use Braverman's appropriate term, not only destroys the material foundations of cooperative social relations, but also permeates even the most private domain of personal life, setting husband against wife, neighbor against neighbor.[37] 'In short', as Engels observed over a century ago, 'everyone sees in his neighbor an enemy to be got out of the way, or, at best, a tool to be used for his own advantage'.[38]

Crime as rebellion?

There is a tendency within the New Left to glorify crime as 'primitive rebellion' and interpret it as a form of spontaneous, anticapitalist revolt. There is definitely some support for this position when we examine previous historical eras.

According to Eric Hobsbawm's well-known study of criminality in precapitalist and agrarian societies, 'social banditry' was a form of class struggle and often a precursor or accompaniment to peasant revolutions. 'The point about social bandits', he writes, 'is that they are peasant outlaws whom the lord and state regard as criminals, but who remain within peasant society, and are considered by their people as heroes, as champions, avengers, fighters for justice, perhaps even leaders of liberation, and in any case as men to be admired, helped and supported.' This respect for 'social bandits' was based on their defense of the oppressed and their selective theft of the oppressor's crops and property.[39]

'Social banditry' or its equivalent persisted throughout at least two hundred years of primitive accumulation, as displaced peasants asserted their traditional communal rights to subsistence through poaching, smuggling and ship-wrecking against bourgeois claims to the supremacy of capitalist private property.[40]

But not all criminality was a blow to class rule in agrarian and early capitalist societies. Peasant society was also victimized by 'professional' criminals and 'common robbers' who did not make any class distinctions between their victims; and the rural and urban poor in eighteenth-century England were regularly demoralized by theft, robbery and other types of *intra-class* victimization.

Criminality as an effective, though limited, method of waging class warfare began to decline with the development of industrial capitalism. There were two important reasons for this. First, modernization reduced the means of protection and survival. The technology of communications and rapid forms of transportation, combined with economic development, public administration and the growth of the state, deprived banditry of the technical and social conditions under which it flourishes. Second, and more importantly, the organized working class developed collective, political associations which were far superior to individual criminality or even the organized self-help of banditry. As Engels observed:

> The earliest, crudest, and least fruitful form of rebellion was that of crime . . . The workers soon realized that crime did not help matters. The criminal could protest against the existing order of society only singly, as one individual; the whole might of society was brought to bear upon each criminal, and crushed him with its immense superiority. Besides, theft was the most primitive form of protest, and for this reason, if no other, it never becomes the universal expression of the public opinion of the working-man, however much they might approve of it in silence.[41]

Under monopoly capitalism, 'street' crime bears little resemblance to the social banditry of Sicilian peasants, of the pastoral nomads of Central Asia or even of the rural poor in mercantile England. Contemporary 'bandits' are more likely to rip off their neighbor or rob the local mom and pop store than to hold up a bank or kidnap a corporate executive. And they are more likely to be regarded as pariahs in the community than to be welcomed as heroes. Nor can theft from supermarkets and chain stores (which is widespread) be considered a modern equivalent of banditry, because bourgeois rule is not weakened by such activity, and the cost of such theft is generally passed on to the consumer in the form of higher prices or inferior commodities. It is only among ultra-leftist sects, which have no base of support within working-class communities, that such banditry is still practised and glorified.

Conclusion

The political solution to 'street' crime does not lie in *mystifying* its reality by reactionary allusions to 'banditry', nor in *reducing* it to a manifestation of 'lumpen' viciousness. The former is utopian and dangerous because it defends practices that undermine the safety and solidarity of the working class (and glorifies spontaneity and putschism); the latter objectively legitimates the bourgeoisie's attack on superexploited workers, especially black and brown workers.

While 'street' crime is associated with the most demoralized sectors of the working class, we must be careful about making mechanical and ahistorical generalizations about the 'lumpen' and 'dangerous class'. As Paul Hirst has correctly pointed out, Marx and Engels took a very harsh and uncompromising attitude to 'street' crime, not from a moralistic perspective, but out of concern for building a disciplined and principled workers' movement. 'Their standpoint', notes Hirst, 'was uncompromisingly political and based on the proletarian class position. Marx and Engels ask of any social class or sociopolitical activity, what is its effectivity in the struggle of the proletariat for socialism, does it contribute to the political victory of the exploited and oppressed?'[42]

Marx and Engels based their evaluation on both a class analysis of criminality and a concrete investigation of the role of the 'lumpenproletariat' in specific political struggles. Thus, they argued that the 'lumpen' weakens the workers' movement by living off the workers' productive labor, for example by theft, as well as by serving the bourgeoisie as informers, spies, collaborators and adventurists.[43]

The contemporary workers' movement must take an equally uncompromising stand against organized, parasitical forms of victimization and against 'criminals' and prisoners who become 'snitches' and agents of the political police. Pimping, gambling rackets, illegal drug operations, etc., are just as damaging to working-class communities as any 'legal' business which profits from people's misery and desperation.

But we must be careful to distinguish organized criminality from 'street' crime and the 'lumpen' from the superexploited sectors of the working class. Most 'street' crime is not organized and not very profitable. Most theft, for example, is committed by individuals, and each incidence of 'street' theft amounts to much less than $100.[44] Moreover, there is typically no direct economic advantage associated with crimes of personal violence – rape, homicide, assault, etc.

The conditions of life in the superexploited sectors create both high levels of 'street' crime *and* political militancy. The urban black community, for example, is hit the hardest by 'street' crime, but it is also the locus of tremendous resistance and struggle – as witnessed by the civil rights movement, the ghetto revolts of the 1960s, and the antirepression struggles of today. Moreover, of the thousands of blacks who annually go to prison for serious crimes of victimization, many have become transformed by the collective experience of prison life and participate in numerous acts of solidarity, self-sacrifice and heroism – as witnessed by the conversion of Malcolm X, George Jackson and countless other anonymous militants in the strikes and uprisings at Soledad, San Quentin, Attica, etc.

While the link between 'street' crime and economic conditions is clearly established, we must guard against economism. Crime is not simply a matter of poverty, as evidenced by the unparalleled criminality and terrorism of the ruling class. Nor is 'street' crime explained by poverty, for petty bourgeois youth in the United States are probably just as delinquent as their working-class counterparts, and there are many impoverished nations in the world that do not in any way approach the high level of criminality in this country. The problem of 'street' crime should be approached not only as a product of the unequal distribution of wealth and chaotic labor market practices, but also as an important aspect of the demoralizing social relations and individualistic ideology that characterize the capitalist mode of production at its highest stage of development.

Notes

1. Center for Research on Criminal Justice, *The Iron Fist and the Velvet Glove* (San Francisco: Institute for the Study of Labor and Economic Crisis, 1977) 14.

2. *Christian Science Monitor*, 13 November 1973; *New York Times* (16 April 1977; 21 July 1977); *San Francisco Chronicle* (25 January 1978). According to the *Law Enforcement News* (3 January 1978), the Law Enforcement Assistance Administration is now funding some 600 anticrime projects at a cost of $37 million.

3. Karl Marx and Friedrich Engels, *The Communist Manifesto* (New York: Appleton–Century–Croft, 1955) 20–1.

4. 'The Politics of Street Crime', *Crime and Social Justice*, 5 (Spring–Summer, 1976) 1–4.

5. *San Francisco Chronicle*, 20 February 1978.

6. Michael Hindelang *et al.*, *Sourcebook of Criminal Justice Statistics: 1974* (Washington, D.C.: U.S. Government Printing Office, 1975) 233.

7. Center for Research on Criminal Justice, 14.

8. Jay Williams and Martin Gold, 'From Delinquent Behavior to Official Delinquency', *Social Problems*, 20, 2 (Fall, 1972) 209–29.

9. James Garofolo, *Public Opinion About Crime* (Washington, D.C.: U.S. Government Printing Office, 1977) 28.

10. 'The Management of Police Killings', *Crime and Social Justice*, 8 (Fall–Winter, 1977) 34–43.

11. 'The Management of Police Killings', 42.

12. *U.S. News and World Report*, 10 October 1977.

13. *San Francisco Chronicle*, 22 December 1977.

14. Law Enforcement Assistance Administration, *Criminal Victimization in the United States: A Comparison of 1973 and 1974 Findings* (Washington, D.C.: U.S. Government Printing Office, 1976).

15. *San Francisco Chronicle*, 20 February 1978.

16. Law Enforcement Assistance Administration, *Criminal Victimization in the United States: 1973* (Washington, D.C.: U.S. Government Printing Office, 1976).

17. See note 16 above.

18. John E. Conklin, *The Impact of Crime* (New York: Macmillan, 1975) 26.

19. Law Enforcement Assistance Administration, *Criminal Victimization Surveys in the Nation's Five Largest Cities* (Washington, D.C.: U.S. Government Printing Office, 1975).

20. LEAA, *Criminal Victimization in the United States: 1973*.

21. Friedrich Engels, *The Condition of the Working Class in England* (Moscow: Progress Publishers, 1973) 168.

22. Yongsock Shin, Davor Jedlicka and Everett Lee, 'Homicide Among Blacks', *Phylon*, 38, 4 (December, 1977) 398–407.

23. For data on the high homicide rate among Native Americans, see Charles Reasons, 'Crime and the Native American', in Reasons and Kuykendall (eds), *Race, Crime and Justice* (Pacific Palisades, Ca.: Goodyear, 1972) 79–95; for data on alcohol-related deaths among blacks in Georgia, see George Lowe and Eugene Hodges, 'Race and the Treatment of Alcoholism in a Southern State', *Social Problems*, 20, 2

(Fall, 1972) 240–52; for a discussion of the high rates of rape, robbery and assault among blacks, albeit from a cultural and 'racial' perspective, see Michael Hindelang, 'Race and Involvement in Common Law Personal Crimes', *American Sociological Review*, 43, 1 (February, 1978) 93–109.

24. See, for example, Edward Green, 'Race, Social Status, and Criminal Arrest', in Reasons and Kuykendall: 103–23.
25. Karl Marx, *Capital*, Vol. I (New York: International Publishers, 1975) 632.
26. Marx, 734.
27. Dario Melossi, 'The Penal Question in *Capital*', *Crime and Social Justice*, 5 (Spring–Summer, 1976) 26–33.
28. See, for example, Douglas Hay *et al.*, *Albion's Fatal Tree: Crime and Society in Eighteenth-Century England* (New York: Pantheon, 1975).
29. Engels, 168.
30. United Nations Social Defense Research Institute, *Economic Crises and Crime* (Rome, UNSDRI, 1976).
31. Marx, 645.
32. LEAA, *Criminal Victimization in the United States: 1973*.
33. Williams and Gold, 209–29; Martin Gold and David Reimer, 'Changing Patterns of Delinquent Behavior Among Americans 13 Through 16 Years Old: 1967–1972', *Crime and Delinquency Literature*, 7, 4 (December 1975) 483–517.
34. Williams and Gold, 215–18. These findings have been confirmed by Paul Takagi in a current (unpublished) study of delinquency among Chinese youth in San Francisco. For a methodological critique of the Gold studies, see Hindelang, 'Race and Involvement in Common Law Personal Crimes', 103–4.
35. See, for example, David Harvey, *Social Justice and the City* (London: Johns Hopkins University Press, 1973).
36. Herman Schwendinger and Julia Schwendinger, 'Delinquency and the Collective Varieties of Youth', *Crime and Social Justice*, 5 (Spring–Summer, 1976) 7–25.
37. Harry Braverman, *Labor and Monopoly Capital* (New York: Monthly Review Press, 1974) 271–83.
38. Engels, 170–1.
39. Eric Hobsbawm, *Bandits* (New York: Delacorte, 1969) 13–23.
40. See, for example, Douglas Hay *et al.*
41. Engels, 250–1.
42. Paul Hirst, 'Marx and Engels on Law, Crime and Morality', in Taylor, Walton and Young (eds), *Critical Criminology* (London: Routledge and Kegan Paul, 1975) 203–32.
43. See note 42 above.
44. LEAA, *Criminal Victimization in the United States: 1973*.

2
Intellectuals for Law and Order

A Critique of the New 'Realists'

Tony Platt and Paul Takagi

Introduction

> Crime will always remain with us, just as fires will be with us, or
> weeds . . . Those less favored by nature or society are more
> tempted to violate laws and therefore suffer punishment for doing
> so more often . . . There has been a worldwide decline in punish-
> ment and therefore of respect of law.[1]

When Ernest van den Haag's *Punishing Criminals* (quoted above)
appeared in 1975, it was regarded as a criminological aberration, a
radical departure from the prevailing liberal consensus.[2] Filled with
factual and methodological errors, a curious stylistic mixture of old-
fashioned *Reader's Digest* moralism and literary pretensions,
Punishing Criminals advocates the death penalty, longer sentences,
'post-punishment incapacitation', banishment, exile, house arrest
and other less imaginative weapons in the 'war against crime'.

Stylistically, van den Haag stands apart from other intellectuals.
The candor of his viciousness is unusual. No sheep's clothing for him.
Substantively, however, he is in the mainstream of a new school of
'realist' thought. While there are considerable tactical and procedural
differences among the 'realists', they are united around their demand
for tougher state repression against the working class in general and
blacks in particular.

The forum for this conservative propaganda is far-ranging: in
1975, the *American Sociological Review* published an article which
argues that penal sentences are unrelated to class and race;[3] this was
followed two years later by Hirchi and Hindelang's claim in the *ASR*
that 'the weight of the evidence is that IQ is more important than race
and social class' in determining delinquency;[4] similarly, the most
prestigious economic journals, including the *Journal of Political
Economy* and the *American Economic Review*, regularly publish

articles proposing that crime is rationally calculated behaviour that can be deterred if the 'cost' is made sufficiently high.[5]

Political scientists such as Edward Banfield and James Q. Wilson extensively rely on this economistic model in their hard-line analysis of crime.[6] Wilson's *Thinking About Crime* is currently perhaps the most widely distributed popular book on the subject. This apology for social eugenics and intensified repression (discussed further in this chapter) is highly recommended by *Fortune* magazine and can be bought at the airport or your local bookstore. Similarly, a highly publicized book dealing with crime, Freda Adler's sexist *Sisters in Crime*, attributes the so-called rise in violent crime to the women's liberation movement.

Professional journals in criminology now routinely carry this kind of analysis: *Federal Probation* printed Wilks and Martinson's nonsense plea for state-supervised surveillance of 'criminals' in the community;[7] a recent lead article in *Crime and Delinquency* clinically proposes that the death penalty can only be made an effective deterrent if 3000 executions per year are carried out.[8] Popular magazines also carry the 'realists' analysis of crime. Wilson's work, for example, has been published in the *New York Times Magazine, Commentary* and *Atlantic Monthly*. In addition, *Time, Newsweek, Washington Monthly, Village Voice* and *U.S. News and World Report* have contained similar reports.[9] The *New York Times*, typifying this kind of coverage, provided a column to sociologist Jackson Toby's proposal that 'incorigibles' should be subjected to 'internment, a long-lasting deprivation of liberty without duration fixed in advance'.[10]

These ideas, which represent the dominant trend in criminology today, are not the product of 'backward' practitioners or unqualified academics. On the contrary, this is the work of the 'best and brightest' intellectuals teaching at such elite universities as Harvard and Chicago, supported by large grants from the federal government and the major (Rockefeller, Ford, etc.) foundations. Although there is opposition within the profession from utopian advocates of the 'justice model' and prison moratorium,[11] the new 'realists' have had a profound impact on legislative policy and the mass media.

In this chapter, we will attempt to place the new 'realists' in the context of an expanding criminal justice apparatus, the contradictions of monopoly capitalism and the impact of the current economic and political crisis on petty bourgeois intellectuals. While Wilson, van den Haag, Martinson and others all claim to be, and sometimes even believe that they are, objectively detached experts, they cannot function outside class relations and they are no more independent than the corporate foundations, boards of trustees and government agencies which sponsor and regulate their work. 'In class society', observes Mao Tse-tung, 'everyone lives as a member of a particular class, and every kind of thinking, without exception, is stamped with the brand of a class'.[12] Before examining the class position of the new 'realists' we will discuss the material context in which their ideology flourishes.

Expansion of criminal justice apparatus

During the last ten years there has been an unprecedented growth in the cost, personnel and scope of the U.S. criminal justice apparatus. In 1955, criminal justice expenditures at all levels of government – local, state and federal – amounted to about one half of 1 per cent of the Gross National Product; by 1971, it had risen to about 1 per cent and the rate of increase since 1966 was about five times as great as it had been in the previous decade.[13] From 1971 to 1975, spending on criminal justice increased 55 per cent from $11 billion to $17 billion. During the same period, the number of full-time criminal justice employees jumped 22 per cent from 862,000 to 1,051,000.[14]

This expansion has especially affected the police. In 1974, over $8.5 billion (about 57 per cent) was spent on the police, eight times more than was allocated ten years earlier.[15] The total number of police in the U.S. went up from 273,000 to 371,000 between 1955 and 1965. Between 1965 (the beginning of the period of urban rebellions) and 1971, the total number of police increased by over 200,000 to 575,000, and by 1975 to 653,000. In short, the number of police officers in this country very nearly doubled in the decade between 1965 and 1975. At the present rate of increase, there will be about 900,000 police (excluding a comparable number of private security personnel) in the United States in 1984. In Colorado, spending on the police increased 80 per cent between 1971–74. The Los Angeles police force doubled in size in the ten years between 1964–74, while Chicago's force increased by about two-thirds. At a time when many areas of social service spending are being cut back due to the fiscal crisis of the 1970s, the police are a booming institution in the public sector.[16]

While most criminal justice expenditures are supported by city and county taxes, the share of the states and the federal government is rising fast. Since its inception in 1968, LEAA has become one of the fastest-growing agencies in the federal government. Its budget has increased from $63 million in 1969 to $1,015 million for fiscal year 1976. Though federal expenditures for the criminal justice apparatus only represent a small percentage of the overall budget, they have nevertheless played a major role in influencing and attempting to standardize policy. Through consolidation of planning and administration, for example, LEAA has the responsibility for rationalizing the internal security network. It has also supplied over $3 billion to fund projects and research, and to subsidize the purchase of equipment, technology, weaponry and computerized information and intelligence systems.[17]

Recent authoritative studies, based on empirical data collected nationwide, indicate that this massive investment in criminal justice has neither reduced the level of crime nor improved the quality of justice. According to a systematic evaluation of LEAA by the Center for National Security Studies, 'the evidence is overwhelming: the federal government has greatly increased its expenditures to combat crime, but these expenditures have had no effect in reducing crime'.[18] Beginning in 1972, LEAA annually invested $160 million in eight 'target' cities with a view to reducing serious crimes by 5 per cent in two years and 20 per cent in five years. Except for two of the cities where there was little change, the crime rates (as recorded by the FBI) in the other six cities increased considerably.[19] A more sophisticated and accurate survey of crime victims nationwide showed no significant change in victimization for violent crimes and slightly higher rates for property crimes during 1973–74, a period when the federal programs were supposedly having their greatest impact.[20]

Aside from the vast array of bourgeois and state crimes which the police either ignore or help to reproduce, the police have proved totally ineffective in protecting working-class communities from intra-class crimes of personal and economic victimization. This conclusion is clearly supported by the Kansas City Preventive Patrol Experiment, by Thomas Pogue's analysis of police expenditures and by an evaluation by Seidman and Couzens of crime-control efforts in Washington, D.C.[21]

At a time when the criminal justice apparatus is being funded and streamlined at an unprecedented high level, it is evident that the level of serious 'street' crime has not diminished. On the other hand, police stations, detention centers, jails and prisons are being filled beyond capacity. The latest correctional census reports its grim findings with dispassionate neutrality:

> A larger number of prisoners sentenced to a maximum term of more than a year were being held in State and Federal correctional facilities on the last day of 1975 than on that day in any other year since the annual count of such inmates was begun in 1926. Moreover, the increase of 24,284 prisoners during 1975 was the largest ever recorded in any year since the series began . . . Between 1968 and 1972, the count, even though known to have been under-enumerated for 1968, 1969, and 1970, showed a general upward movement. Clearly, however, the inmate population has been rising since 1972. The total on December 31, 1975, 242,750, was some 11 percent higher than 12 months earlier.[22]

This trend is apparently also the case for juveniles. According to a definitive study by the National Assessment of Juvenile Corrections, it is estimated that about 500,000 juveniles are imprisoned in *adult* jails each year and that another 500,000 are held in detention centers:

> Rates [of imprisonment] generally exceed those of other industrialized nations for which data are available. Although the proportion of youth who were held in jail and detention manifested a steady decline during the nineteenth and first half of the twentieth century, this trend appears to have been reversed in recent years.[23]

Despite various efforts to lower the crime rate and reduce imprisonment through such experiments as 'target hardening', diversion, team policing, methadone, etc., the rate of crime remains relatively stable while the prison and death row population grows.

The accumulation of misery

The current trend to intensify penal repression – in the form of restoring capital punishment in 40 states, legislating mandatory sentences, lengthening terms of imprisonment for certain categories of crime, etc. – must be considered in a broader context. With the deepening crisis in U.S. capitalism, in which 1976 *official* rates of 5.5 per cent inflation and almost 8 per cent unemployment were acknowledged by government economists, the real value of workers' wages has declined severely, social services have been drastically cut

back and the ranks of the unemployed and under-employed have
grown by the millions.[24] Not taking into account the more than half
million young men and women who were neither in school nor
'actively looking' for jobs in 1974, teenage unemployment for 16 to 19
year olds was officially 16 per cent.[25]

Unemployment and inflation are part of the general fiscal crisis of
monopoly capitalism in the 1970s. The burden of this crisis is being
primarily carried by the working class, especially national minorities.
Black and brown unemployment rates are at least double those of
white workers. A recent study by the National Urban League reports:

> By the first quarter of 1975, official black unemployment reached
> 1.5 million – the largest number of blacks out of work since the
> Great Depression of the 1930's. And, based on the National Urban
> League's Hidden Employment Index, which incorporates the
> discouraged workers, the actual black unemployed was 3 million
> or 26 per cent of the black labor force . . . In inner-city poverty
> areas, an estimated 50 per cent or more of blacks were
> unemployed – with the unofficial unemployment rate for black
> teenagers in poverty areas going much higher.[26]

According even to conservative government estimates, the Labor
Department reported a 40.4 per cent unemployment rate for black
youths aged 16 to 19 years old in July 1977. Comparable rates are to
be found in Chicano and Puerto Rican communities.[27]

The current high levels of unemployment, demoralization and
criminal victimization among national minorities can be best understood in the context of the capitalist labor market. The creation of
'the relative surplus population' or 'the industrial reserve army' is
continuously reproduced as 'a necessary part of the working
mechanism of the capitalist mode of production'. The relative surplus
population takes a variety of forms in modern society, 'including the
unemployed; the sporadically employed; the part-time employed; the
mass of women who, as houseworkers, form a reserve for the "female
occupations"; the armies of migrant labor, both agricultural and
industrial; the black population with its extraordinarily high rates of
unemployment; and the foreign reserves of labor'.[28]

For Marx, the relative surplus population is not an aberration or
an incidental consequence of the capitalist economy but rather the
'lever of capitalist accumulation, nay, a condition of the existence of
the capitalist mode of production. It forms a disposable industrial

reserve army that belongs to capital quite as absolutely as if the latter had bred it at its own cost. Independently of the limits of the actual increase of population, it creates, for the changing needs of the self-expansion of capital, a mass of human material always ready for exploitation'.[29] Through replacing human labor by machines and technology, increasing the productivity of existing labor, displacing skilled labor with unskilled and maintaining competition between the employed and unemployed for scarce jobs – the industrial reserve army, in Marx's words, 'furnishes to capital an inexhaustible reservoir of disposable labor power. Its conditions of life sink below the average normal level of the working-class; this makes it at once the broad basis of special branches of capitalist exploitation'.[30] This analysis led Marx to formulate the 'absolute general law of capitalist accumulation' that:

> In proportion as capital accumulates, the lot of the laborer, be his payment high or low, must grow worse. The law . . . that always equilibrates the relative surplus population . . . to the extent and energy of accumulation, this law rivets the laborer to capital more firmly than the wedges of Vulcan did Prometheus to the rock. It establishes an accumulation of misery, corresponding with accumulation of capital.[31]

This 'absolute general law of capitalist accumulation' was generally regarded by bourgeois economists as an indication of the weakness of Marxist theory during the 1940s and 1950s when the U.S. economy appeared strong and growing. 'Now that the consequences of this cycle of accumulation have worked themselves out more fully', notes Harry Braverman, 'the matter takes on a somewhat different appearance.'[32] With soaring unemployment rates and welfare rolls, a persistently high level of inflation and a general attack on the wages and health and safety conditions of the working class, there can be little doubt about the proposition that the 'accumulation of wealth at one pole is, therefore, at the same time accumulation of misery . . . at the opposite pole'.[33]

In the current crisis, there has been a growth of what Marx called the *stagnant* relative surplus population, whose employment is irregular and marginal.[34] This sector merges with the 'sediment', as Marx called it, of the relative surplus population which, as a product of capitalist development, exists in the world of welfare and prison, available for exploitation in times of labor shortage (for example, during World War II).

During periods of economic stagnation, which are increasingly and routinely the case, 'capital knows how to throw these (surplus populations), for the most part, from its own shoulders on to those of the working class and the lower middle class'.[35] The working class is victimized both by the anarchy of the capitalist labor market and by a system of taxation which requires it to shoulder the main burden of welfare and prisons. Harry Braverman vividly describes this process as follows:

The human detritus of the urban civilization increases, not just because the aged population, its life prolonged by the progress of medicine, grows even larger; those who need care include children – not only those who cannot 'function' smoothly but even the 'normal' ones whose only defect is their tender age. Whole new strata of the helpless and dependent are created, or familiar old ones enlarged enormously: the proportion of 'mentally ill' or 'deficient', the 'criminals', the pauperized layers at the bottom of society, all representing varieties of crumbling under the pressures of capitalist urbanism and the conditions of capitalist employment or unemployment. In addition, the pressures of urban life grow more intense and it becomes harder to care for any who need care in the conditions of the jungle of the cities. Since no care is forthcoming from an atomized community, and since the family cannot bear all such encumbrances if it is to strip for action in order to survive and 'succeed', in the market society, the care of all these layers becomes institutionalized, often in the most barbarous and oppressive forms. Thus understood, the massive growth of institutions stretching all the way from schools and hospitals on the one side to prisons and madhouses on the other represents not just the progress of medicine, education, or crime prevention, but the clearing of the marketplace of all but the 'economically active' and 'functioning' members of society, generally at public expense and at a handsome profit to the manufacturing and service corporations who sometimes own and invariably supply these institutions.[36]

It is not surprising, then, to find a relationship between the severity of penal practices and the size of the prison population on the one hand and conditions of the capitalist labor market on the other. In their classic analysis of *Punishment and Social Structure*, Rusche and Kirchheimer criticized the idealist assumptions of bourgeois penology and proposed that 'the transformation in penal systems cannot be explained only from changing needs of the war against crime, although this struggle does play a part. Every system of production tends to discover punishments which correspond to its productive relationships'. In particular, Rusche and Kirchheimer argued that the modern prison was an important instrument for training, regulating and exploiting labor during the early stages of capitalist accumulation.[37]

The use of the prison for the direct exploitation of labor declined for the most part[38] under monopoly capitalism due to the permanent over-supply of labor and the necessity of a working class 'free' to sell its labor power in exchange for a wage. But, as Ivan Jankovic points out, the 'persistent use of imprisonment in the most advanced capitalist societies in the final quarter of the twentieth century' suggests that the criminal justice apparatus plays an important role in containing and manipulating the marginalized sectors of the labor force. Jankovic found that, irrespective of changes in the rate of criminal activity, 'as the total number of unemployed persons increases, the total number of persons present in and admitted to prisons also increases' (*Crime and Social Justice*, Fall–Winter 1977).

This conclusion is supported by at least two other important studies. A report prepared by Harvey Brenner for the Joint Economic Committee finds that a 1 per cent increase in the unemployment rate sustained over a period of six years is associated with, inter alia, 3340 state prison admissions.[39] Similarly, William Nagel's recent study reports that 'States with a high incidence of persons living below the poverty line tend to have a *lower* crime rate but a *higher incarceration* rate . . . There is no significant correlation between a state's racial composition and its crime rate but there is a very great positive relationship between its *racial composition* and its *incarceration* rate'. These findings lead Nagel to conclude that 'the causes of crime in this country are deeply rooted in its culture and in its economic and social injustices. The massive use of incarceration has not contributed and will not contribute significantly to the abatement of crime or to correction of the flaws in our social fabric'.[40]

As the multinational corporations successfully use wage controls, inflation and other attacks on working people to stabilize their 10 to 15 per cent profit margin (which had slipped below 10 per cent during the late 1960s) and the ranks of the industrial reserve army swell by the millions, the criminal justice apparatus becomes increasingly important and necessary. The astronomic growth of the police and criminal justice budgets, subsidized in the main by the working class, make sense only in the context of the overall crisis of capitalism. In order to legitimate the growth of the criminal justice apparatus and cut back in desperately needed social services, the capitalist state needs 'law and order' ideologues to depict the horrors of 'street crime' and devise new methods of punishment. And they have the 'best and brightest' criminologists on their payroll, directly and indirectly, who are eager to perform this service and prove their loyalty. But before we examine the rise to prominence of these new 'realists' it is necessary to first understand the demise of penal liberalism.[41]

The demise of liberalism

Liberalism in penal policy triumphed during the first half of this century. While a study of its long-term development remains unwritten, we know that liberalism accepted crime as a social phenomenon related to the political economy. Sociological studies demonstrated that when unemployment and wage cuts or inflation (or both, as in the present period) create a sharp decline in the living standards of broad sections of the population, there is a corresponding increase in the penal population. This recognition resulted in changes in penal policy, stemming primarily from a concern for the smooth and efficient administration of the criminal justice apparatus.

Liberalism, for example, examined punishment from the situation of the offender or the perspective of individualized punishment, evaluated the prospects for rehabilitation and elaborated the balancing of sentencing alternatives based upon the risk to 'society'. These concerns did not suggest a rejection of policies of repression, but rather reflected an effort to provide long-term solutions to the problem of burgeoning penal populations during crises in the political economy. Thus, sentencing policies were modified by the extensive use of probation, local jail terms and fines. The indeterminate sentence and parole were adopted principally by the industrialized states to provide flexibility in the management of the prison.

Similarly, in the area of juvenile delinquency, programs such as the Chicago Area and Cambridge–Somerville projects sought to ameliorate the personal and social conditions which were considered responsible for crime. Significantly, it was during the 1930s Depression that programs in re-education and delinquency prevention proliferated; these included vocational training, recreation and social casework. Many of these programs, however, were privately funded; not until the post-World War II era did the state formally adopt a penal policy of corrections.

It is instructive to examine the practical consequences of this policy in California because it was here that liberal reforms and the treatment ideology were first institutionalized. California has the distinction of having one of the largest penal systems in the world. The prisons were reorganized and their administration centralized during the 1940s. The newly created Department of Corrections rapidly expanded the prison system to accommodate the increase in prisoners from 5501 in 1945 to 13,896 in 1955 and to over 17,000 in 1960.

The 1950s were a relatively prosperous period, due to the stimulation of the economy by defense and defense-related spending. However, prison officials had recognized as early as the mid-1940s that massive unemployment and marginalization were a long-term feature of the postwar economy. During this period, the ranks of the surplus army of labor increased dramatically, especially among the thousands of blacks and Chicanos who had been recruited during the war to work in the shipyards, steel plants and agricultural industries. Many of these workers were replaced by returning servicemen, but many more became technologically unemployed. While they were welcome to live in temporary housing units so long as their labor increased capital, they were thrown out at the end of World War II and cast aside as so much surplus population into the new and old ghettos.

During the 1950s, in apparent response to a growing heroin epidemic and an increase in crimes of violence, prisoners in California were subjected to longer and mandatory sentences for specific crimes. By 1965, for example, the total prison population, including juveniles and women, reached 26,483. Plans to construct new prisons were shelved as the economy began to deteriorate again. Despite a decline in commitment rates (due to the extensive use of probation, local jail sentences and fines) pressures on the prison system increased as the penal population climbed to over 28,000 in 1968. Here, then, we begin to find cracks in the liberal strategy.

The Department of Corrections attempted several solutions to the growing penal population. (1) Early parole release to small caseloads was introduced. (2) Subsidies were given to the counties to encourage local supervision as an alternative to imprisonment. (3) Distinctions were made between different levels of criminal activity (for example, marijuana from heroin use, possession from sale of drugs, etc.) with a view to keeping less serious offenders out of prison. (4) Within the prison system itself, treatment programs were intensified.

Experimental programs in treatment were introduced in 1951. While evaluation studies of the treatment model produced equivocal findings, it quickly spread to other operations in the prison system: parole, vocational training, housing units, half-way house programs, etc. Although treatment programs were never implemented on a system-wide basis, the treatment ideology was employed to legitimate and facilitate the bureaucratic management of prisoners.[42] The Department of Corrections vigorously promoted a rhetoric of treatment even though, as early as the mid-1950s, research findings discredited the effectiveness of rehabilitative efforts.[43]

While these short-term solutions slowed down the growth of the resident penal population, they could not avert the growing crisis. The urban rebellions of the early 1960s, the increase in prison revolts, the failure of treatment programs and the killing of prisoners by 'correctional officers' in the most 'innovative and progressive' penal system in the United States – all of this jarred the sensibilities of even the most liberal penologists and demonstrated once and for all the bankruptcy of liberalism.

Meanwhile, these developments in California were being closely observed by the National Council on Crime and Delinquency, a liberal technocratic organization, supported by corporate and government funds. In 1963, Milton Rector, director of the NCCD, recommended adoption of their Model Sentencing Act which attempted to distinguish 'dangerous' from 'non-dangerous' offenders. The purpose of the Act was to develop new sentencing procedures whereby the majority of offenders could be routed into some form of noninstitutional supervision, thus taking some pressure off the prisons. Only a few states adopted the Model Sentencing Act. After the prison rebellions in California and New York, Rector called for a moratorium on prison construction and observed that 'the recent riots and strikes that were reactions to repressive treatment would not have occurred' if these states had adopted the Model Sentencing Act.[44] This was wishful thinking on Rector's part. While the Act appeared in the short run to reduce prison populations, the evidence indicates that states which adopted the Act are well above the national median in their incarceration rates.

By 1971, a number of liberal organizations began to comment on the horrors of the prison system. Perhaps the most influential critique, based on the number of citations it has received in other books, is *Struggle for Justice*, written by the American Friends Service Committee. This book, written with a utopian faith 'in the ability of groups and individuals to grow and perfect the quality and conditions of their lives together',[45] advocates a 'justice model', which was later more fully developed by David Fogel as a prescription for a new penal practice.[46] The 'justice model' assumes that democratic ideals and a just social order can be achieved through the 'rule of law'; and that the problems in criminal justice – especially the arbitrary acts of functionaries which 'trigger' prison rebellions – can be ameliorated by legislating precise legal and administrative guidelines for officials.

At the national level, the National Moratorium on Prison Construction, with interlocking ties with the NCCD, is perhaps the most important liberal organization opposed to the building of new prisons. The Moratorium group, primarily church-based, while humanistic in its analysis of crime and punishment, naively advocates increased employment as an alternative to imprisonment. The creation of new jobs is, of course, a reasonable demand, but the National Moratorium does not understand the necessity of unemployment and repression under capitalism, nor the iron law governing the relationship between the accumulation of capital and the accumulation of misery.[47]

At the same time that the NCCD and National Moratorium have taken public positions against further construction of new prisons, they continue to advocate and legitimate internal reforms of existing prisons. NCCD, through its director Milton Rector, and the National Moratorium, through spokesperson William Nagel, both participated in the National Advisory Commission on Criminal Justice Standards and Goals. The Commission's publication, *Corrections*, basically rationalizes the elaboration of penal powers into a familiar criminal justice model. It portrays the prison as a self-contained phenomenon, arguing that its conflicts and contradictions can be resolved through administrative intervention. It recommends a 'non-discriminatory, just and humane foundation that honors the legal and social rights of its clients' – in short, a justice model and 'system solution', to be achieved by excluding sociomedical problem cases from corrections, by developing community-based programs, by manpower training and by increased citizen involvement.[48] It is not only a familiar refrain but also one which has the support of leading 'realists' such as Norval Morris and Gordon Hawkins.[49] Unlike the utopian liberals, however, the 'realists' have no illusions about reforming the criminal justice apparatus. Moreover, they have very concrete proposals for dealing with crime, 'street' criminals and prisoners.

The new 'realists'

Van den Haag, Wilson and other new 'realists' are indignant and outraged at the ineffectiveness and sloppiness of the police, courts and prisons. Contemptuous, on the one hand, towards the state bureaucrats who administer the criminal justice apparatus, on the other hand they are not to be outdone for bloodthirstiness or calculated viciousness. Some common themes and assumptions give the new 'realists' a unity of interest and purpose.

1. Focus on 'street' crime

The new 'realists' focus almost exclusively on those crimes which are either specific to or concentrated primarily within the working class. The 'crime problem' is defined almost exclusively as 'street' crime, i.e., working-class crime, i.e., black community crime in particular. Norval Morris and Gordon Hawkins put it this way:

> We must get our priorities clear: violent and predatory crime are what matter most. The police and the courts must be set free [*sic*] to concentrate their resources on dealing with such crime . . . This is not only because these crimes harm particular individuals and represent the citizens' prime fears. It is also because they threaten our cities and destroy our sense of community.[50]

James Q. Wilson limits his book to 'predatory crime for gain, the most common forms of which are robbery, burglary, larceny, and auto theft'. Here is his justification:

> This book deals neither with 'white-collar crimes' nor, except for heroin addiction, with so-called 'victimless crimes'. Partly this reflects the limits of my own knowledge, but it also reflects my

conviction, which I believe is the conviction of most citizens, that predatory street crime is a far more serious matter than consumer fraud, antitrust violations, prostitution, or gambling, because predatory crime . . . makes difficult or impossible the maintenance of meaningful human communities.[51]

Van den Haag dispenses with any justification and treats street crime as if it was the only kind. 'Corporate crime', 'business crime', 'white-collar crime', etc., are not listed in the index, not even under 'crime'. Wilks and Martinson at least admit that their proposal for hiring citizens to spy on convicted felons might not be appropriate for persons convicted of stock swindles and tax frauds. 'The realistic threat of punishment', they suggest, 'and a high degree of certainty of punishment plus restraint (resulting from surveillance), tools which we use successfully every day to control our children, our co-workers, and those we encounter on the street, might be effectively used as methods for controlling *street crime* within the framework of a democratic value system.'[52]

What is remarkable in this literature is that the authors dogmatically assert their definition of crime without apology or explanation. They take the most backward, the most reactionary and the most ignorant attitude to crime, justify it as a popular mancare ('these crimes . . . represent the citizens' *prime* fears'), and don't even bother to discuss the overwhelming evidence relating to corporate and state crimes.

We agree, however, that street crime is a serious and demoralizing problem which depreciates the quality of life in working-class communities, and fosters racism and other divisions in such communities. We do not wish to glorify or romanticize street crime as a form of primitive political rebellion. Unlike the 'realists', on the other hand, we do not think that street crime is the 'prime' reason why the cities are threatened or urban life is not 'meaningful'. Nor can street crime be set apart from the historical processes which marginalize millions of people into unemployment and dead-end jobs. 'While crime of course predates modern capitalist development', we noted earlier, 'the systematic reproduction of exploitative social relations (which is at the heart of criminal conduct) flourishes under advanced capitalism in a far more extensive and brutalizing form than was possible in pre-capitalist society.'[53]

2. *Anti-intellectualism*

The new 'realists' are basically uninterested in the causes of crime. For them, it's a side issue, a distraction and a waste of their valuable time. 'Fascinating as they are, there is little need here to go further into theories of crime causation', writes van den Haag. 'They do help to make the occurrence and frequency of criminal conduct intelligible. But none promises to tell much that can be applied to crime control . . . '[54] Morris and Hawkins's opportunistically titled *Letter to the President on Crime Control* notes in the introduction that crime and delinquency 'respond to deeper social, cultural, and political currents beyond the substantial influence of the criminal justice system'.[55] This is their *only* statement on the causes of crime. In the next 89 pages, there are numerous proposals for crime control but not a word about those 'deeper currents'. Similarly, James Q. Wilson dismisses as utopian the search for the causes of crime:

I have yet to see a 'root cause' or to encounter a government program that has successfully attacked it, at least with respect to those social problems that arise out of human volition rather than technological malfunctions. But more importantly, the demand for causal solutions is, whether intended or not, a way of deferring any action and criticizing any policy . . . Though intellectually rewarding, from a practical point of view it is a mistake to think about crime in terms of its 'causes' and then to search for ways of alleviating those causes. We must think instead of what it is feasible for a government or a community to do . . .[56]

While unabashedly pragmatic and anti-intellectual in their approach, the new 'realists' feel some obligation and necessity to destroy the nexus between poverty and crime. If, as they claim, crime is not related to class or race, then they cannot be accused of being anti-working class or racist. Van den Haag, with typical disregard for the facts, conveniently solves the problem by asserting that poverty is on the decline while crime is on the rise:

The trend toward equalization has pervaded the income structure as a whole, although its steepness has varied in different periods and in different segments of the structure. There is less relative poverty, less poverty, and a smaller proportion of poor than twenty, fifty, or a hundred years ago . . . Crime rates have risen as poverty and inequality have declined.[57]

Not surprisingly, van den Haag is unable to document this fantasy.[58]

James Q. Wilson's approach is slightly more sophisticated but just as ignorant. He too is irritated by the economic reformers. 'Crime rose fastest in this country at a time when the number of persons living in poverty or squalor was declining . . . Early in the decade of the 1960s, this country began the longest sustained period of prosperity since World War II [*sic*] . . . Crime soared.'[59] And just in case Wilson's argument is disputed, he adds for good measure the following undocumented comment, which is completely unsupported by the available evidence:

> The theory that crime is an expression of the political rage of the dispossessed, rebelling under the iron heel of capitalist tyranny, leaves one wondering why virtually every nation in the world, capitalist, socialist, and communist, has experienced in recent years rapidly increasing crime rates.[60]

Having thus extracted 'crime' from the political economy, Wilson then argues that 'lower-class' (as opposed to 'lower-income') persons are inherently criminal because they 'attach little importance to the opinion of others', are 'preoccupied with the daily struggle for survival', and are 'inclined to uninhibited, expressive conduct'.[61]

Given that this statement is made under the heading of 'Poverty, Race and Community', it is fair to assume that Wilson is talking about blacks. He is quick to point out, however, that he would like to give the good blacks a chance to escape from the bad blacks. 'The real price of segregation, in my opinion, is not that it forces blacks and whites apart but that it forces blacks of different class positions together.'[62] If 'lower-*income*' blacks are allowed to move to the suburbs, concludes Wilson, the process of 'acculturation' into the superior cultural values of the white suburbs will mean a lower crime rate.[63] For those who voluntarily remain 'lower-*class*' and incorrigible, Wilson and the other 'realists' propose a tiered and systematic program of punishments.

3. Punishing criminals

There is general agreement among the new 'realists' that 'wicked people exist. Nothing avails except to set them apart from innocent people. And many people, neither wicked nor innocent, but watchful, dissembling, and calculating of their opportunities, ponder our reaction to wickedness as a cue to what they might profitably do. We have trifled with the wicked, made sport of the innocent, and encouraged the calculators'.[64] There is also general agreement that the criminal justice apparatus is chaotic and ineffective. For van den Haag, this is the result of a 'worldwide decline in punishment and therewith of respect for law',[65] for Wilson, it's a combination of ignorance and soft-heartedness; for Morris and Hawkins, it's the federal government's failure to understand 'predatory crime' as 'the most potent threat to the American way of life';[66] and for Wilks and Martinson, it's because the 'treatment and incarceration' apologists are always bickering.

While sharing a unity of moral outrage and contempt for criminal justice bureaucrats, the 'realists' promote their own particular remedies. They range from uncompromising advocates of capital punishment to cost-benefit proponents of penal sanctions. The former camp includes van den Haag, who would like some criminals to be permanently imprisoned ('post-punishment incapacitation') and others banished, exiled or held under house arrest,[67] and Marlene Lehtinen, who proposes that capital punishment can only be an effective deterrent if at least 3000 persons are executed a year:

> The system has operated to execute men, blacks, the ignorant, and the poor. A system designed to apply the death penalty non-discriminatorily would probably execute a far greater number of such persons, simply because the crimes that call for execution are most frequently committed by them.[68]

The latter camp seems to include a number of criminologists who secretly always aspired to be accountants. For them, it's all a matter of 'cost-benefit ratios' and calculating cheap and effective deterrents. The technocratic literature on this topic has grown enormously within the last few years.[69] Prompted by overcrowded prisons, an unprecedented wave of prisoner rebellions and the impact of the fiscal crisis on public sector spending, there has been a revival of interest in strategies of deterrence, in methods of breaking up the prison population (e.g., 'adjustment centers', methadone, diversion, etc.) and in cutting costs (e.g., decriminalization of 'victimless' crimes, capital punishment, community surveillance, etc.). As Wilson puts it, 'we can confine a larger proportion of the serious and repeat offenders and fewer of the common drunks and truant children. We know [sic] that confining criminals prevents them from harming society, and we have grounds for suspecting that some would-be criminals can be deterred by the confinement of others'.[70] Similarly, Morris and Hawkins advocate increased diversion for youthful 'status' offenders and the construction of more 'experimental' prisons like Butner for 'serious' offenders.[71]

Class position

We have described the emergence and parameters of a new 'realist school' in criminology which, in a relatively short period of time, has come to dominate the professional literature and influence legislative policy. Though the 'realists' have met with opposition from utopian advocates of the 'justice model' and prison moratorium, the two groups share a basic acceptance of the capitalist mode of production and the necessity for technocratic solutions to the current penal crisis. And, as we have shown, there is considerable agreement between the 'realists' and liberals on specific proposals such as decriminalization of 'victimless' crimes, standardizing correctional programs and making 'treatment' in prison voluntary.[72]

It is not surprising that the leading intellectuals in criminology are articulating and promoting racist and anti-working-class policies. The social sciences in North American universities have *always* legitimated the ruling ideology of monopoly capital and ruthlessly excluded or repressed any serious study of Marxism.[73] Criminology, with its particularly close ties to the state apparatus, was originally developed as a science of repression,[74] and the long-standing collaboration between criminology and the state has been even more strongly cemented in recent years with the help of massive investments and subsidies from the federal government and corporate think tanks.[75]

But these material forces do not *by themselves* adequately explain why criminology has taken such a sharp and decisive turn to the right, why the traditionally liberal search for the *causes* of crime is being abandoned, or why the wolves have discarded their sheep's clothing and pious bleatings. The reason perhaps for this qualitative shift lies in the increasing irreconcilability between capitalism and liberalism. Liberal ideology traditionally assumes that capitalism can ultimately provide both a minimum level of material benefits (housing, food, health care, etc.) and political freedoms (equality, justice, speech, etc.) for all its citizens. But, as we have discussed earlier, the crisis in the political economy has generated unprecedented levels of misery and a deterioration in the quality of life at a time when capitalism has reached its highest level of maturity.

The demise of liberal penal policy is a reflection of the failure of the liberal democratic state to manage the crisis in the political economy and a recognition by high-level state functionaries (and their surrogates in the academy) of capitalism's limitations. This contradiction between the realities of capitalism and the professed ideals of liberalism can no longer be mystified; the state is required to develop new strategies of coercion which, while superficially aimed at street crime, serve as a warning against both political dissent and attacks on existing property relations. New measures of exploitation and repression require new rationales; it is in this context that we can make sense of the ideological content and class position of the new 'realists'.

There are at least three important, unifying elements in the 'realists'' ideology: (1) promotion of the state; (2) moral outrage and cynicism; and (3) elitism and hatred of the working class.

1. Promotion of the state

Throughout the writings of the new 'realists' can be found criticisms of and impatience with the state, occasional attacks on the privileges of the ruling class and a concern for preserving democratic, i.e., constitutional, values. Morris and Hawkins, for example, begin their *Letter to the President* with a critique of the federal government's failure to control crime. Wilson complains that 'the rise in power of organized police and correctional officers and the continued power of tenured judges, powers which, though for many purposes quite desirable, have come to constitute a serious impediment to progress'.[76] Wilks and Martinson go to great lengths to defend their proposal against charges of 'big brotherism':

> Is it 'big brother' to expect offenders to obey duly enacted laws? . . . Relief from punishment can be gained as long as the offender avoids criminal behavior. Relief from punishment is not determined by his successful completion of treatment (e.g., learning to read, keeping a job). His behavior relative to criminal law, and this behavior alone, would determine whether the State will punish him. This, after all, is the essence of democracy.[77]

Since the 'realists', like intellectuals in general, regard themselves as *independent* critics of the social order, they have harsh words for everybody, including criminal justice functionaries. But beneath this veneer of negativism lies a deep appreciation and promotion of the capitalist state. All the 'realists' recommend an expansion and refinement of the repressive apparatus. 'Our program', write Morris and Hawkins, 'is designed primarily to ensure that [criminal justice] agencies *as presently constituted* operate more efficiently as instruments of social protection.' To this end, they recommend increased involvement by the federal government and more police for the ghettos and barrios.[78] Van den Haag believes that the state, once unshackled from the constraints of legal niceties, can restore order and respect for law. And even Wilks and Martinson, for all their contempt for criminal justice bureaucrats, would like the government to hire 'restraining agents' to report 'to the police whenever a restrainee is observed committing a criminal offense'.[79]

Whatever reservations the 'realists' may have about the competency and intelligence of criminal justice functionaries, they have a basic faith in the state's ability to restore social stability. As members of the petty bourgeoisie, intellectuals identify their own class interests with those of the state, whose 'neutrality it supposes to be akin to its own, since it sees itself as a "neutral" class between the bourgeoisie and the working class, and therefore a pillar of the State – *its* State. It aspires to be the "arbitrator" of society, because, as Marx says, it would like the whole of society to become petty-bourgeois'.[80] Thus, the 'realists' attempt not only to bring order to what for them is a precarious world but also to promote a program of law and order in which they will play a key role.

2. Moral outrage and cynicism

The 'realists' are morally outraged at the forces of crime and disorder which threaten *their* safety. 'If we represent anyone other than ourselves', write Wilks and Martinson, 'it is the residents of the Central Park Precinct who feel compelled to place police locks on their doors and safety grates over their windows.'[81] In a similar vein, Morris, Hawkins, Wilson and others lament the breakdown of neighborhood controls and the passing of 'the community'.[82] At the same time, however, the 'realists' typically express a cynicism and futility about the possibility of change. As an 'intermediate' class with close ties to the bourgeoisie, they understand a great deal about the realities of power and their dependency on the ruling class for all significant economic and political decisions.

Stephen Zelnick, writing in another context about disillusioned literary intellectuals, accurately captures the vacillation and confusion of the new 'realists'. 'Because of its identification with the ruling class to which it does not belong', he writes, 'it produces the most illusory thinking, the most wayward imagination, and experiences the most intense neurotic problems. The petty bourgeoisie is especially likely to think, imagine, and feel in a fantastic manner because it does not participate directly in determining the essential course of reality . . . It perceives the world through exhilarating fantasy alternating with nervous anticipation of doom.'[83]

Look, for example, at how the 'realists' appreciate the futility of their proposals:

> We cannot alter the number of juveniles who first experiment with minor crimes. We cannot lower the recidivism rate, though within reason we should keep trying. We are not yet certain whether we can increase significantly the police apprehension rate. We may be able to change the teenage unemployment rate, though we have learned by painful trial and error that doing this is much more difficult than once supposed.[84]

> Many of our recommendations, although desirable, will make no more than a marginal difference to the incidence of crime or juvenile delinquency.[85]

> Crime always will remain with us . . . The issue is how best to control and minimize crime . . .[86]

It is this basic cynicism, coupled with grandiose schemes of punishment, that often leads the 'realists' to bizarre and irrational solutions. Van den Haag, for example, nostalgically calls for the return of exile and banishment, presumably in anticipation of settling new territories in space.[87] Similarly, Wilks and Martinson, despite their reputation as rigorous empiricists, would like to put offenders under secret surveillance by 'restraining agents . . . equipped with a camera in order to obtain meaningful evidence'.[88]

3. Elitism and hatred of the working class

Since the 'realists' blame the working class (and not capitalism) for the rise in crime, it is not surprising that they oppose even token concessions to 'participatory democracy'. Wilson finds it absurd that prisoners might be allowed to organize unions and participate in 'decisions as to whether any changes are to be made in the purposes and methods of prisons'.[89] And van den Haag is convinced that the penal crisis is caused in large part by the 'laissez-faire' attitude of prison officials who allow prisoners to run the institutions![90]

The anti-working-class attitudes of the 'realists' are also revealed in their paternalistic approach to state workers. Wilson, for example, emphasizes the need for the careful training of the police and the screening out of 'bad apples', as though the most brutal and racist police officer or guard could even approach the level of viciousness advocated by the 'realists'. Wilson, through his work for the Police (Ford) Foundation, has supported the 'Taylorization' of police work: the concentration of all phases of control of police work in the hands of high-level administrators at the expense of the rank and file. This increases the state's ability to dominate all aspects of police work through highly rewarded and loyal managers, rather than trusting the officers on the beat who face long hours, irregular shifts, poor working conditions, job insecurity and a justifiably angry citizenry.

The rhetoric of the 'war on poverty', with its emphasis on 'maximum feasible participation', has been replaced by the cult of technological efficiency, in which the intellectual occupies a central position. All the 'realists' advocate an expanded role for the technical–professional strata and further research and experimentation. This self-serving attitude reveals a deep fear of being displaced or replaced by the proletariat. For them, there is no belief in the potentiality for human freedom, no enthusiasm for the militant struggles and sacrifices of a defiant working class, and no inspiration from the great revolutionary movements of our time. On the contrary, there is simply a grim determination to hold the line and add new fortifications to the garrison state.

Conclusion

The ideological repertoire of the new 'realists' is typical of the petty bourgeoisie in crisis. Faced on the one side by an increasingly militant and organized working class, and on the other by the pressures of inflation and rising unemployment in the professional strata, the 'new middle class' feels itself 'beleaguered and pressed from all sides'.[91] In the absence of resolute control by the working-class movement, the discontent and alienation of the petty bourgeoisie is more likely to be exploited by the bourgeoisie, as the history of fascism reveals.[92]

There are many elements of the new 'realists'' ideology which recall fascist trends in penal policy in Germany at the beginning of the 1930s depression. Under fascism, 'considerable effort is spent in cultivating a moral distinction between those who are poor but honest and the strata which have become criminal'. The purpose of this tactic is to create divisions within the working class and to encourage the working class to accept a lower standard of living, necessitated by inflation and economic crisis. Under fascism also, punishments became more brutal, in the form of increasing use of the death penalty and longer and more severe sentences. As Rusche and Kirchheimer noted, 'the judge is subjected to strong pressure from above to intensify punishments on the grounds that the authority of the state must be defended . . . Increasing severity of punishment is in the first instance a change in criminal policy conditioned by economic crisis'. Finally, penal policy in fascist Germany eliminated sociological considerations from criminal procedure so that information about a defendant's social milieu and personal history were *not* considered in determining the form of punishment.[93]

These developments in fascist penal policy have their parallel today in Wilson's and van den Haag's efforts to classify and isolate the 'criminal' strata; in the legislation of mandatory punishments, definite sentences and the death penalty; and in the adoption of formal, mechanistic models of sentencing, typified by California's new laws and the National Council on Crime and Delinquency's Model Sentencing Act.

While contradictions exist among leading criminologists and they are by no means organized or monolithic, there is increasing programmatic unity between the utopian liberals and the new 'realists', their rhetorical antagonisms to the contrary. The economic and political crisis of the 1970s has forced liberal criminologists to make a choice. In the past, liberals typically argued that crime is related to economic conditions and that it is possible to reduce the level of crime through economic and social reforms. This presumed that capitalism had the capacity to both solve fundamental social problems and avoid crisis.

With deteriorating economic conditions and widespread political dissent in the 1970s, the liberals' faith in stability and progress has been profoundly shaken. Writing in *Society*, Isidore Silver observes that liberalism (the 'belief that government can mediate between rich and poor') and the 'liberal democratic state' are under attack from the left and right. 'The rest of us', he complains, 'are caught in the middle. Yet there should be no illusions. We are still wed to working out our criminal justice problems within that broad middle.'[94]

Yet this is precisely the voice of illusion, self-deception and nostalgia. It desperately assumes the independence of liberals as a 'middle' force; it totally ignores the reality of a criminal justice apparatus moving rapidly to the right; and it incorrectly argues that 'radicals' are responsible for the current crisis. While Silver exhorts his colleagues to hold on in the middle, there are realistically only two choices. As criminologists we can join the new 'realists' in blaming the working class, especially black and brown people, for the crime problem (as the bourgeoisie blames the working class for the economic crisis) and help to devise new methods of punishment and control. Or we can continue to investigate the relationship between crime and the political economy, and put our skills in the service of working-class struggles against exploitation and repression.

It would be a mistake to write off the 'realists' as aberrant cranks. They are a decisive influence in criminology and their ideas and programs are very much on the rise. With the deepening crisis of world capitalism and increasing militancy and organization within the U.S. proletariat, the petty bourgeoisie assumes crucial functions of legitimation and administration. While very much preoccupied with defending *their own* class privileges from the terrors of the 'proletarian abyss', the petty bourgeoisie can only be successful in this enterprise (albeit in the short run) if they operate as 'loyal subordinates' and 'transmission agents' of the bourgeoisie.[95] The 'realists' represent that fraction of the petty bourgeoisie whose 'frenzied desperation' propels them toward 'fascist forms of reaction in the bitter illusion that the material comfort and security of the past can be restored'.[96] Intellectuals for law and order are not a criminological fad. They are an indication of the changing form of class relations and class struggle in the United States.

Notes

1. Ernest van den Haag, *Punishing Criminals* (New York: Basic Books, 1975).
2. See, for example, Clarence Schrag's review of *Punishing Criminals* in *Criminology*, 14 (February, 1977) 569–73.
3. Theodore Chiricos and Gordon Waldo, 'Socioeconomic Status and

Criminal Sentencing: An Empirical Assessment of a Conflict Proposition', *American Sociological Review*, 40 (1975) 753–72.

4. Travis Hirchi and Michael Hindelang, 'Intelligence and Delinquency: A Revisionist Review', *American Sociological Review*, 42 (1977) 571–87.

5. Many of these articles (including those by Gary Becker and Isaac Ehrlich) are collected in Lee McPheters and William Stronge (eds), *The Economics of Crime and Law Enforcement* (Springfield: Charles C. Thomas, 1976).

6. Edward Banfield, *The Unheavenly City* (Boston: Little, Brown, 1972); James Q. Wilson, *Thinking About Crime* (New York: Vintage, 1977).

7. Judith Wilks and Robert Martinson, 'Is the Treatment of Criminal Offenders Really Necessary?', *Federal Probation*, 40 (March 1976) 3–9.

8. Marlene Lehtinen, 'The Value of Life: An Argument for the Death Penalty', *Crime and Delinquency*, 23 (July 1977) 237–52.

9. See, for example, 'Kids Who Kill for Kicks', *Time* (11 July 1977); 'Criminals Belong in Jail', *Washington Monthly* (January 1976); and 'Big Change in Prisons: Punish – Not Reform', *U.S. News and World Report* (25 August 1975).

10. Jackson Toby, 'Open-Ended Sentence', *New York Times* (15 January 1973).

11. See 'The Demise of Liberalism' ahead.

12. Mao Tse-tung, *Four Essays on Philosophy* (Peking: Foreign Languages Press, 1966) 2–3.

13. Center for Research on Criminal Justice, *The Iron Fist and the Velvet Glove* (Berkeley: Center for Research on Criminal Justice, 1977) 7–9.

14. U.S. Dept. of Justice, *Trends in Expenditure and Employment Data for the Criminal Justice System, 1971–1975* (Washington, D.C.: U.S. Government Printing Office, 1977).

15. Center for Research on Criminal Justice, op. cit., 7.

16. Ibid.

17. Ibid., 50.

18. Center for National Security Studies, *Law and Disorder IV* (Washington, D.C.:Center for National Security Studies, 1976) 4.

19. Ibid., 30.

20. U.S. Dept. of Justice, *Criminal Victimization in the United States: A Comparison of 1973 and 1974 Findings* (Washington, D.C.: U.S. Government Printing Office, 1976).

21. George Kelling *et al.*, *The Kansas City Preventive Patrol Experiment* (Washington, D.C.: The Police Foundation, 1974); Thomas Pogue, 'The Effect of Police Expenditures on Crime Rates', *Public Finance Quarterly*, 3, 1 (January 1975); Robert Seidman and Michael Couzens, 'Getting the Crime Rate Down: Political Pressure and Crime Reporting', *Law and Society Review* (Spring 1974).

22. U.S. Dept. of Justice, *Prisoners in State and Federal Institutions on*

December 31, 1975 (Washington, D.C.: U.S. Government Printing Office, 1977) 1.

23. Rosemary C. Sarri, *Under Lock and Key: Juveniles in Jails and Detention* (University of Michigan: National Assessment of Juvenile Corrections, 1974) 65.

24. Irwin Silber, 'Will the "Recovery" End up on the Rocks?', *Guardian* (27 October 1976) 4.

25. Robert B. Carson, 'Youthful Labor Surplus in Disaccumulationist Capitalism', *Socialist Revolution*, 9 (May–June 1972) 37, 40.

26. National Urban League, *Black Families in the 1974–1975 Depression* (Washington, D.C.: National Urban League, 1975).

27. Kevin Kelley, 'Poverty: Worse for Minorities', *Guardian* (27 October 1976) 7.

28. Harry Braverman, *Labor and Monopoly Capital: The Degradation of Work in the Twentieth Century* (New York: Monthly Review Press, 1974) 386.

29. Karl Marx, *Capital*, Vol. I (New York: International Publishers, 1975) 632.

30. Ibid., 643.

31. Ibid., 644–5.

32. Braverman, op. cit., 389.

33. Marx, op. cit., 645. For a more extensive discussion of this proposition for contemporary capitalism, see Braverman, op. cit., 386–402.

34. According to Marx, op. cit., 640–8, the relative surplus population also includes the *floating* sector, who are 'attracted' to and 'repelled' from the labor force according to movements of technology and capital, and the *latent* sector, who are made redundant by changes in agricultural technology and compelled to seek employment in the centers of capitalist industry.

35. Ibid., 644.

36. Braverman, op. cit., 279–80.

37. Georg Rusche and Otto Kirchheimer, *Punishment and Social Structure* (New York: Russell and Russell, 1967).

38. For a discussion of the persistence of this mode of punishment in the South, see Thorsten Sellin, *Slavery and the Penal System* (New York: Elsevier, 1976).

39. Harvey Brenner, *Estimating the Social Costs of National Economic Policy* (Washington, D.C.: U.S. Government Printing Office, 1976).

40. William G. Nagel, 'On Behalf of a Moratorium on Prison Construction', *Crime and Delinquency*, 23, 2 (April 1977) 154–72.

41. Much of the following discussion is based on unpublished research by Paul Takagi.

42. See, for example, Richard Speiglman, 'Prison Psychiatrists and Drugs: A Case Study', *Crime and Social Justice*, 7 (Spring – Summer 1977) 23–39.

43. See, for example, Helen Witmer and Edith Tuft, *The Effectiveness of*

Delinquency Prevention Programs (Washington, D.C.: Children's Bureau, 1954); W. C. Bailey, 'Correctional Outcome: An Evaluation of 100 Reports', *Journal of Criminal Law, Criminology and Police Science* (1966), originally presented to the California Department of Corrections in 1959.

44. Milton Rector, 'Model Sentencing Act', *Crime and Delinquency*, 18 (October 1972) 337.

45. American Friends Service Committee, *Struggle for Justice* (New York: Hill and Wang, 1971) v.

46. David Fogel, *We Are the Living Proof . . .* (Cincinnati: W. H. Anderson, 1975).

47. See, for example, the newsletter of the National Moratorium on Prison Construction, *Jericho* (May – June 1977) Washington, D.C.

48. National Advisory Commission on Criminal Justice Standards and Goals, *Corrections* (Washington, D.C.: U.S. Government Printing Office, 1973).

49. Norval Morris, *The Future of Imprisonment* (Chicago: University of Chicago Press, 1974); Norval Morris and Gordon Hawkins, *Letter to the President on Crime Control* (Chicago: University of Chicago Press, 1977).

50. Morris and Hawkins, op. cit., 8, 13–14.

51. Wilson, op. cit., xx.

52. Wilks and Martinson, op. cit., 8. Emphasis added.

53. 'The Politics of Street Crime', *Crime and Social Justice*, 5 (Spring–Summer 1976) 1–4.

54. Van den Haag, op. cit., 77–8.

55. Morris and Hawkins, op. cit., 7.

56. Wilson, op. cit., xv, 233.

57. Van den Haag, op. cit., 91, 102.

58. For an alternative and thoroughly documented analysis, see Harry Braverman, *Labor and Monopoly Capital*, loc. cit.

59. Wilson, op. cit., xiii–xiv, 4.

60. Ibid., xiii.

61. Ibid., 41–2.

62. Ibid., 39.

63. Ibid., 42–4.

64. Van den Haag, op. cit., 235–6.

65. Ibid., 155.

66. Morris and Hawkins, op. cit., 7–8.

67. Van den Haag, op. cit., 241–61.

68. Lehtinen, op. cit., 247.

69. For an overview of this literature, see Jan Palmer, 'Economic Analysis of the Deterrent Effect of Punishment: A Review', *Journal of Research in Crime and Delinquency*, 14 (January 1977) 4–21.

70. Wilson, op. cit., 234.

71. See, for example, Norval Morris, *The Future of Imprisonment* (University of Chicago Press, 1974).
72. See, for example, *Corrections*, loc. cit.
73. See, for example, Herman and Julia Schwendinger, *The Sociologists of the Chair* (New York: Basic Books, 1974); Marlene Dixon, 'Professionalism in the Social Sciences', *Sociological Inquiry*, 46 (1976) 251–62.
74. Tony Platt, 'Prospects for a Radical Criminology in the United States', *Crime and Social Justice*, 1 (Spring–Summer 1974) 2–10.
75. Center for Research on Criminal Justice, *The Iron Fist and the Velvet Glove*, loc. cit.
76. Wilson, op. cit., xix.
77. Wilks and Martinson, op. cit., 8–9.
78. Morris and Hawkins, op. cit., 13–14. Emphasis added.
79. Wilks and Martinson, op. cit., 6.
80. Nicos Poulantzas, *Fascism and Dictatorship* (London: NLB, 1974) 241.
81. Wilks and Martinson, op. cit., 3.
82. See, for example, Wilson, op. cit., 27–8.
83. Stephen Zelnick, 'The Incest Theme in "The Great Gatsby": The False Poetry of Petty Bourgeois Consciousness', in Norman Rudich (ed.), *Weapons of Criticism* (Palo Alto: Ramparts Press, 1976) 329.
84. Wilson, op. cit., 233–4.
85. Morris and Hawkins, op. cit., 7.
86. Van den Haag, op. cit., 19–20.
87. Ibid., 256–7.
88. Wilks and Martinson, op. cit., 6.
89. Wilson, op. cit., xix.
90. Van den Haag, op. cit., 257–61.
91. Marlene Dixon, 'Proletarian versus Petty Bourgeois Socialism', *Synthesis*, 1 (Summer, 1976) 6.
92. See, for example, Poulantzas, op. cit., 237–46 and R. Palme Dutt, *Fascism and Social Revolution* (San Francisco: Proletarian Publishers, 1974), originally published in 1934.
93. Rusche and Kirchheimer, op. cit., 'New Trends in Penal Policy Under Fascism', 177–92.
94. Isidore Silver, 'Crime and Conventional Wisdom', *Society*, 14 (March–April 1977) 9–19.
95. Braverman, op. cit., 406.
96. Dixon, 'Proletarian versus Petty Bourgeois Socialism', op. cit., 18.

3
Social Class and the Definition of Crime

Herman Schwendinger and Julia Schwendinger

James Petras (1977) has analyzed bourgeois crimes that destabilized and then destroyed the democratic Chilean government.[1] He noted that these crimes were essentially class crimes and hence that 'no single group or groups acted [alone] to bring Allende down'. By distinguishing the 'three step flow' of organizations, events and criminal engagements, preparing the way for the fascist seizure of power, Petras performs a service for radical criminology.[2] His article also affirms certain historical generalizations. First, the struggle for socialism is confronted inevitably with counter-revolutionary bourgeois violence. Second, in light of the Chilean experience, reliance on bourgeois legality to defend socialist achievements is suicidal.

Petras's observations, about the judiciary and the police, support these generalizations. The criminal justice agencies, during Allende's presidency, did not vigorously prosecute or sanction the waves of crimes by bourgeois organizations against persons, property, and the state. Thus, while Allende called for the rule of law, the very agencies that were responsible for upholding this rule encouraged further crimes by their inaction.

Such observations remind us that the class composition and class functions of the state apparatus are not automatically transformed whenever a rising class and its allies are successful politically. The class struggle continues within the apparatus as well as outside of it. Consequently, whether the resources commanded by the state can be utilized effectively in favor of an ascendent class depends upon the outcome of the struggle for power within the state. In that struggle socialists may control one part of the government but not another. In Allende's case, socialists controlled the executive office; nevertheless, the police, judiciary and armed forces were still commanded by bourgeois functionaries. As a result, the class loyalties of police, judges and military commanders restricted Allende's ability to stabilize the country in the face of massive political crimes.

Therefore, when Allende called upon the nation to respect the rule of law in order to defend the democratic government, his words were ineffective. Legality, which is not always voluntaristic, is not backed by mystical forces; it is secured by the criminal justice system and the military. These vital centers of organized political violence embody dictatorial powers, and ultimately are predicated upon the dictatorship of the bourgeoisie or the proletariat. Under stable political conditions, such powers are signified by criminal laws and sanctions. Under unstable conditions, they include the full panoply of 'emergency powers' directly exerted by the armed forces as well as by the criminal justice system.

But Allende's emergency powers, which would have introduced martial law, preventive detention, and other measures, could not be exercised without the cooperation of the criminal justice system and the military. Allende, moreover, could not invoke emergency powers without risking civil war with substantial segments of the bourgeoisie, including elements in the military. Under these conditions, the requisite power to administer the government might have been maintained by reconstituting the social basis on which organized political violence is founded. Such a reconstitution would have involved the mobilization of popular justice movements, of progressive elements in the military and police, and of armed detachments of workers and their allies. This mobilization might then have provided the armed forces necessary for maintaining the integrity of his democratically elected government. But the refusal at the height of his powers to mobilize decisively such armed forces sealed off any possibility of successfully maintaining the government. In order to avoid civil war, Allende appears to have done little more than affirm the virtue of bourgeois legality.

Additional lessons, based on the realities rather than the myths of legality, are revealed by the Chilean developments. The rule of law, under varying circumstances, can serve different aims. For example, it is often regarded as a bulwark of democratic rights. On the other hand, as long as bourgeois property rights reign supreme, the rule of law is also a means for defending bourgeois property, the liberties based on this form of property, and the principles of state sovereignty that secure the political preconditions for the capitalist mode of production. Consequently, the rule of law is a means to 'higher' ends; and full dictatorial powers are invoked whenever bourgeois legality is considered inadequate for maintaining the foundations of bourgeois order.

Furthermore, whenever the defense of bourgeois property, liberties, etc., cannot be conducted legally, because of the balance of class forces within the state, then the robust, bourgeois 'civil society' – the realm of 'private interests' – which normally stands behind the state (Gramsci, 1971) moves vigorously to rectify this situation. The Chilean terrorists who defended bourgeois property, liberties, and political sovereignty, were part of such a civil society. Their acts were justified and reinterpreted in the name of *Fatherland and Liberty*. Therefore, such terrorist groups, for all their reactionary violence, are also ideological entities. Their political crimes repeatedly demonstrate the existence of a class morality that places certain economic and political rights and duties above democratic ideals.

The Chilean counter-revolutionaries regarded their violations of law to be morally justified by higher ends. By what standards can we then consider them criminals? Petras's article offers two criteria. The first is legalistic: the bourgeois terrorists are criminals because they violated the laws of a democratic government. The second criterion involves the relations between social harms and class interests: the bourgeois political acts are crimes because they are harmful to the interests of the working class.

These criteria raise a number of key questions. Is the criterion of legality generally necessary for delineating crimes – bourgeois political acts or, for that matter, any other crimes? We must not forget that under certain political circumstances the criterion of legality is ambiguous and even contradictory. There are genocidal and other social harms that are not legally classified as crimes because state power resides in the hands of a national bourgeoisie. Does this absence of a legal violation make these social harms less criminal?

In addition, there are certain bourgeois crimes, such as capitalist exploitation, that are prohibited by law in socialist societies. The designation of such acts as legal crimes certainly introduces important consideration into the analysis and control of social harms. Further, does the absence of socialist legal distinctions from bourgeois laws exclude these bourgeois harms from the roster of crimes within capitalist societies?

Answering these questions will be the central focus of this article. First, however, we must review some fundamentals about legal relations in bourgeois societies. The historical review that follows will place the definition of crime in a context that will clarify these and other issues posed by the downfall of the Allende government. This context involves such previously mentioned relationships as class control of the state or of its parts, the organized violence underlying legality, the independence of civil society from the state, the relation between individual liberties and class morality, and the role of individual rights in bourgeois society.

Legal relations and the bourgeoisie

Historically, the state originated because of the formation of class relations, and therefore every comprehensive system of laws is essentially determined by class factors. Legal or state definitions of crime are especially important because they maintain the interests of ruling classes by force. Such general interests are above all sustained by laws that guard the economic infrastructure of a political order. First and foremost, the infrastructure requires guarantees that a dominant set of social production relations will be reproduced.

In addition, although bourgeois production relations are generally identified with the ascending dominance of wage labor and capital, other social production relations were also secured by law in early bourgeois societies. For example, early bourgeois production relations were characterized by the exploitation of numerous and varied forms of labor including slave labor, forced labor and bonded labor as well as wage labor (Schwendinger and Schwendinger, 1976:11; Petras, 1976:22). Commodity production, which was based on slavery at that time, was introduced on a wide scale in the Caribbean and in the southern part of North America by the growth of world mercantile relations. Thereupon, colonial laws were written to guard production by slaves; moreover, later, though it was the first to recognize the universal rights of man, the American Constitution still protected slavery. In fact, slavery in the United States was guarded well into the Civil War until 1863 when the Emancipation became effective. Despite the legal status of slavery, Eugene V. Debs (1970) once remarked, 'The history of the Negro in the United States is a history of crime without a parallel'.

One can say that bourgeois laws themselves have undermined pre-existing production relations together with the customs, laws, and lives of people everywhere. For example, not only were slave relations secured by such laws but treaties were imposed on American Indian tribes legalizing the wholesale and violent theft of natural resources, and the transformation of these resources into bourgeois property. Other forced legal relations sustained the uneven terms of trade that favored the ruling classes in the United States and undermined class relations based on native industries in South America.

The reproduction of a class society guards the relations of production but it also secures another level of relationships based upon production relations. Since major institutions, such as the family and the state, are derived from and react back on production relations, they must also be protected and regulated by legal relations. Similarly, prohibitions against such acts as killing, rape, and incest are interrelated with the protection of these major institutions even though these acts appear to be based on characteristics that exist everywhere and always. Doubtless 'elementary rules of social life have been known for centuries', but they are not based on natural social-laws about fundamental properties of social organizations.[3] To the contrary, these rules are subordinated to social organizations (e.g., bourgeois family relations) that are created and modified by changes in modes of production as well as other relationships. Furthermore, such changes have substantially altered the contents of virtually all of these elementary rules. The greater proportion of contemporary killings take place during imperialist wars and in the course of 'business' (e.g., at the workplace) and are not prohibited by law at all (e.g., Swartz, 1975).

A few final points about the intricacies of class relations and legal definitions of crime are in order. Since civil and criminal laws generally secure the conditions for reproducing class relations, they represent state authority that is imposed by ruling classes upon social classes, tribal groups and colonial nations. Yet, although laws are generally instruments of a ruling class and/or its fractionated groups, the most important class interests that are fulfilled by legal relations cannot be defined by reference to the arbitrary will of sovereign powers or the special interests of ruling class fractions. The most relevant class interests are based on the conditions that reproduce the class system as a whole. Therefore, these class interests can only be represented by the general interests of a ruling class, which transcend the particular interests of ruling individuals or groups.

Legal relations when taken as a whole also have general characteristics that transcend their particular aspects. Individual laws are part of a system of laws that has core elements, sometimes called 'basic laws of the land' (e.g., constitutional laws), because they guard the economic and political foundations of the social order. Such elements correspond to general ruling class interests; consequently, they too are determined by structural necessities, by the socio-economic trends that created the foundations of society.

Lastly, legal systems are not without contradictions. When regarded generally, they are instruments of ruling classes, but certain laws that safeguard personal property, security of the person, economic and political rights, etc., may at any given time also be in the interests of working clases. Some of these particular laws are in the interests of ruling classes because they guard certain relations, such as wage relations, that gratify needs institutionalized among workers and their families by the capitalist relations of production or the relations based on them. On the other hand, other laws of this type (e.g., recognizing the right to strike and the democratic rights of political dissidents) may contradict ruling interests in a limited way.

Within this general analytic context, bourgeois legal systems are relevant because they were developed to secure generalized commodity production and exchange, based on the capitalist mode of production. Consequently, as we have seen, early bourgeois laws buttressed the primitive accumulation of capital by violence, and legitimated the consolidation of landed and merchant capital that was being generated by market forces (Marx, 1959:713ff). These laws suppressed self-earned property relations based on small farming and the artisanry. They also demolished the customary relations that offered free and common access to natural resources, to pasturage, timber, fish and game. Bourgeois laws thereby accelerated the annihilation of economic relations that had provided millions of people with the necessities of life. These necessities were still obtained through labor, but the power to labor was now being organized within the capitalist mode of production.

Today, generalized commodity relations set the stage for legal relations in bourgeois democracies. In such societies, wage labor and capital prevail; hence, the forms of legal relations are ordered by illusions and realities associated with commodity fetishism. Such illusions and realities include, among other things, the universality of individual rights and duties, and the free will of countless numbers of persons who, motivated by personal advantage, voluntarily exchange equivalences in commodity markets. Also included here is the formal equality of every commodity holder – the owner of capital equally with the laborer who has nothing to sell but labor power.

Particularly in western bourgeois democracies, such illusions and realities have played an important role juridically although they are anchored historically in simpler commodity relations. Prior to our current socio-economic formations based on the extended reproduction of capital, individual right and duty coexisted with customary rights of groups and collective forms of responsibility. These rights and duties were largely based on modes of production dominated by feudal estates or joint-family groupings. But capitalism undermined such modes of production and, as the capitalist state evolved, civil and criminal laws oriented toward individuals displaced customary norms oriented toward collectivities (Kennedy, 1970; Ayre, 1974).

For the capitalist mode of production, certain individual rights (and hence duties) are more significant than others. Legal rights involving respect for a worker's claim to possess his or her labor power are significant, because the exchange of labor power for wages enters into the terms for capitalist exploitation. Equally significant are the legal rights involving respect for the capitalist's claim to possess the means of production, to appropriate labor power by payment in wages or in kind, and to control both of these commodities to generate surplus value. Added to these significant rights are those securing circulation relations wherein commodities realize their values.

Among the rising bourgeoisie in early capitalism, it was claimed that such proprietory rights were derived from natural forces of the universe that transcended human will. Consequently, it was further said that these rights could not be alienated from individuals by a sovereign power, because such a power only represented the will of a ruling prince or a parliament but not God. Finally, since these proprietory rights were considered inalienable, they were morally appropriate and, in spite of any laws restricting certain economic liberties, e.g., freedom of trade, they were correct.

The struggle for these significant rights engendered a demand for political rights and finally produced a catalogue of rights called 'the rights of man'. After the bourgeois revolutions, furthermore, the standards of right and duty, of justice, and hence criminality, were incorporated into the fundamental laws of the land. However, this legal transformation of the category of right does not detract from the fact that bourgeois conceptions of justice had emerged prior to, and were instrumental to, the revolutionary transformation of the political order. Thus, bourgeois class struggles confirm the revolutionary importance of the concepts of right, duty, crime and justice that are independent of criteria based on prevailing legal relationships.

But this confirmation should not imply that bourgeois justice necessarily defended the welfare of laborers in early bourgeois societies. In such societies, procedural rights, for instance when instituted in criminal courts, were hardly available to the poor who could not afford an attorney, who were unable to make bail, and who were tried by judges and juries that were generally men of property. On the other hand, the ownership of property by itself did not ensure standards of justice that were favorable to the rising bourgeoisie. Since the bourgeoisie did not dominate all parts of the state apparatus and, in fact, had to create a new type of state, it also formalized criminal law procedures along lines that encouraged the independence of the judiciary from the remnants and traditions of feudalism within the state apparatus (e.g., on administrative levels and in civil bureaucracies). Conflicts among the various bourgeois fractions (i.e., 'interest groups') gave rise to other reasons for an independent judiciary. Procedural laws were also needed to support the general interests of the new ruling class in the face of the particular interests of its fractions.

During the latter half of the 19th century, the disappearance from the western democracies of these feudal remnants, the expansion of industrial capitalism, and the accommodations between the agrarian and industrial bourgeoisie, ended the chief antagonisms that had necessitated the formalization of criminal law procedures to guarantee the bourgeoisie their rights. The liberalism that characterized many judges in the first half of the century gave way to strict conservatism, and the ideology of the independence of the judiciary became a camouflage for the struggle against the proletariat. Eventually, the once-political question of protecting legal rights became largely a question of mere legal technique (Rusche and Kirchheimer, 1968: 142–3).

On the other hand, in the struggle between the bourgeoisie and the proletariat with its allies, criminal law procedures, when unrestrained, at times become obstacles to bourgeois aims. Such occasions occur after political dissension has been repressed by reactionary state officials. Sometimes, when this happens, bourgeois legality protects the struggle for democratic rights and socialism. For the most part, however, this legality and its armament of procedural laws remain a superb means for guarding the bourgeois consolidation of economic power.

Legal definition of crime

Equipped now with information about the historical changes in the validity of bourgeois rights, we can again turn to the legal definition controversy. It will be recalled that according to most criminologists, crimes are considered to be social harms that are prohibited by law and are therefore sanctioned by the state. But first, it should be emphasized that their definition is a very special conception; it is not the simple, descriptive definition of an illegal act as found in criminal codes. The codes refer to *discrete* acts of crime such as burglary, homicide, extortion, etc. The codes do not signify the *common* characteristics that cut across all crimes; for example, crimes are anti-social acts, crimes are forbidden by law, etc. Criminologists, legal scholars, and other intellectuals, however, formulate definitions of crime on the basis of such common characteristics. These definitions are then used when intellectuals communicate ideas about crime to each other or to the population at large.

Thus, numerous criminologists in their education of other professionals and of the population at large claim that crime refers only to acts stipulated by law and sanctioned by the state. Such information, however, tacitly delegitimates references to those crimes not stipulated by law and not sanctioned by the state. Consequently, from a legalistic standpoint, Clarence Darrow (1920) would be denounced as professionally incompetent as well as an ideologue for his declaration:

> The man on the outside [of prison] who has committed no crime may have done something. For instance: to take all the coal in the United States and raise the price two dollars or three dollars when there is no need of it, and thus kill thousands of babies and send thousands of people to the poorhouse and tens of thousands to jail, as is done every year in the United States – this is a greater *crime* than all the people in our jails ever committed; but the law does not punish it. Why? Because the fellows who control the earth make the laws (our emphasis).

As indicated, criminologists inform the population that legally defined crimes commonly refer to anti-social acts and thus are harmful to society. Yet, the selection of social harm as a common characteristic of such crime is open to serious doubt in a class society. We certainly agree that a great many crimes are socially harmful.

However, since the control of state power enables ruling classes to legally sanction acts that oppose their own interests, such as strikes,[4] political dissent, and affiliation with left-wing political parties, any definition that accepts the corollary that legal crimes are social harms implicitly legitimates such criminal laws and sanctions regardless of their repressive contents. Workers' strikes, political dissents and left-wing affiliations are not social harms; instead, the laws that repress these acts in the interest of a ruling class are socially injurious. Consequently, when legal definitions equate crime with social harm, they assume the rectitude of legal order and are inherently apologetic.[5]

Proletarian definitions of crime

Several years ago, we wrote (1970) that a definition of crime, based on human rights, would avoid state-imposed restrictions on the study of criminal behavior. Our proposal noted that great harms inflicted on the people of many nations have been excepted from legal classification simply because the perpetrators of these harms can manipulate the law in their own interest. The imperialist war against the Indo-Chinese people was still raging at the time, and to this day culprits, who were at the highest levels of government, have not been prosecuted for their crimes against humanity.[6] Nor have thousands of criminologists shown professional concern with these crimes. Their reasoning is simple: the perpetrators have not been defined or sanctioned as criminals by the state.

Thus, our discussion of the legal definition of crime emphasized its restrictive effect on scientific and political practice.[7] Legal definitions are ideological instrumentalities which shape and develop the language and objectives of science in such a way as to strengthen class domination. By restricting the definition of the domain and nature of criminology, for instance, the legal definition reproduces the bourgeois division of labor among scientific workers and directly subordinates criminological inquiries to state policies and legal practices.[8]

Upon proposing a human rights perspective toward crime, however, we *firmly* rejected natural-law definitions of human rights even though such definitions use criteria that are independent of the state. At that time, we pointed (1970: 145) to the limitations of such definitions: 'By delineating the naturally intrinsic qualities of men, philosophers have attempted to transcend the politically controversial issues posed by the abrogation of human rights. Their natural-law principles, however, cannot be substituted for a substantive and historically relevant interpretation of human rights which takes into account the political ideals men have, as well as the kinds of social institutions which can nullify or realize these ideals.' Thus, our interpretation of human rights obviously rejected ahistorical moral criteria warranted by natural laws and applicable to societies everywhere and always.

When answering a thoughtful criticism of our perspective, written by Clayton Hartjen (1972), we further indicated (1972:81) that certain nonlegal definitions of crime arise out of struggles against class oppression. Citing Angela Davis (1971), for instance, we noted her distinction between those violations of the law reflecting the selfish interests of individuals and violations in the interest of a class or a people being oppressed by the law. In the former instance, the violator can be considered a criminal, but, in the latter, he or she is a reformer or a revolutionary. The reformer or revolutionary is certainly called a criminal by the state, but this is an ambiguous label since it symbolizes moral as well as legal culpability. The reformer or revolutionary has violated a law but morally the act represents the interests of a working class and its allies.[9]

From the arrests of the members of the Paris Commune (Waldman, 1973) onward, and perhaps even earlier, state officials have utilized the category of crime to obscure the differences between the illegal practices of reformers or revolutionaries and those of ordinary criminals. In our time, the tacit acceptance of legalistic perspectives toward crime often performs the same function. But radicals have generally demystified these perspectives in their practice of analyzing the foundations of legal order in class societies and by emphasizing the double standards and the ruling class interests that underly legal conceptions of crime. *Yet, there still remains the vital task of delineating from a proletarian point of view a moral and scientific basis for correctly applying the category of crime to harmful social relationships.*

Until the task of delineating the basis for correctly applying the category of crime is substantially completed, radicals, to some degree, will continue to struggle on the terrain of bourgeois ideology and within a bourgeois problemmatic. They too will remain frozen in the single moment of analysis, forgetting Marx's (1845) injunction: 'The philosophers have *interpreted the world in various* ways; the point, however, is to *change* it.'

Going beyond the terrain of bourgeois ideology first requires a scientific account of the antagonistic class relationships giving rise to alternative class moralities and their respective conceptions of crime. In mature capitalist societies, such antagonistic classes are above all represented by the bourgeoisie and the proletariat. Corresponding to these social classes are ideological relationships, including those based on bourgeois morality and on proletarian morality. These moralities contain conceptions of good and evil, right and duty, justice and criminality that differ according to class perspectives.

Furthermore, progressive features of bourgeois morality are included in proletarian morality. In this sense, proletarian morality evolves from and transcends bourgeois morality. Qualitative transformations in class relationships introduce changes in the historical development of morality. Thus, bourgeois morality represents ideological conditions that reproduce capitalist relationships; however, with the emergence of the proletariat, an antagonistic class, moral ideas change. As the proletariat actively moves to transform the present to conform to its own interest, it develops its own morality. It selectively carries forward moral traditions which enable it· to change the existing order as well as to maintain itself. In the process of change, in the vicissitudes of class struggle, new moral elements are added and moral traditions are reconstituted within a new class-conscious framework. There emerges a qualitatively new morality that signifies the ideological effort required of people to change themselves, to bring about the revolutionary transformation of society (Engels, 1939: 104– 5).

Therefore, at this stage, proletarian morality does not signify proletarian relations as they *are*; but it signifies what they can and will necessarily *become*, because of objective trends in class society. Furthermore, proletarian morality attains its qualitative distinctions in the class struggle; but this attainment does not exclude its allies. The peasantry, petty bourgeois intellectuals, small shopkeepers, etc., may anticipate or participate (e.g., through the struggle for democratic rights) in the development of this morality. Because of structural tendencies, however, the proletariat is the only *class* that is objectively capable of fully developing and instituting the most advanced forms of morality, including the most advanced definitions of crime.

The advanced definitions of crime identify the crimes against collectivities such as nations and exploited classes as well as against all individuals. Here, therefore, are the imperialist acts of aggression which annihilate, oppress, or exploit an entire people. Here also are the social harms resulting from class exploitation, from the forcible appropriation by capital of the surplus value created by labor.

Hence underlying the advanced definitions are criteria for judging crimes that refer to the laws of imperialism and social class development; that justify the right of self-determination and non-interference in the internal affairs of a nation; that refer to the right of the proletariat to control, appropriate, and administer surplus value in its own collective interest; and that delineate 'system crimes' based on criminogenic conditions inherent in the most general properties of a socio-economic formation.[10] Since they in part rely on collective rights and duties, such criteria go beyond and yet include the notion of individual right and responsibility.

Doubtless, similarities exist between bourgeois and proletarian notions of criminality and justice. These similarities are due to the necessity of protecting the forms of social coexistence (e.g., wage relations, family relations, etc.) in which every class is equally interested. Nevertheless, there are many differences between these ideas which are related to the definition of crime. There are various social harms that are criminal and that vitally affect the interests of the working class and its allies, yet they are not designated as unlawful, while those social harms that affect the general interests of the bourgeoisie are made illegal.[11] Certainly the categories that involve systemic capitalist relationships, such as capitalist exploitation and imperialist relations, will hardly be given legal expression in capitalist societies. Such categories, on the other hand, are progressively reflected in the evolution of socialist laws by the dictatorship of the proletariat. They are also expressed by the recognition and support given by socialist governments to oppressed nations and national liberation struggles.

For these reasons, the socialist morality developed under socialist conditions springs originally from that portion of the morality of the proletariat already created under bourgeois conditions. Furthermore, as indicated, even though the proletarian ideas about criminality are important in the struggle for a better life, very few of these conceptions are given legal expression as long as state power remains more or less in the hands of the bourgeoisie. When state power is in the hands of the working class and its allies, however, these ideas should be expressed by the state in either its legal, ideological or planning capacity or in all of these capacities. Consequently, the advanced definitions of crime emerging under capitalism should, to some degree, prefigure state practices in socialist societies.

Objective criterion for moral judgments

Generally, as indicated, moral judgments about crime in bourgeois societies are related to class interests. But, does this mean that the truthfulness of such judgments is merely relative? Does it mean that irreconcilable judgments are both true and false depending upon one's standpoint, and that what is true for one class under these conditions is false for the other?

A Marxist answer to this possibility goes against moral relativism. The truthfulness of moral judgments about crime can only be warranted by objective criteria based on scientific knowledge about right, duty, justice and crime, originating in socially determined relationships rather than in natural laws. The criteria for such judgments are related to the interests of social classes, but any act which is alleged to serve these interests objectively must also be consistent with the laws of social development.[12] Thus, the actions of individuals or groups may be appraised as good or evil according to whether they promote or hinder the interests of a social class as a whole, but such an appraisal can only be properly made in light of a scientific understanding of the social trends in society and of the objective consequences of human activities under given historical conditions.

Furthermore – and here is the crux of the argument – the objective criterion for moral judgments indicates that the interests of all humanity can be served no longer unless the interests of the working class are advanced at the expense of the ruling class. At this stage of world-wide social developments, moreover, such an advance cannot be fully achieved by providing working people a more equitable share of resources allocated among the classes. The demand for class equality, from a proletarian standpoint, finds its fullest expression in the abolition of classes (Engels, 1939:117–18). Hence, working-class interests are fully satisfied when the conditions that reproduce the class system as a whole are eliminated.

For these reasons, the objective criterion of social development raises any discussion pertaining to the truthfulness of moral judgments about crime and social justice to a level of analysis that transcends the subjective differences between classes. When restricted to such differences alone, the conflicts between moral judgments are irreconcilable. An objective evaluation of the validity of moral judgments, however, is dependent upon scientific knowledge about the organized methods for establishing desirable social relations. Such social relations among other things will terminate social harms forever, promote freedom for all humanity through control over nature as well as society, and realize human potentialities through unparalleled development of the productive forces.

Thus, it is concluded on objective grounds that, to serve the interests of all humanity, it is necessary to advance the interests of the working class at the expense of the ruling class by abolishing capitalism. Such a conclusion, however, is contradicted by bourgeois humanism, a moral philosophy about individualism and private property, expressed classically by natural-law conceptions of the irreducible essence of man, by libertarian doctrines about free labor and free trade, and by universal ideals about the dignity, rounded development and welfare of individuals. Utilizing their utilitarian ethics, bourgeois humanists distinguish needs common to all individuals. Then, relying on bourgeois social science, they assume that the common human needs can be fully implemented in capitalist societies.

But this humanist assumption is mistaken and bourgeois humanism as a consequence has become ineffectual. Doubtless, the liberal judgments of bourgeois humanists did condemn class injustice under the ancient regime and in colonial societies. And they were historically progressive because they supported the conditions that led to the demise first of feudal servitude and then slave labor. But, the individualism and liberties of the capitalist class today cannot be upheld without undermining the dignity, rounded development and well being of the working class. As a result, the utilitarian injunctions of bourgeois humanism cannot be implemented successfully because of the conflicting nature of humanistic ideals, and the objective contradictions between these ideals and capitalist reality.[13]

Because of such conflicts and contradictions, the phrase 'human rights', among proponents of proletarian morality, classifies rights that are clearly distinguished apart from those necessary for the reproduction of capital. Such a distinction is identified with socialist conceptions of human rights. (These conceptions incorporate certain democratic rights into a larger ensemble of social, cultural economic and political rights, such as the right to employment, to safe working conditions, to sexual and racial equality, to child care, education, housing, medical care, etc.)[14] Such a distinction, however, does not eliminate the necessity for a scientific analysis of the methods, to be organized by revolutionary parties and other working-class organizations, for achieving these rights in bourgeois societies. Generally such an analysis indicates that only class-conscious struggles for human rights and socialism will achieve the rights which are at most promised by bourgeois humanists but of which working people have been practically deprived.

Again, class struggles cannot succeed without repressing the rights of capitalists and prohibiting as criminal the exploitative relations secured by these rights. The material conditions that render human rights possible can hardly be established until the working class as a whole can, in its own interest, planfully allocate the surplus value created by its labor power. Consequently, the class rights that reproduce capitalists must be prohibited and the class rights of the proletariat must be affirmed, before any socialist society can begin to secure the satisfaction of common individual needs universally.[15]

Conclusion

The paragraph above refers to the definitions of crime established under socialist conditions, but the struggle for human rights and socialism usually requires definitions that refer to the types of crime occurring during prior stages of development. During these earlier stages, the implementation of proletarian definitions requires flexible strategies that are sensitive to concrete conditions. Certain conditions and definitions may only warrant long-term educational implementation initiated and carried out by a revolutionary party. Other conditions may encourage struggles to change the law here and now. Still further conditions may call for mass political struggles against such basics as imperialist, racist, and sexist relations and policies. Finally, some conditions may call for implementation based on social and economic planning, and on social reforms that support higher living standards and democratic rights. Radical proposals, which systematically relate definitions of crime to flexible strategies based on concrete instances, are sorely needed.[16]

Under such prior conditions, furthermore, the inclusiveness and relative importance of definitions of crimes also depend upon circumstances. It will be recalled that definitions of crime require objective warrants; therefore, before indiscriminately labelling all harms as crimes, priorities must be established in light of a revolutionary praxis. Where coalitions among working-class groups and a national bourgeoisie are necessary for instance, in the struggle against imperialism, then strategic distinctions between the harms generated by a national bourgeoisie and the bourgeoisie of an imperialist nation become significant. Proletarian categories of crime, though politically independent, should not be heedlessly elevated by sectarian principles without concern for the concrete conditions that effect the development of national class struggles and that warrant the creation of the categories. If dogmatism prevails, such categories, when used, will divide the working class from its allies, including the petty bourgeoisie, and they will provide capital with the social base for fascism.[17]

Chilean events indicate that the absence of politically independent definitions of crime among the great popular classes can set the stage for fascism. The political crimes against the Allende government and its supporters among the people were not vigorously repressed by the police and the judiciary. But neither did broad coalitions mobilize massively and decisively to create popular centers for social defense and to oust the government officials who were derelict in their duty. Clearly then, the Chilean experience suggests that bourgeois legal ideologies are influential especially when socialist movements succeed in electoral struggles.

The Chilean tragedy does not simply involve a failure of leadership and Allende's overreliance on the ideology of bourgeois legality. The Chilean working class and its allies did not force Allende to rectify his policies, because they were not prepared ideologically to recognize the necessity for moving independently to alter the balance of power within the state apparatus. Despite the public outcry against the political crimes of the bourgeoisie, organizations that were rooted in the Chilean working class and the petty bourgeoisie may also have been neutralized somewhat by bourgeois mythologies that base the definition of crime and its implementation on law and the state alone.

There is a class strategy for preparing the way for the political confrontation between classes for state power. This class strategy, called 'a war of position' by Antonio Gramsci (1971), involves a long-term struggle for hegemony in all spheres of life. In the ideological sphere, in our opinion, the struggle requires the creation of a proletarian perspective toward crime, law, and the state that will counter bourgeois, legalistic ideologies and that will direct the moral energies of the working class and its allies in defense of socialist achievements. Ideology, after all, also structures the moments when great masses of people become active historical agents taking conscious part in political struggles and thereby becoming fully engaged in revolutionary change.

Notes

1. Space restrictions force us to side-step many of the complexities related to the definition of crime. Fortunately, a series of articles, authored by Richard Ayres and Anatol Anton, is being written for publication. From our communication it appears that they will deal comprehensively with the issues posed by Marxist ethics and its relation to crime, law, and the state. Finally, we would like to thank Greg Shank, Paul Takagi, Richard Ayres, Gene Grabiner and Virginia Engquist-Grabiner for their critical and editorial suggestions.

2. Petras's article in this regard provides a model for radicals interested in developing strategies for aborting or preventing the incipient fascist conditions that arise in bourgeois democracies, when national self-determination or socialist movements become strong. Such a model is in contrast with the advice given by bourgeois social scientists helping intelligence agencies subvert democratic governments, for instance in Guatemala, Brazil, Chile, Greece, etc. Andreas Papandreou (1972:19) rhetorically asks about the 1967 military coup in Greece, 'How do five men take over a government overnight?' His answer,'. . . they did so on the basis of a NATO plan with the code name Prometheus. The plan was on computer tape, prepared in Washington and revised there in February 1967. The tapes contain the names of the people who would be arrested, as well as the names of the officers who would be arresting them. It was programmed by an M.I.T. graduate computer scientist . . . [and was implemented on the basis of a decision] made, by a subcommittee of the U.S. National Security Council in February 1967 under the chairmanship of . . . W. W. Rostow'.

3. For the relations between the natural law tradition and natural social-laws, see Schwendinger and Schwendinger (1974:7–14).

4. Staughton Lynd's article on law and the right to strike indicates the pressures subverting this right by modifying the law. See, in particular, the discussion about legal precedents that support voluntary alienation of this right in collective bargaining agreements (Lynd, 1977:10–14).

5. Such criticism is not only made by radicals. Upon reviewing *The Subculture of Violence* by Marvin Wolfgang and Franco Ferracuti, Edward Glover (1969) notes the apologetic function of the category of social harm in this type of definition. Glover states that Wolfgang and Ferracuti 'quote with indulgent condescension from Gillin, who said that crime is "an act that has been shown to be actually harmful to society or is *believed* to be harmful by a group of people that has the

power to enforce its beliefs and that places such an act under the ban of positive penalties", a proclamation which, taken literally enough, would act not only as a stumbling block to the investigation of larval criminality but would seriously undermine the constitutional law of the most democratic country. It would, incidentally, provide a complete justification for the policies of Goebbels and his Nazi confreres under which the opponents of their regime were treated as capital criminals, thereby following the engaging habit, current in an earlier century, of British Whigs and Tories who were accustomed when in office to impeach, exile, or execute on Tower Hill their most venomous and influential opponents'.

6. For this reason, Robert Scheer (1972) in an extraordinary article, 'The Language of Torturers', wrote, 'Ellsberg could have written his cautious articles against the war and stayed in the club but by releasing the [Pentagon] Papers he turned not just against the war but also against the system behind it . . . But, after all, the criminals are still in power'.

7. Other writings, including the sophisticated article by Gene Grabiner (1973), have critically distinguished positivistic and idealistic perspectives underlying this controversy.

8. As indicated by Tony Platt's (1974: 2, 5–6) classic article on radical criminology, the awareness of this restriction underlies a profound break with conventional, liberal criminology. Today, in our opinion, definitions of crime that transcend legalistic definitions represent one of the central pillars of radical criminology in the United States. Such definitions justify professional services directed against repressive relations that are not necessarily prohibited by law. (They in fact are frequently engendered by the state.) Consequently, one of the possibilities addressed by a new definitional perspective is the creation of a radically different social distribution of labor services among criminologists.

9. Later, it will become obvious that acts in the interest of the working class and its allies must be judged objectively. The good intentions of reformers and revolutionaries are not objective warrants for such acts.

10. Our original article (1970: 147–8) proposed ' . . . that the *social conditions* themselves must become the *object* of social policy and that it is not an individual or a loose collection of atomistic individuals which is to be controlled, but rather the social relationships between individuals which give rise to criminal behavior . . . In this context, the term crime as a label for social systems becomes a warrant, not for controlling atomistic individuals, or preventing an atomistic act, but rather the regulation or elimination of social relationships, properties of social systems, or social systems taken as a whole'. Capitalist exploitation is seen in this framework; it is 'a system crime'.

11. Also to be considered is that the limited laws in areas such as workers'

health and safety are hardly implemented. For example, Murray Kempton (1973:15) reports, 'For more than thirty-five years, the Nader study reminds us, the Department of Labor has been empowered by Congress to void any government contract whenever the contract fails to meet adequate health and safety standards. Its jurisdiction covers 75,000 firms. In 1969, the Labor Standards Bureau managed to inspect barely 5 per cent of them, discovered safety violations in 95 per cent of the few it covered, and ended up withdrawing the government's sanction from just two contractors. Under the Johnson Administration, the . . . Bureau had inspected only 3 per cent of the contractors, but . . . ended up voiding three contracts'.

12. This objective criterion is derived from Franz Loeser (1958).Added writings dealing with this criterion and other Marxist ethical issues include William Ash (1964,1966), M.Levitas (1958), John Shaw (1958), John Lewis (1958), George Burgher (1958), and Gerschorn Freyer (1964). For a general view of Marxist ethics, we recommend William Ash's writings for clarity, coverage and depth.

13. This contradiction is reflected in a speech made by Harris Dole, head of the Bureau of Mines, who, in a speech to mine inspectors, stated, 'You must avoid at all costs the pointless, futile, self-defeating game of cops and robbers with mine management . . . You must reconcile the requirements of mine safety with the need for efficient production . . . For the law not only specifies diligent attention to mine health and safety; it demands as well that private enterprise be fostered and encouraged to develop the mineral resources of the nation for the benefit of the people' (reported in *The Wall Street Journal* [3 January 1973] and cited by Kempton [1973:15]).

14. For information about socialist conceptions of human rights see Bernhard Graefrath (1970) and Imre Szabo (1966).

15. Just as the essential features of a socio-economic system are not reducible to its political functions, the class conceptions of crime are not to be reduced to state relations alone. Though the state is vitally important to proletarian definitions of crime, it is among a number of organized methods for dealing with crimes, particularly under bourgeois conditions.

16. Similar considerations apply to the rights of a people, an oppressed nation for example. Ash (1966:329), therefore, properly observes: 'The thesis of the "permanent core of morality", which would link Marxism with the European ethical tradition, is rejected quite categorically by Marx himself as early as the writing of *The Poverty of Philosophy* in 1846. "Communists preach no morality. They do not put to people the moral demand: Love one another, be not egoists, because they know very well that egoism is under certain conditions the necessary form of the individual struggle for survival." In other words, there is no morality

which applies equally to capitalist and socialist society; and, as Lenin
... states quite clearly, no moral standards,"over and above", the class
struggle to change society by which that struggle can be regulated. "Our
morality is entirely subordinated to the interests of the class struggle of
the proletariat . . . Morality is what serves to destroy the old exploiting
society and to unite all the toilers around the proletariat, which is
creating a new, Communist society." Indeed, the attempt to establish a
humanistic ethic for the working class *prior* to their creating the
conditions for building socialism could be a way of disarming them
before they can make a revolution – like white liberals urging non-
violence on the Afro-American people.'

17. In transitions to socialism, such preparation would aim at the independence of the police and judiciary (as well as armed force elements)
from those who continue to guard capital within the state itself.
Therefore, it would consider organized methods for recomposing and
formalizing the police, judiciary, criminal law procedures, etc. Note that
similar problems were faced by the early bourgeoisie, when they were
confronted by remnants and traditions of feudalism within the state
apparatus.

References

Ash, William (1964) *Marxism and Moral Concepts* (New York: Monthly
Review Press).
—— (1966) 'Marxist Ethics and the European Tradition', *Science and
Society*, 30 (Summer) 325–34.
Ayre, Richard (1974) 'Studies in the Historical Origins of Deviance in
Capitalist Society', Unpublished Master's Thesis (University of
Colorado).
Burgher, George (1958) 'Marxism and the Moral Law', *Marxism Today*, 2
(April) 127–8.
Darrow, Clarence (1920) 'Address to the Prisoners in Cook County Jail'.
Davis, Angela (1971) *If They Come in the Morning* (New York: Third Press).
Debs, Eugene (1970) 'On Race Prejudice', *Eugene V. Debs Speaks*, ed.
Jean Y. Tussey (New York: Pathfinder Press) 90–104 (originally pub-
lished in *International Socialist Review*, 1903).
Engels, Frederick (1939) *Herr Eugen Duhring's Revolution in Science (Anti-
Duhring)* (New York: International Publishers).
Freyer, Gerschorn (1964) 'Morality and the Historical Process', *Science and
Society*, 28 (Fall) 409–31.
Glover, Edward (1969) 'Criminological Reviewers Reviewed', *Psychiatry
and Social Science Review*, 3 (August) 21–30.
Grabiner, Gene (1973) 'The Limits of Three Perspectives on Crime: "Value-

Free Science", "Objective Law" and "State Morality"', *Issues in Criminology*, 8 (Spring) 35–48.

Graefrath, Bernhard (1970) *The Economic, Social and Cultural Human Rights in the GDR* (Berlin: The German Democratic Committee on Human Rights).

Gramsci, Antonio (1971) *Selections from the Prison Notebooks* (New York: International Publishers).

Hartjen, Clayton (1972) 'Legalism and Humanism: A Reply to the Schwendingers', *Issues in Criminology*, 7 (Winter) 59–69.

Kempton, Murray (1973) 'Blue Collar Blues', *New York Review of Books* (8 February 1973).

Kennedy, Mark (1970) 'Beyond Incrimination', *Catalyst*, 6 (Summer) 1–37.

Lenin, V. I. (1920) 'The Task of the Youth Leagues', *Selected Works*, Vol. IX (New York: International Publishers) 467–83.

Levitas, M. (1958) 'On Marxism and Morals', *Marxism Today*, 2 (June) 184–6.

Lewis, John (1958) 'Reply to Discussion on Marxism and Morals', *Marxism Today*, 2 (June) 187–90.

Loeser, Franz (1958) 'The Objective Criterion in Ethics', *Marxism Today*, 2 (May) 152–6.

Lynd, Staughton (1977) 'Workers' Control in a Time of Diminished Workers' Rights', *Radical America*, 10 (September–October) 5–19.

Marx, Karl (1959) *Capital*, I (Moscow: Foreign Languages Publishing House).

——(1845) *Thesis on Feuerbach* (the Thesis is published on pp. 659–662 of *German Ideology* [1968] Moscow: Progress Publishers).

Mintz, Robert (1974) 'Interview with Ian Taylor, Paul Walton, and Jock Young', *Issues in Criminology*, 9 (Spring) 33–53.

Papandreou, Andreas (1972) 'The Takeover of Greece', *Monthly Review*, 24 (December).

Petras, James F. (1976) 'Class and Politics in the Periphery and the Transition to Socialism', *The Review of Radical Political Economics*, 8 (Summer) 20–35.

——(1977) 'Chile: Crime, Class Consciousness and the Bourgeoisie', *Crime and Social Justice*, 7 (Spring – Summer).

Platt, Tony (1974) 'Prospects for a Radical Criminology in the United States', *Crime and Social Justice*, 1 (Spring – Summer) 2–10.

Rusche, Georg and Otto Kirchheimer (1968) *Punishment and Social Structure* (New York: Russell and Russell).

Scheer, Robert (1972) 'Language of Torturers', *Sundance* (August–September).

Schwendinger, Herman and Julia R. Schwendinger (1970) 'Defenders of Order or Guardians of Human Rights?', *Issues in Criminology*, 5 (Summer) 123–57.

——(1972) 'The Continuing Debate on the Legalistic Approach to the Definition of Crime', *Issues in Criminology*, 7 (Winter) 71–81.

——(1973) 'The Report to the Florence Conference', Unpublished paper delivered at the Florence Conference sponsored by the European Group for the Study of Deviance and Social Control.

——(1974) *Sociologists of the Chair* (New York: Basic Books).

——(1976) 'Collective Varieties of Youth', *Crime and Social Justice*, 5 (Spring – Summer) 7–25.

Shaw, John (1958) 'The Moral Law', *Marxism Today*, 2 (April) 186–7.

Swartz, Joel (1975) 'Silent Killers at Work', *Crime and Social Justice*, 3 (Summer) 15–20.

Szabo, Imre (ed.) (1966) *Socialist Conception of Human Rights* (Budapest: Akademiai Kiado).

Taylor, Ian, Paul Walton and Jock Young (1973) *The New Criminology* (London: Routledge and Kegan Paul).

Waldman, Martin R. (1973) 'The Revolutionary as Criminal in the 19th Century France: A Study of the Communards and Deportes', *Science and Society*, 38 (Spring) 31–55.

Wolfgang, Marvin and Franco Ferracuti (1967) *The Subculture of Violence* (New York: Barnes and Noble).

Part II
Crime

4

Karl Marx, the Theft of Wood and Working-class Composition

A Contribution to the Current Debate

Peter Linebaugh

The international working-class offensive of the 1960s threw the social sciences into crisis from which they have not yet recovered. The offensive was launched in precisely those parts of the working class that capital had formerly attempted to contain within silent, often wageless reserves of the relative surplus population, that is, in North American ghettos, in Caribbean islands, or in 'backward' regions of the Mediterranean. When that struggle took the form of the mass, direct appropriation of wealth, it became increasingly difficult for militants to understand it as a 'secondary movement' to the 'real struggle' that, it was said, resided only in the unions and the plants. Nor could it be seen as the incidental reactions of 'victims' to an 'oppressive society', as it was so often by those organizations left flat-footed by the power of an autonomous Black movement and an autonomous women's movement.

This is not the place to elaborate on the forms that the struggles have taken in the direct appropriation of wealth, nor how these were able to circulate within more familiar terms of struggle.[1] We must note, however, that they thrust the problem of crime, capital's most ancient tool in the creation and control of the working class, once again to a prominent place in the capitalist relation. As the political recomposition of the international working class threw into crisis the capitalist organization of labor markets, so that part of traditional social science, criminology, devoted to studying one of the corners in the labor market, 'criminal subcultures' and street gangs, had to face a crisis of its own. George Jackson recommended burning the libraries of criminology. Young criminologists began to question the autonomous status of criminology as a field of study (Hirst, 1972:29; Phillipson, 1973:400; Melossi, 1976:31; Currie, 1974:113). Accompanying both the internal and external critique of criminology has been a recovery of interest in the treatment of crime within the Marxist tradition. Yet, that tradition is by no means accessible or complete and in fact contains contradictory strains within it, so that one cannot be completely unqualified in welcoming it.

In stating our own position let us try to be as clear as possible even at the risk of overstatement. We wish to oppose the view that fossilizes particular compositions of the working class into eternal, even formulaic, patterns. We must, in particular, combat the view that analyzes crime (or much else indeed) in the nineteenth-century terms of a 'lumpenproletariat' versus an 'industrial proletariat'. It is to be regretted that despite the crisis of criminology and the experience of struggle that gave rise to it, some militants can still speak of the 'lumpenproletariat' *tout court* as though this were a fixed category of capitalist relations of power. When neither the principle of historical specification nor the concept of class struggle is admitted there can be no useful analysis of class strategy, howsoever exalted the methodology may be in other respects.[2]

In the rejection of various idealist interpretations of crime including their 'Marxist' variants, there is, perforce, a revival of interest in the situation of the problem within specified historical periods, that is, within well constituted phases of capitalist accumulation. In this respect the recent work that discusses the problem in terms of original accumulation must be welcomed (Melossi, 1976:26ff). At the same time we must express the hope that this analysis may be extended to the discussion of the appropriation of wealth and of crime at other periods of the class relation. The contribution of those whose starting point in the analysis of crime is the concept of 'marginalization' (Crime and Social Justice Collective, 1976:1 – 4; Herman and Julia R. Schwendinger, 1976: 7 – 26) leads us to an analysis of the capitalist organization and planning of labor markets, certainly an advance in comparison with those for whom capital remains de-historicized and fixed in the forms of its command. On the other hand one cannot help but note the unilateral nature of the concept, the fact that it entails an approach to the question that must accept capital's point of view without adequately reconstituting the concept with working-class determinants. One remembers that the life and works of Malcolm X and George Jackson, far from being contained within incidental 'marginal sectors', became leading international reference points for a whole cycle of struggle.

The recent publication of the English translation of Marx's early writings on the criminal law and the theft of wood provides us with a propitious moment for another look at the development of Marx's thinking on the question of crime.[3] We hope that some suggestions for placing those articles within the context of the real dynamics of capitalist accumulation may not only allow us to specify the historical determinants of class struggle in the 1840s, but – what is of far greater importance – may make a contribution to the present debate, a debate which in its abandonment of 'criminology' as traditionally constituted in favor of an analysis of the political composition of the working class has more than a few similarities with Marx's own development after 1842.

It would not be much of an exaggeration to say that it was a problem of theft that first forced Marx to realize his ignorance of political economy, or to say that class struggle first presented itself to Marx's serious attention as a form of crime. Engels had always understood Marx to say that it was the study of the law on the theft of wood and the situation of the Moselle peasantry that led him to pass from a purely political viewpoint to the study of economics and from that to socialism (Cornu, 1958:ii, 68). Marx's own testimony is no less clear. In the 1859 preface to his *Contribution to the Critique of Political Economy* he wrote:

> In 1842–43, as editor of the *Rheinische Zeitung*, I found myself embarrassed at first when I had to take part in discussions concerning so-called material interests. The proceedings of the Rhine Diet in connection with forest thefts and the extreme sub-division of landed property; the official controversy about the condition of the Mosel peasants into which Herr von Schaper, at that time president of the Rhine Province, entered with the *Rheinische Zeitung*; finally, the debates on free trade and pro-tection, gave me the first impulse to take up the study of economic questions (Marx, 1904 edn: 10).

Faced with his own and Engels's evidence, we must therefore beware of those accounts of the development of Marx's ideas that see it in the exclusive terms of either the self-liberation from the problematics of Left Hegelianism or the outcome of a political collision that his ideas had with the French Utopian and revolutionary tradition that he met during his exile in Paris. The famous trinity (French politics, German philosophy, and English political economy) of the intellectual lineages of Marx's critical analysis of the capitalist mode of production appears to include everything but the actual, material form in which class struggle first forced itself to the attention of the young radical in 1842.

Our interest, however, is not to add the footnote to the intellectual biography of Marx that his ideas, too, must be considered in relation to their material setting. Our purpose is different. We wish to find out why, as it was his inadequate understanding of crime that led him to the study of political economy, Marx never again returned to the systematic analysis of crime as such. As we do this we shall also find that the mass illegal appropriation of forest products represented an important moment in the development of German capitalism, and that it was to the partial analysis of that moment that a good part of the work of some founders of German criminology was devoted. The same moment of struggle in German agrarian relations produced contradictory results among those attempting to understand it: on the one hand, the formation of criminology, and on the other, the development of the revolutionary critique of capitalism.

Between 25 October and 3 November 1842, Marx published five articles in the *Rheinische Zeitung* on the debates about a law on the theft of wood that had taken place a year and a half earlier in the Provincial Assembly of the Rhine.[4] The political background to those debates has been described several times (Cornu, 1958: ii,72–95; Mehring, 1962:37ff). Here we need only point out that the 'liberal' emperor, Frederick William IV, following his accession, attempted to make good on a forgotten promise to call a constitutional convention, by instead re-convening the provincial assemblies of the empire. Though they had little power, their opening, together with the temporarily relaxed censorship regulations, was the occasion for the spokesmen of the Rhenish commercial and industrial bourgeoisie to stretch their wings in the more liberal political atmosphere. The *Rheinische Zeitung*, staffed by a group of young and gifted men, was their vehicle for the first, hesitant fights against the Prussian government and the landed nobility. Characterized at first by 'a vague liberal aspiration and a veneration for the Hegelian philosophy' (Treitschke,1919:vi, 538), the journal took a sharper turn under Marx's editing and it was his articles on the theft of wood that caused von Schaper to write the Prussian censorship minister that the journal was now characterized by the 'impudent and disrespectful criticism of the existing government institutions' (Marx, 1842:747).

Though containing passages of 'exhilarating eloquence' (Wilson,

1940:124), the articles as a whole suffer from an uncertainty as to their central subject. Is it the appropriation of wood, legal or illegal? Is it the equity of the laws of property governing that appropriation? Or, is it the debates with their inconsistencies and thoughtlessness that took place in the assembly before the law was passed? Marx is least confident about the first subject; indeed, we learn little about the amounts and types of direct appropriation. He really warms to the second as it allows him to expound on the nature of the state and the law. On the third his characteristic wit and sarcasm come into full play. Despite these ambiguities, the articles as a whole are united by the theme of the contradiction between private self-interest and the public good. He objects, in particular, to nine provisions in the new law:

1. It fails to distinguish between the theft of fallen wood and that of standing timber or hewn lumber.
2. It allows the forest warden to both apprehend wrongdoers and evaluate the stolen wood.
3. It puts the tenure of the appointment of the forest warden entirely at the will of the forest owner.
4. Violators of the law are obliged to perform forced labor on the roads of the forest owner.
5. The fines imposed on the thief are remitted to the forest owner (in addition to compensation for damaged property).
6. Costs of defense incurred at trial are payable in advance.
7. In prison, the thief is restricted to a diet of bread and water.
8. The receiver of stolen wood is punished to the same extent as the thief.
9. Anyone possessing wood that is suspected must prove honest title to it.

Young Marx was outraged by the crude, undisguised, self-interested provisions of punishment established by this law. He was no less indignant with its substantive expansion of the criminal sanction. His criticism of the law rested upon an *a priori*, idealist conception of both the law and the state. 'The law', he wrote, 'is the universal and authentic exponent of the rightful order of things.' Its form represents 'universality and necessity'. When applied to the exclusive advantage of particular interests – the forest owners – then 'the immortality of the law' is sacrificed and the state goes 'against the nature of things'. The 'conflict between the interest of forest protection and the principles of law' can result only in the degradation of 'the idea of the state'. We stress that this criticism applied to both the substantive and the procedural sections of the law. In the latter case, 'public punishment' is transformed 'into private compensation'. 'Reform of the criminal' is attained by the 'improvement of the percentage of profit' devolving on the forest owner. The attack on the substantive part of the law rests on similar arguments. 'By applying the category of theft where it ought not to be applied you exonerate it.' 'All the organs of the state become ears, eyes, arms, legs, and means by which the interest of the forest owner hears, sees, appraises, protects, grasps and runs.' 'The right of human beings gives way to the right of trees.' As he stated this, Marx also had to ask, which human beings? For the first time he comes to the defense of the 'poor, politically and socially propertyless' when he demands for the poor 'a customary right'.

On what basis is the demand made? Some confusion results as Marx, only a few years away from his Berlin studies of the pandects and jurisprudence, attempts to solve the problem. First, he justifies it on the basis that the law must represent the interests of all 'citizens', that is, he refers to the classical arguments of natural justice. Second, and not altogether playfully, he says that 'human poverty . . . deduces its right to fallen wood' from the natural fact that the forests themselves present in the contrast between strong, upright timber to the snapped twigs and wind-felled branches underneath an 'antithesis between poverty and wealth'. Third, in noting that the inclusion of the appropriation of fallen wood with that of live and hewn timber under the rubric of the criminal sanction is inconsistent with both the sixteenth-century penal code and the ancient 'Germanic rights' (*leges barbarorum*), he suggests the greater force of these feudal codes.

It is true that Marx understands that these changes of law correspond, over the centuries, to changes in property relations: 'all customary rights of the poor were based on the fact that certain forms of property were indeterminate in character, for they were not definitely private property, but neither were they definitely common property, being a mixture of private and public right, such as we find in all the institutions of the Middle Ages.' Accumulation has in these articles no separate existence apart from the law which indeed determines it as Marx implies when he says that it was the introduction of the Roman law that abolished 'indeterminate property'. Powerless to resist, as it were, the tide of a millenium of legal development, Marx seeks to defend the 'customary right' by fleeing the seas of history altogether and placing his defense upon the *terra firma* of nature itself. There are objects 'which by their elemental nature and their accidental mode of existence' must defy the unitary force of law which makes private property from 'indeterminate property', and the forests are one of these objects.

Appeal as he might to the 'universal necessity of the rightful order of things' or to the bio-ecology of the forest, neither of these lofty tribunals could so much as delay, much less halt, the swift and sharp swath that the nobility and burgomasters in Dusseldorf were cutting through the forests of the Rhineland. Fruitless as such appeals had to be, Marx could not even understand, by the idealist terms of his argument, *why* it was that the rich Rhenish agriculturalists found it necessary to pass such a law at that time, thus expanding the criminal sanction. Nor – and this was far dearer to his interests – could he analyze the historical forces that propelled the Rhenish cotters to the direct appropriation of the wood of the forests. To be sure, we know from passing remarks made in other articles of the 1842–43 period that Marx understood that the parcelling of landed property, the incidence of taxation upon the vineyards, the shortages of firewood, and the collapsing market for Moselle wines were all elements of a single situation that he could, however, only see from the partial, incomplete standpoint of natural justice.

When looking at these articles from the standpoint of Marx's later works, we can see that he analyzes only the contradictory appearance of the struggle. Having no concept of class struggle or capitalist accumulation, he treats the Rhenish peasantry with a democratic, egalitarian passion, but still as an object external to the actual forces of its development. Unable to apprehend the struggle as one against capitalist development, he assumes that a reasoned appeal to the agrarian lords of the forest, or to their sympathetic brethren in Cologne, will find sympathetic ears. Thus real development occurs, he thought, at the level of the state which only needed to be reminded of its own inherent benevolence to reverse the course of the law and of history.

Precisely this viewpoint, though in an inverted form, dominated the work of the early German criminologists. Like the young Marx, they separated the problem of the state and crime from the class relations of accumulation. They saw crime from a unilateral, idealist viewpoint. However, for them it was less a question of state benevolence than it was of the malevolence of the working class. They sought to determine the 'moral condition of the people' by the classification, tabulation, and correlation of 'social phenomena'. The work produced in this statistical school sought to find 'laws' that determined the relative importance of different 'factors' (prices, wages, extension of the franchise, etc.) that accounted for changes in the amounts and types of crime. Like the young Marx, they were unable to ask either why some forms of appropriation became crimes at specified periods and others not, or why crimes could at some times become a serious political force imposing precise obstacles to capitalist reproduction.

The problem of the historical specification of class relations, and in particular those as they were reflected in Marx's articles, can be solved only from the standpoint of his later work, especially the first volume of *Capital*. There we learn that in discussing the historical phases of the class relation it is necessary to emphasize the forms of divisions within the working class that are created by combining different modes of production within the social division of labor. This is one of the lessons of Chapter XV. The effect of the capitalist attack managed by means of the progressive subordination of living labor to machines is to extend and intensify 'backward' modes of production in all of their forms. This is one of the weapons capital enjoys in establishing a working class articulated in a form favorable to it. Another is described in Chapter XXV of *Capital*, a chapter that is often read as a statement of a dual labor market theory, i.e., that capital in maintaining both an active and a reserve front in its social organization of labor power creates the mechanism for reducing the value of necessary labor. In fact, the 'relative surplus population' is maintained in several different forms, forms determined precisely by the combination of different modes of production. With the reproduction of capital and the struggles against it, that combination constantly changes. The chapter begins with a difficult, apparently technical, section on the value composition of capital that reminds us that the configuration of the working class cannot be analyzed exclusively in terms of its attachments to different 'sectors' or 'branches' of the social division of labor. Even while accounting for divisions in the class that rest upon its relation to capitals with variant compositions, the political composition of the working class must always be studied from the additional viewpoint of its ability to use these divisions in its attack upon capital. These are divisions whose determinations are not merely the relation to the labor process (employed or unemployed), but divisions based upon the quantitative and qualitative form of the value of labor power.

Lenin, in his analysis of the development of capitalism in Russia and, generally, in his polemics with the 'legal Marxists' of the 1890s, was forced to cover much of this ground. 'As for the forms of wage-labor, they are extremely diverse in a capitalist society, still every-where enmeshed in survivals and institutions of the pre-capitalist regime' (Lenin, 1899:590). In contrast to the Narodnik economists who considered the size of the proletariat exclusively as current factory employment, Lenin was forced to remind militants that the working class must be considered only in its relation to capital and in its ability to struggle against capital, regardless of the forms in which capital organizes it within particular productive settings. From a quantitative point of view the timber and lumber workers of post-Reform Russia were next in importance only to agricultural workers. The fact that these belonged to the relative redundant population, or that they were primarily local (not migratory) workers, or that a proportion of their income did not take the form of the wage made them no less important from either the standpoint of capitalist accumulation or from that of the working-class struggle against it. Although 'the lumber industry leaves all the old, patriarchal way of life practically intact, enmeshing in the worst forms of bondage the workers left to toil in the remote forest depths', Lenin was forced to include his discussion of the timber industry in his section on 'large-scale machine industry'. He did so not on the grounds of the quantitative scale of lumber workers within the proletariat as a whole, but because the qualitative extension of such work remained a condition of large-scale industry in fuel, building, and machine supplies. Under these circumstances it was not possible to consider the two million timber workers as the tattered edges of a dying 'feudalism'. Forms of truck payment and extra-economic forms of bondage prevailed not as mere remnants from a pre-capitalist social formation, but as terms of exploitation guaranteeing stability to capitalist accumulation. This was made clear in the massive agrarian unrest of the years 1905–7 when the illicit cutting of wood was one of the most important mass actions against the landowners (Perrie, 1972:128–9).

Let us return, at this point, to the development of capitalism in the Rhineland and, in sketching some elements of the class relation, see if we can throw some light upon the historical movement of which Marx's articles were a partial reflection.

Capitalist development in Germany, at least before 1848, is usually studied at the level of circulation as the formation of a national market. In 1818, 1824, and 1833, at the initiative of Prussia, a series of commercial treaties were signed creating a customs union, the Zollverein, that sought to restore the larger market that Napoleon's 'continental system' had imposed. The treaties removed restrictions on communications and transport. They abolished internal customs, established a unified external tariff, and introduced a common system of weights and measures. 'In fact', as a British specialist stated in 1840, 'the Zollverein has brought the sentiment of German nationality out of the regions of hope and fancy into those of positive material interests' (Bowring, 1840:1). In 1837 and 1839 treaties with the Netherlands abolishing the octroi and other Dutch harbor and navigation duties established the Rhine as the main commercial artery of western Prussia (Henderson, 1939:129–30). Indeed, the Zollverein was only the most visible aspect of the offensive launched by German capital, providing as it did the basis for a national banking and credit market, a precondition of the revolutions in transportation of the 1830s and 1840s, and the basis of the expansion in trade that found some of its political consequences in the establishment of Chambers of Commerce, the consolidation of the German bourgeoisie, and the liberal initiatives of the young Frederick William IV.

The reforms in internal and foreign commercial arrangements, together with the reforms of the Napoleonic period that created a free market in land and 'emancipated' the serfs, provided the foundations not only of a national market but laid the basis within a single generation for rapid capitalist development. Older historians, if not more recent ones, clearly understood that those changes 'far from bringing into being the anticipated just social order, led to new and deplorable class struggles' (Treitschke, 1919:vii, 201). The expropriation of the serfs and their redeployment as wage laborers are of course logically and historically distinct moments in the history of capital. During the intermediating period the articulation of the working class within and without capitalist enterprises must present confusions to those attempting to analyze it from the framework established during other periods of working-class organization. A consideration of the working class that regards it only when it is waged or only when that wage takes an exclusively monetary form is doomed to misunderstand both capitalist accumulation and the working-class struggle against it. To consider our period alone, those who find class struggle 'awakened' only after the 1839 strike of gold workers at Pfortsheim and the Berlin cotton weavers' and Brandenburg railway workers' strikes will not be able to understand why, for all their faults, Marx's articles on the theft of wood expressed an important moment in the dynamics of accumulation and class relations. In the following pages we can only suggest some elements of those dynamics.

The recomposition of class relations in the Rhineland during the 1830s and 1840s was not led, as in England at the time, by the introduction of large-scale machinery. German manufacture was nevertheless deeply affected. From the point of view of class relations, manufacturing capital was organized in two apparently opposite ways. On the one hand the changes in transportation required massive, mobile injections of labor willing to accept short-term employments. Under state direction the great railway boom of the 1830s more than quadrupled the size of the railway system. River transport also changed – steam-powered tugs replaced the long lines of horses pulling laden barges on the Rhine. These changes provided, as it were, the material infrastructure to the possibilities made available by the Zollverein. On the other hand, the capitalist offensive against traditional handicraft and small workshop production met setbacks that were partially the results of workers' power in the detail of the labor process or of the obstacles remaining in the traditional, often agrarian, relations that engulfed such productive sites.

What Banfield, the English free-trader, wrote of the foremen of the Prussian-owned coal mines of the Ruhr applied equally well to most forms of Rhenish manufacture in the 1840s: 'Their business they generally understand, but the discipline, which is the element by which time is played off against money, and which allows high wages to co-exist with large profits, does not show itself' (Banfield, 1848:55–6). Only a visitor from England with two or three generations of experience in the organization of relative surplus value could have so clearly enunciated this fundamental principle of capitalist strategy. In Prussia the height of political economy stopped with the observation that the state organization of the home market could guarantee accumulation. In the silk and cotton weaving districts of Elberfeld where outwork and task payments prevailed, workers' power appeared to capital as short-weighting of finished cloth, 'defective workmanship', and the purloining of materials. The handworkers of the Sieg and Ruhr (wire-drawers, nail-makers, coppersmiths, etc.) prevented the transition to large-scale machinery in the forge industries. Linen workers and flax farmers prevented the introduction of heckling and scutching machines. Alcoholism and coffee addiction were regarded as serious impediments to the imposition of higher levels of intensity in work. Of course, another aspect of this power to reject intensification in the labor process was a stagnation that brought with it low wages and weaknesses in resisting the prolongation of the working day which, in cotton textiles, had become sixteen hours by the 1840s. Such were the obstacles to accumulation throughout Rhenish manufacture – the Lahn valley zinc works, the sugar refineries of Cologne, the rolling mills and earthenware factories of Trier and Saarbrucken, the fine steel trades of Solingen, as well as in coal, weaving, and forge work.

These apparently opposite poles of the labor market in Rhenish manufacturing – the 'light infantry', mobile, massive, and sudden, of railway construction and the stagnant, immobile conditions of small-scale manufacturing – were in fact regulated by the rhythms of agrarian relations. The point needs to be stressed insofar as many tend to make an equivalence between agriculture and feudalism on one hand and manufactures and capitalism on the other, thus confusing a primary characteristic of the social (and political) division of labor under capitalism with the transition to capitalist dominance in the mode of production as a whole. Both the form of the wage and the labor markets of manufacture were closely articulated to agrarian relations. Remuneration for work in manu-facturing was in part made either by the allotment of small garden plots or by a working year that permitted 'time off' for tending such plots. Other non-monetary forms in compensation, whether tradi-tional perquisites in manufacture or common rights in forests, provided at once an obstacle to capitalist freedom in the wage and, at the pivot of the capitalist relation, a nodal point capable of uniting the struggles of workers in both agrarian and manufacturing settings. This mutual accommodation between manufacturing and agriculture could sometimes present bottlenecks to accumulation, as in the Sieg valley, where village control over the woodlands guaranteed that timber exploitation would remain more an aspect of working-class consumption than an industrial fuel in the metal trades. Macadamization of the roads to the foundries allowed owners to buy and transport fuels, at once releasing them from the 'parsimony' of village-controlled wood supplies and providing the basis for the re-organization of the detail of the labor process (Banfield, 1846:142). Thus we can begin to see that technical changes in transportation are as much a weapon against the working class as they are adjuncts to the development of circulation in the market.

The progressive parcelling of arable and forest lands in the Rhine, the low rates of agricultural growth, as well as the mixed and sometimes sub-subsistence forms of compensation provided a dispersed and extensive pool for the intensive and concentrated labor requirements of the railway and metallurgical industries, and concurrently established (what was well known at the time) a form of agrarian relations wherein political stability could be managed (Palgrave, 1912:ii, 814–16; and Lengerke, 1849). The 'latent' and 'stagnant' reserves of proletarians were regulated, in part, by the institutions designed to control mendicity and emigration.

The emigration of German peasants and handicraft workers doubled between 1820 and 1840. Between 1830 and 1840 it actually tripled as on average forty thousand German-speaking emigrants a year jammed the main ports of embarkation (Bremen and Le Havre) awaiting passage (Droz, 1957:78). The areas with the most intense emigration were the forest regions of the upper Rhine (Milward and Saul, 1973:147). A lucrative business existed in Mainz for the factors who organized the shipping of the peasants of the Odenwald and the Moselle across the Atlantic to Texas and Tennessee. Pauperization records are no less indicative of active state control of the relative surplus population than they are of the magnitude of the problem. Arrests for mendicity increased between 1841 and 1842 in Franconia, the Palatinate, and Lower Bavaria by 30 per cent to 50 per cent (Mayr, 1867:136–37). In the 1830s one in four people in Cologne were on some form of charitable or public relief (Milward and Saul, 1973:147).

Emigration policies and the repression of paupers alike were organized by the state. The police of western Prussia were directed to prevent the accumulation of strangers. The infamous Frankfurt Assembly of 1848 devoted much of its work to the encouragement and regulation of emigration. What early German criminologists were to find in the inverse relation between the incidence of emigration and that of crime had already become an assumption of policy in the early 1840s. The agrarian proletariat of the Rhine was thus given four possible settings of struggle during this period: emigration, pauperization, the immiseration of the 'dwarf economy', or the factory. Its history during that period is the forms of its refusal of the last, the least favorable terrain of struggle. Of course to many contemporaries these problems appeared to be the result of 'over-population' whose solution might have been sought in Malthusian remedies were it not for the fact that the struggles of the Rhenish proletariat for the re-appropriation of wealth had already forced the authorities to consider them as a major problem of 'crime and order'.

The organization of agriculture in the Rhineland during the 1830s and 1840s was characterized by the open-field system regulated by the *Gemeinde* or village association on the one hand, and by the progressive parcelling (or even pulverization) of individual owner-ship on the other (Milward and Saul, 1973:82). Friedrich List called it the 'dwarf economy' (ibid.). Since the time of the French occupation of the Rhine when cash payments replaced labor dues, the first historic steps were taken in the 'emancipation of the peasantry'. The two forms of agrarian relations were complementary: the *Gemeinde* tended to encourage parcelling, and thus one would be mistaken to consider the property relation of the *Gemeinde* opposed to the development of private property. Parcelling and the concurrent development of a free land-market in Rhenish Prussia wrought 'devastation among the poorer peasantry' (Treitschke, 1919:vii, 301).

The village system of farming, still widespread in the 1840s, was the 'most expensive system of agriculture' according to one of its nineteenth-century students. It was argued that the distance separat-ing the individual's field from his dwelling caused a waste of time, and that the tissue of forest and grazing rights and customs caused a duplication of effort, constituting an impediment to 'scientific' farming. Similarly, common rights in the mill were an inefficient deployment of resources and an obstacle to innovations. Side by side with the *Gemeinde* existed the enormous number of small allotment holders who, living at the margin of subsistence, were intensely sensitive to the slightest changes in prices for their products and to changes in interest rates at seeding or planting time. On ten million arable acres in the Rhineland, there were eleven million different parcels of land (Cornu, 1958:ii, 78–9). As a result of the opening of the Rhineland to competition from east Prussian grain and the extension of the timber market, small allotment holders could neither live on the lower prices received for their products nor afford the higher prices required for fuel. Under this progressive erosion of their material power, a life and death struggle took place for the re-appropriation of wealth, a struggle that was endemic, highly price sensitive, and by no means restricted to timber and fuel rights.

'In summer many a cow is kept sleek on purloined goods' (Banfield, 1846:157). In the spring women and children ranged through the fields along the Rhine and its tributaries, the Mosel, the Ahr, and the Lahn, cutting young thistles and nettles, digging up the roots of couch-grass, and collecting weeds and leaves of all kinds to turn them to account as winter fodder. Richer farmers planted a variety of lucerns (turnips, swedes, wurzel), but they had to be ever watchful against the industrious skills of their neighbors, skills that often 'degenerated into actual robbery'. It must be remembered that a good meal in the 1840s consisted of potato porridge and sour milk, a meal that depended upon the keeping of a cow and on access to fodder or grazing rights that had become increasingly hard to come by.

The terms of cultivation among the orchards were similar to conditions of grazing and foraging – operose work and a suspicious eye. The size of orchards was determined not by the topography of the land but by the walking powers of the *gardes champêtres* who provided 'inefficient protection against the youth or loose population of the surrounding country'. At harvest time cherries, apples, pears, walnuts, and chestnuts were guarded by their owners who rested on beds of straw during evening vigils. The expansion of the field police in the 1830s did nothing to reduce the complaints of depredations. A 'man of weight' in the Moselle valley provides us with this description:

> The disorderly habits that have such an influence in after life, it may safely be asserted have their root in the practice of sending children to watch the cattle on the (uninclosed) stubbles. Big and little meet here together. The cattle are allowed to graze for the most part on other people's lands; little bands are formed, where the older children teach the younger their bad habits. Thefts are discussed and planned, fighting follows, then come other vices. First, fruit and potatoes are stolen, and every evening at parting the wish is entertained that they may be able to meet again the next. Neither fields, gardens, nor houses are eventually spared, and with the excuse of this employment it is scarcely possible to bring the children together to frequent a summer day-school, or to attend on Sundays to the weekly explanation of the Christian doctrines (quoted in Banfield, 1846:159).

We note that in these observations no fine distinction can be drawn between the struggle to retain traditional common rights against their recent expropriation and the endemic depredations that were executed without cover of that appeal to legitimacy. Nor should we expect it. In viticulture, garden, and orchard farming the transformation of the market, the fall of prices, the stringencies of credit, especially during the period of 1839–42, intensified the immiserations of the Rhenish agrarian population which still accounted for about 73 per cent of employments.

Traditionally, one of the most important cushions to natural and cyclical disaster was the widespread existence of common rights in private and corporate forests. Despite the relatively high levels of population density and manufacturing development in western Prussia, the proportion of forest to arable lands was three to four, in contrast to Prussia as a whole where it was about one to two. The riches of the forests could provide not only fuel, but also forage, materials for houses, farm equipment, and food. The crisis hitting the Rhenish farming population made these riches all the more necessary to survival. At the same time, access to them was becoming progressively restricted with the inexorable expropriation of forest rights.

The forest, one knows, had supported a complex society both within its purviews and in the neighboring terrain: woodcutters, charcoal burners, coopers, sabot makers, basket makers, joiners, tanners, potters, tile makers, blacksmiths, glass makers, lime burners – the list is limited only by the limits of the uses of wood. Particular use-rights in the traditional forest economy had a social life of their own prescribed in a 'tissue of customary rights' that defy the norms and clarities of private property. All rights were governed by two principles. First, that 'no Man can have any Profit or Pleasure in a Forest which tends to the Destruction thereof', in the words of a sixteenth-century treatise (Manwood, 1717:2). Second, the forms of human appropriation were designed to guarantee and preserve the stability and hierarchy of class relations which guaranteed to the lord his liberty in the hunt and mastery of the chase and to the poor particular inalienable usages. Assart of the forest, rights of agistment, rights of pannage, estovers of fire, house, cart or hedge, rush, fern, gorze and sedge rights, rights to searwood, to windfalls, to dotards, rights of lops and tops – in all, the overlapping vocabulary of natural and social relations recall a forgotten world, easily romanticized by those first criticizing the simplicities of *meum et tuum*. Indeed such romanticism is provoked by the harshness of the opposite view that said the existence of such rights 'hindered intensive sylviculture, disturbed the progress of orderly cutting, prevented natural regeneration of the forest and depleted the fertility of the forest soil' (Heske, 1938:241).

Forest relations in the Rhineland had already changed considerably by the time that Karl Marx took up his angry pen in 1841. The parcelling off of large forest estates, the buying and selling of woodlands, the expropriation of forest usufructs had all well progressed by the 1840s. The movement to abolish forest rights really began with the French Revolution. The Prussian agrarian edict of 1811 removed all restrictions that encumbered the free, private exploitation of forest properties.

The first forty years of the century were characterized by a secular appreciation in the value of timber relative to the value of other agrarian products. This may be attributed to the markets encouraged by the Zollverein, to the demands of railway construction, to the increasing demand for machinery (oak was still widely used), and to the burgeoning market for both individual and productive fuel consumption, itself the result in part of the expropriation of forest usufructs. Dutch shipbuilding, traditionally dependent on the wide rafts of oak brought down the Rhine, remained active. British shipbuilding relied in part on Rhenish hardwoods – oak, elm, cherry and ash – for its supply of spars, masts, yards, staves, and knees (Bowring, 1840:137). Industrial and commercial building in Cologne and the Ruhr was dependent on Rhenish timber. The discovery of the deep seams in 1838 that launched the great expansion of the Ruhr coalfields brought with it an equally sudden rise in the demand for mining timbers (Henderson, 1975:54). Timber prices rose no less in the fuel market where beech was extensively used as an industrial firing fuel, and where timber remained the main source of working-class fuel consumption despite the growing importance of coal. The price of beech tripled between the beginning of the century and 1841. Between 1830 and 1841 it doubled, rising in part due to the demand for railway ties (Banfield, 1846:109). Constructional timber prices rose by 20 per cent during the same period.

This secular trend in forest prices and the struggle of the 'peasant proletariat' against it (Noyes, 1966:23) brought about a real crisis in legitimate appropriation that required the active intervention of the state. That which exports to Belgium and Holland started, the wind and the sun completed, and hundreds of years of soil and mulch in the Rhenish broadleaf forests were destroyed in the first part of the century (U.S. Government, 1887:74). The free alienation of forest lands, their subdivision and parcelling, and the violent, unplanned clearing of the woods threatened both part of the livelihood of an entire class in the Rhineland and sound principles of sustained yield management. Without succumbing to the romanticism of the forest which seems everywhere to accompany its destruction (e.g., Chateaubriand – 'forests preceded people, deserts followed them'), we must note that on the vanguard of the movement to 'preserve' the German woods was the Prussian state anxious to socialize the capital locked up in private forest acres.

For a start, the state reduced the clearing of its own forests and expanded the proportion of forests it owned relative to private, corporate and village forests. By the summer of 1841 more than one half of the Rhenish forests were Prussian owned or controlled. Under state encouragement an apparatus, independent of particular capitalists, was developed for the scientific study and management of timber. G. L. Hartig (1764–1837), organizer of the Prussian Forest Service, and Heinrich Cotta (1763–1844), founder of the Forest Academy at Tharandt (the oldest such school in the world), pioneered the development of scientific sylviculture. Partially under their influence, the free assart and clearing of the forest was subjected to state supervision in order to prevent the further depredation of the woods. The schools established in this movement produced a forest police expert in soil rent theory, actuarial calculations, afforestation scheduling, and cutting according to age–class composition. Not until the end of the century had the Germans lost their pre-eminence in sustained yield management.[5]

Enforcing the plans developed by these specialists in sustained yield and capital turnover against a working population increasingly ready to thwart them stood the cadres of the police and the instruments of law. 'No state organization was more hated', a Prussian sylviculturist wrote, 'than the forest police' (quoted in Heske, 1938:254). At the end of the nineteenth century the mere listing of the manuals and books of the Prussian forest police filled 61 pages in a standard bibliography (Schwappach, 1894). The law that these cadres enforced, in state *and* corporate and village forests, was the result of some centuries of development. Nothing could be more misleading than to regard the legislation criticized by Marx as law that with a single stroke cut through the thicket of feudal rights in order to establish the property law of the bourgeoisie. That process had been going on for a long time, at least since the forest ordinances of 1515 which, more than anything else, had abolished the unwritten, communal norms of the Carolingian period. The revisions of the law which Marx criticized were modifications of the main legal instrument concerning Prussian forests, the Forestal Theft Act of 1837

(U.S. Government, 1887:53). Several other German states had recently reorganized their forest police and revised their written codes. That of Baden, for example, enacted in 1833, contained 220 sections establishing rules and punishments for nearly every detail of forest appropriation. In Thuringia and Saxe-Meiningen similar codes were established. Written permits were required for berry and mushroom gathering. Dead leaves and forest litter could be gathered for fodder only 'in extreme cases of need'. The topping of trees for May poles, Christmas trees, rake handles, wagon tongues, etc., was punishable by fine and prison. By the 1840s most forests of Prussia had become subject to the police and deputies of the *Forstmeister* of the Ministry of Interior in Berlin (Banfield, 1846:115). The moment of class relations reflected in Marx's articles was not that of the transition from feudalism to capitalism or even one whose reflection in the law marked a transition from Teutonic to Roman conceptions of property. Each of these had occurred earlier. Nevertheless, it was an important moment in class relations which is to be measured not only by its intensity for which there is ample evidence, but also by its victories, an aspect of which must be studied in the obstacles placed upon the creation of a factory proletariat in the 1840s.

The countryman had a tenacious memory. 'The long vanished days when there in the teeming forests anyone who wished might load his cart with wood, remained unforgotten throughout Germany' (Treitschke, 1919:vii, 302). Of course, *anyone* could never have loaded his cart with wood. That some could think so is testimony to the power of the movement in the 1830s and 1840s that was able to confuse the issue of lost rights with the direct appropriation regardless of its ancient legitimacy. Lenin in a similar context warned against accepting those 'honeyed grandmothers' tales' of traditional 'paternal' relations, a point that must be stressed even while we note that such tales have a way of becoming a force in themselves.

One need not be a specialist in nineteenth-century German folklore to recognize that much of the imagination of the forester expressed hostility to the forces transforming the forests and their societies. In these imaginary worlds the trees themselves took sides with the cotters against their oppressors. Michael the Woodman roamed the forests of the Odenwald selecting trees destined for export on which to place his mark. Such trees were fated to bring misfortune upon their ultimate users: the house built of them would burn, the ship would sink (Hughes, 1910:36). Knorr in the Black Forest played pranks on travellers. The wild Huntress in the same place gave strangers wrong directions. Particular trees were endowed with marvelous powers. A cherry whose loose boughs provided the cradle of a lost infant, a walnut that withstood the sieges of tumultuous gales, these could confer unexpected generosities upon neighboring peasants. Others exercised capricious malevolence against wayfarers, travellers or others strange to the woods. The legends and stories of the forests testified to the fact that poor woods-people and the peasants of the purlieus could find friends in the densest regions of the forest against the oppressions not only of princes and seigneurs but also of their more recent enemies – the tax collector, the forest police, and the apostles of scientific forest management.

By the end of the 1830s the forests of the Rhineland were haunted by more effectual dangers than the evil spirits of popular imagination. Thus in 1842 a Prussian guidebook warned travellers:

> Keep as much as possible to the highways. Every side path, every woodway, is dangerous. Seek herbage in towns when possible, rather than in villages, and never, or only under the most urgent necessity, in lonely ale-houses, mills, wood-houses, and the like. . . . Shouldst thou be attacked, defend thyself manfully, where the contest is not too unequal; where that is the case, surrender thy property to save thy life (quoted in Howitt, 1842:89–90).

The real dangers in the forests before the revolution of 1848 were not those that Michael the Woodman might effect upon wayfarers but those that a mass movement for the appropriation of forest wealth placed upon capitalist accumulation. In 1836, of a total of 207,478 prosecutions brought forward in Prussia, a full 150,000 were against wood pilfering and other forest offences (Cornu, 1958:ii, 74; Wilson, 1940:41). In Baden in 1836 there was one conviction of woodstealing for every 6.1 inhabitants. In 1841 there was a conviction for every 4.6 inhabitants, and in 1842 one for every four (Banfield, 1846:111).

So widespread was this movement that it would not be much of an exaggeration to say that German criminology cut its teeth in the tabulation of this movement. From the standpoint of later bourgeois criminology their works appear crude methodologically and in their substance, so many trivialities. Dr. G. Mayr, for instance, one of the first academic statisticians of criminology and the Zollverein, discovered that the more difficult it is to gain a livelihood in a lawful manner, the more crimes against property will be committed. Hence property crimes will vary directly with the price of provisions and inversely with the level of wages. He discovered that wood pilfering was likely to be greater in regions where privately owned forests prevailed over corporate and communal forests (Mayr, 1867: chapter 4). W. Starke studied the theft of wood in Prussia between 1854 and 1878. He concluded that the theft of wood was greater during the winter than the summer, and greater in cold years than in warm ones (Starke, 1884:88). L. Fuld made painstaking calculations to show that in Prussia between 1862 and 1874 there was a significant positive correlation between the price of rye and the number of convictions for the theft of wood. Valentini, the director of prisons in Prussia, discovered that within the eight districts of Prussia that he studied, the amount of crimes recorded varied according to the forms of land tenure prevalent in each. He found that in the 'dwarf economy' of the Rhineland, where the parcelling of land had been carried to its extremes, pauperism was highest and the pilfering of wood the greatest, though these high rates did not hold for other types of crimes 'against property' (Valentini, 1869:58). However, objectionable as such work may appear to the more sophisticated calculators of crime, one must stress that it reflects in part a real social analysis of the wage, or a decisive form of income, for a large part of the western Prussian proletariat. It is just as much an indication of that struggle as the 'honeyed grandmothers' tales'. In fact, we could say that the development of scientific sylviculture and of positivist criminology were two sides of the same coin: one studying sustained yield and the other the endemic ('moral', as they would say) obstacles to that yield.

If we take a glance forward to the revolution of 1848 a number of our problems become clarified. First, the great rural jacqueries of March that swept southwestern Germany were in part united by their common attempts to re-appropriate the wealth of the forests, sometimes under the slogan calling for the recovery of lost rights and other times not. The attempts were geographically widespread and common to several juridically distinct sectors of the agrarian population – feudal tenants, day laborers, crofters and cotters alike (Droz, 1957:151–155). Second, this movement defies a rigid separation between a class of 'rural peasants' and 'urban workers', as the coordination and leadership of them was the responsibility of itinerant handworkers, loggers, rivermen, bargemen, teamsters, and wagoners, precisely those categories of workers with a foot both in the 'country' and the 'city'. Furthermore, the working class that was locked within 'backward' settings of manufacture and domestic industry burst out in flashes of destruction against factories and machines, a movement that paralleled the struggle against the forest police, enclosures, functionaries, tax collectors, and forest owners, a movement that in the Rhineland certainly was often united by the same personnel (Adelmann, 1969: *passim*). This is not the place to consider the strengths and weaknesses of the revolutionary working class of 1848 as a whole, nor do we mean to replace as its revolutionary subject the eastern textile workers or the Berlin craftsmen with the south German agrarian masses. We only wish to indicate that the relation between the 'latent' and 'stagnant' labor reserves to capitalist development in the Rhineland, some of whose unities we've tried to suggest, had their political analogues in 1848. The Frankfurt Assembly of 1848 found that the work of its Agriculture and Forestry Commission overlapped with that on Workers' Conditions and that the problems of repression of autonomous rural and urban movements were similar (Noyes, 1966: chapters 9 and 13).

The defeat of these movements, more than anything else, paved the way for the advanced assault of German industrialization. Only after 1848 do those familiar indices of capitalist power against the working class (spindles per factory, number of steam engines employed, output of pig iron, etc.) begin to 'take off'. In light of that it is especially poignant to find that it was not until late into the Nazi period that the full expropriation of forest rights was completed, a time, in other words, when they had long ceased to be a principal terrain of struggle (Heske, 1938:240ff.). It is a fact worth considering nevertheless by those who consider the final expropriation of such rights as the decisive moment in the birth of capitalism!

In sketching the dynamics of the class struggle in western Prussia during the 1840s, we've tried to show that the problem of the theft of wood should be seen neither as a problem of Primary Accumulation in the expropriation of a feudal peasantry nor as a problem of an anarchic, individualized 'lumpenproletariat'. Instead, we've attempted to present the elements of an analysis that cast the problem in a different light. In particular, we've seen in it a struggle to maintain and increase one of the forms of value of the working class, a form that enabled it for a time to reject those terms of work and exploitation that German capital was seeking to make available in the factory. We recall that the detonators of the working-class explosion in the spring of 1848 were precisely various categories of workers, agrarian and urban, within different forms of the relative redundant population. Marginal, to be sure, from the point of view of Siemens or Krupps, but a historic mass vanguard nevertheless. Other recent examples come easily to mind. We may end by noting that the author of *Capital*, the work that is the starting point of the working-class critique of the capitalist mode of production and that provides us with the concepts for at once analyzing the forms of the divisions within the working class and the conditions for using these within the revolutionary struggle against capital, dedicated his work to a Silesian peasant, Wilhelm Wolff, 'the brave, noble fighter in the vanguard of the proletariat'.

Notes

1. I have found the article by Paolo Carpignano, 'U.S. Class Composition in the Sixties' , *Zerowork 1* (December 1975), invaluable in the development of this theme.
2. One thinks here of those 'deviancy specialists' influenced by Althusser (see, for example, Hirst, 1972: 28–56). It may be that Marx 'never developed an adequate philosophical reflection of his scientific discoveries'. However, some account of those discoveries is in order, especially when by Marx's own account one of his most important contributions over the advances made by Adam Smith and David Ricardo was that of the principle of historical specification of the categories of political economy (Marx, 1867: 52–4).
3. I would like to thank E. J. Hobsbawm and Margaret Mynatt at Lawrence and Wishart who kindly assisted me in making available the English translation of these articles before their publication.
4. There does exist a small literature on Marx's articles (see, for example, Cornu, 1958: ii, 72ff., and Vigouroux, 1965: 222–3) but its chief interest is in the intellectual passage of Marx's thought from Kant, Rousseau and Savigny to Feuerbach and Hegel.
5. Even at the end of the nineteenth century the Italian, French and English literature on forestry subjects presented a dearth in comparison with the German. This is the conclusion of the American sylviculturist Bernhard Fernow (1902: 492).

References

Adelmann, Gerhard (1969) 'Structural Change in the Rhenish Linen and Cotton Trades at the Outset of Industrialization' in F. Crouzet, W. H. Chaloner and W. M. Stern, *Essays in European Economic History, 1789–1914* (London: Arnold).

Ainlay, John (1975–6) 'Review of Ian Taylor, Paul Walton and Jock Young, The New Criminology', (1973) in *Telos 26*.

Banfield, T. C. (1846) *Industry on the Rhine: Agriculture* (London: C. Knight & Co.).

—— (1848) *Industry on the Rhine: Manufactures* (London: C. Cox).

Bonger, William Adrian (1905) *Criminalité et Conditions Economiques* (Amsterdam: G. P. Tierie).

Bowring, John (1840) 'Report on the Prussian Commercial Union', *Parliamentary Papers*, XXI.

Cornu, Auguste (1958) *Karl Marx et Friedrich Engels: Leur Vie et leur œuvre*, 3 vols (Paris: Presses Universitaires de France).

Crime and Social Justice Collective (1976) 'The Politics of Street Crime', *Crime and Social Justice*, 5 (Spring – Summer) 1–4.

Currie, Elliott (1974) 'Review: The New Criminology', *Crime and Social Justice*, 2 (Fall–Winter) 109–13.

Deveze, Michel (1961) *La Vie de la Forêt Française au XVIᵉ siècle*, 2 vols (Paris: S.E.V.P.E.N.).

Droz, Jacques (1957) *Les Révolutions Allemandes de 1848* (Paris: Presses Universitaires de France).

Endres, Max (1905) *Handbuch der Forstpolitik* (Berlin: J. Springer).

Fernow, Bernhard E. (1902) *Economics of Forestry: A Reference Book for Students of Political Economy* (New York: T. W. Crowell).

Fuld, L. (1881) *Der Einfluss der Lebensmittelpreise auf dem Bewegung der Strafbaren Handlunger* (Mainz: J. Diemer).

Hamerow, Theodore S. (1958) *Restoration, Revolution, Reaction: Economics and Politics in Germany, 1815–1971* (Princeton University Press).

Henderson, W. O. (1939) *The Zollverein* (Cambridge University Press).

—— (1975) *The Rise of German Industrial Power 1834–1914* (Los Angeles: University of California Press).

Heske, Franz (1938) *German Forestry* (New Haven: Yale University Press).

Hirst, Paul Q. (1972) 'Marx and Engels on law, crime and morality', *Economy and Society*, I, 1 (February).

—— (1973) 'The Marxism of the "New Criminology"', *The British Journal of Criminology*, XIII, 4 (October) 396–8.

Howitt, William (1842) *Rural and Domestic Life in Germany* (London: Longman, Brown, Green and Longmans).

Hughes, C. E. (1910) *A Book of the Black Forest* (London: Methuen).

König, H. (1927) *Die Rheinische Zeitung von 1842–43 in ihrer Einstellung zur Kulturpolitik des Preussischen Staates* (Munster: F. Coppenrath).

Lengerke, A. V. (1849) *Die Landliche Arbeiterfrage* (Berlin: Büreau des Königl. ministeriums für landwirthschaftliche angelegenheiter).

Lenin, V. I. (1899) *The Development of Capitalism in Russia* (Moscow: Foreign Languages Publishing House).

Manwood, John (1717) *Manwood's Treatise of the Forest Laws*, Fourth edition, ed. by William Nelson (London: B. Lintott).

Marx, Karl (1842) 'Proceedings of the Sixth Rhine Province Assembly. Third Article. Debates on the Law of the Theft of Wood', Karl Marx and

Frederick Engels, *Collected Works*, Vol. 1 (New York: International Publishers, 1975).

—— (1859) *A Contribution to the Critique of Political Economy*, translated by N. I. Stone (Chicago: Charles Kerr, 1904).

—— (1867) *Capital: A Critical Analysis of Capitalist Production*, Vol. 1, translated by Samuel Moore and Edward Aveling (London: George Allen and Unwin).

Mayr, G. (1867) *Statistik der Gerichtlichen Polizei im Königreiche Bayern* (Munich: J. Gotteswinter & Mösel).

Mehring, Franz (1962) *Karl Marx: The Story of his Life*, translated by Edward Fitzgerald (Ann Arbor: University of Michigan Press).

Melossi, Dario (1976) 'The Penal Question in *Capital*', *Crime and Social Justice*, 5 (Spring – Summer) 26–33.

Milward, Alan S. and S. B. Saul (1973) *The Economic Development of Continental Europe 1780–1870* (New Jersey: Rowman and Littlefield).

Noyes, P. H. (1966) *Organization and Revolution: Working Class Associations in the German Revolutions of 1848–1849* (Princeton University Press).

Palgrave, R. H. (1912) *Dictionary of Political Economy*, 3 volumes (London: Macmillan).

Perrie, Maureen (1972) 'The Russian Peasant Movement of 1905–1907: Its Social Composition and Revolutionary Significance', *Past & Present*, 57 (November).

Phillipson, Michael (1973) 'Critical Theorising and the "New Criminology"', *The British Journal of Criminology*, XIII, 4 (October) 398–400.

Schwappach, Adam (1894) *Forstpolitik* (Leipzig: C. L. Hirschfeld).

Schwendinger, H. and Schwendinger, J. (1976) 'Collective Varieties of Youth', *Crime and Social Justice*, 5 (Spring–Summer).

Starke, W. (1884) *Verbrechen und Verbecher in Preussen 1854–1878* (Berlin: T. C. F. Enslin).

Stein, H. (1972) 'Karl Marx et le pauperisme rhénan avant 1848', *Jahrbuch des Kölnischen Geschichtsvereins*, XIV.

Taylor, Ian *et al.* (1973) *'Rejoinder to the Reviewers'*, *The British Journal of Criminology*, XIII, 4 (October) 400–3.

Treitschke, H. v. (1919) *A History of Germany in the Nineteenth Century*, translated by Eden and Cedar Paul, 7 volumes (New York: McBride, Nast).

U.S. Government (1887) *Forestry in Europe: Reports from the Consuls of the United States* (Washington, D.C.: Government Printing Office).

Valentini, H. v. (1869) *Das Verbrecherthum in Preussische Staat* (Leipzig).

Vigouroux, Camille (1965) 'Karl Marx et la législation forestière Rhénane de 1842', *Revue d'histoire économique sociale*, XLIII, 222–3.

Wilson, Edmund (1940) *To the Finland Station* (New York: Harcourt, Brace).

5
Delinquency and the Collective Varieties of Youth

Herman Schwendinger and Julia Schwendinger

Introduction

Taken as a whole, the presentation of material in *Delinquency and the Collective Varieties of Youth* is organized on varying levels of abstraction. The first half of the manuscript (the very first section of which is reproduced here) contains fairly abstract discussions of causal relationships while the later sections gradually concretize the analysis, focusing on specific times and places. These conjunctures in time and place will be derived from historical literature on delinquency, but they will emphasize the development of delinquent formations in the Los Angeles area of California. We initially gathered the data about these formations by continuous participant observations between 1959 and 1962. In 1963 a preliminary statement about the research was written and further research, now involving a large research project, was begun. This research, which followed up the previous investigation, lasted until 1967.

In the succeeding years, the research was restricted to data processing and analysis. Simultaneously, we concentrated on a critical evaluation of the last half century of delinquency theory in preparation for the theoretical section of a delinquency manuscript. That study, however, rapidly transformed itself into a wide-ranging evaluation of the formative years of American sociology, important here because modern delinquency theory was found to be seriously influenced by the general orientation toward man, woman and society being constructed from 1883 to 1922 by liberal intellectuals. Delinquency theorists applied the writings of these intellectuals, because they provided the foundations for whole families of adaptable theoretical ideas, including social disorganization theories, mass society theories, pluralism, structural functionalism and conflict theories. Thus, our analysis moved far beyond delinquency theory into other forms of social thought that had structured a host of modern sociological ideas. The unintended consequence of this analysis was *The Sociologists of the Chair,* published by Basic Books in 1974.

The five sections below are from the aforementioned work-in-progress, *Delinquency and the Collective Varieties of Youth,* a theory of adolescence and delinquency. According to this theory, the social forms of delinquency today are produced by economic, political and ideological relationships that have been components of the early development of capitalism. Although these relationships have been undergoing change, they continue to exist in advanced capitalist societies. In socialist societies some of these relationships can be eliminated rapidly. The other relationships, however, require thoroughgoing social transformations.

The Collective Varieties suggests that relatively autonomous, highly variable, stratified adolescent formations, that are not inclusive of all the youth in a community, mediate the relations between (1) the socioeconomic formations among adults and (2) the modal patterns of delinquency among youth. Superficially, the causal conditions underlying the adolescent formations and their delinquency modalities appear to be located in the sphere of commodity circulation and consumption. These causal conditions, which exist within the family and the school because they reproduce the forces and relations of production intergenerationally, are fetishized by bourgeois scholars. Beneath the surface, however, the essential causes of delinquency are embedded in the relations that reproduce and maintain the capitalist mode of production.

If we turn our attention away from delinquency and toward adolescent formations, then social production relations come into view once again. The structures of adolescent formations within a local society of youth are very complex. Certain aspects of these structures, which are organized around fads and fashions, for instance, are extremely unstable. Other aspects, however, are much more durable because they are determined by long-term trends. The study of the structures of adolescent formations thus requires an identification of cause and effect relationships on a number of analytic levels. While a structure in its broadest detail is determined by causal relationships on all levels, on the deepest level there are relationships that are based on social production relations and hence class conditions. These relationships are involved whenever *The Collective Varieties* refers to the components of a 'general structure' or the 'basic structure' of a local society of youth.

The following five sections introduce the reader to the production relations that underlie the development of three types of adolescents, who personify basic structural relations within a local society of youth. Although numerous geographical and temporal variations exist, in Los Angeles during the late 1950s, these types were often named Socialite, Vato, and Intellectual. Future work will indicate that there are other economic relations, as well as other types of adolescent relations, that provide primary reference points for mapping the general structures of adolescent formations. Since crime and delinquency never emerge directly from economic conditions above, subsequent work will contain major sections on the political and ideological relations that determine the variations in delinquent groups, as well as the structural variations within local societies of youth.

Schwendinger　You say that if you haven't got the 'coins' you can burn someone who has the coins and that way you can be equal to him?

Thief　That way you can have what everyone else has.

Schwendinger　What about the guy you burn? What do you say about that guy?

Thief　Tough shit! If you burn him and get away with it – more power to you.

Schwendinger　You mean getting the coins is enough of a justification?

Thief　Yeah, if a guy is fool enough to let himself get fucked – well, then, too bad! Almost anyone who has got coins to start out with, got them somehow. And, in my opinion, I suspect that maybe he didn't burn somebody for those coins, but in a roundabout way those coins were burnt. Otherwise he wouldn't have so much coins. No matter how he lived in the business world – there is always some chicken-shit stuff going on in it. Somebody's burning somebody and one of them is gonna get the coins.

> Fragments of a conversation with
> a white marginal youth from a
> middle-class family

The wild rogues

Every political economy generates its own material causes and legal categories of crime. Youthful lawbreakers certainly existed before capitalism, but the monumental changes that were initiated by the capitalist mode of production created their own causes and definitions of youthful behavior. With regard to the material causes, the historical facts are incontrovertible: capitalist developments from the late fourteenth century onwards ripped apart the ancient regime and introduced new patterns of criminality among the youth. In the wake of these early capitalist developments bourgeois officials instituted new forms of legal repression. Even before the industrial revolution such bourgeois institutions as the asylum, the prison, the workhouse, and the half-way house, had become familiar social landmarks. Further, categories that are central to modern views of young criminality, such as the 'juvenile delinquent' and 'delinquency,' were being added to the rhetoric of social control by bourgeois reformers at the onset of this revolution.

When we examine the beginnings of these developments in England, we find that the historical intersection of capitalism and youthful criminality was presaged in England by the great mid-fourteenth-century bubonic plague. This plague decimated the population, created a scarcity in labor, and weakened the yoke of feudalism. During the succeeding decades, young and old escaped the thrall of serfdom by every possible means. By rising up in fury against their lords, many revolutionary serfs dared to become independent farmers. Some, however, fled fearfully from the mailed fist of a military retainer and huddled together in forest bands. Others put packs on their backs and tramped the roads in all directions. They sustained themselves by working as wage laborers, by squatting on a plot of available land, or by practising the ancient arts of deception and thievery.

Subsequently, a carnival of crime erupted from this swirling decomposition of feudal relations and the rise of early capitalism. New criminal populations soon stabilized and began to reproduce themselves generationally. The children of 'harlots','hedge priests', and 'sturdy beggars' were taught 'evil catches' instead of the skills of the ploughman, spinner, and artisan. Upon reaching adulthood, which, at the time, fell anywhere between the ages of 14 and 17, these youngsters took to the roads singly or in bands. They roamed the countryside by day, slept in barns or in damp fields at night, and stole, pillaged, and begged from the population at large.

Throughout the fifteenth and the sixteenth centuries, these youth, dubbed *Wilde Rogues* and *Wilde Dells*, could still be seen in the countryside. Some, however, traveled to urban centers and became acquainted with pickpockets, gamblers, and confidence men; they joined the ranks of the city prostitutes or apprenticed themselves to the thieving beggars. Others, on leaving their rural communities, quickly found work as casual laborers and were swallowed up in the poorer communities of the larger towns.

Meanwhile, within the cities, the persons in the shadow of the law were also reproducing themselves. In Alsatia, a thieves' quarter centered in the very heart of London, and in the poorer districts on the edge of the city, one found the street prostitutes who were called *Walking Morts,* the genial *Doxies* who were companions of common rogues, and the raucous *Bawdy Baskets* who stole linen while they hawked lace, needles, and pins. Along with others in similar circumstances, these women instructed their little boys, the *Kynchen Coes,* and their younger daughters, the *Kynchen Morts,* to silently 'creep in at windows and cellar doors' and to pursue dilingently a life of crime.[1]

The descendants of prostitutes or thieves, the apprentices to the city rogues, and the young rural vagrants, were not the only youth who were designated criminals. Immediately surrounding the quarters of Walking Morts, Bawdy Baskets and Doxies, there lived a population of working men and women and thier numerous offspring. These children passed the time with one another, laughing, playing, and brawling in streets. Such rowdy and boisterous youth took their own places among the pre-capitalist repertoire of troublesome social types.

Such rowdy behavior was not tolerated for long. As early capitalism evolved, some citizens demanded that every indigent soul be harnessed to the wheels of commerce and industry. These citizens condemned the 'idle' and 'mischievous' lives led by the children of the poor. Thomas Firmin, a seventeenth-century bourgeois philanthropist, claimed to have observed these children 'in whole companies at play' in the out-parts of the city.[2] He indignantly declared that they were forever wrangling, cheating, swearing, and fighting with one another. He alleged that they were a menace to equestrian traffic, that they were fond of throwing stones at the passing coaches, and that they even made horsemen lose their lives by maliciously whipping the horses, causing the hapless riders to be cast to the ground.

To eliminate this idleness, maliciousness and violence, Firmin urged the creation in every parish of a workhouse for destitute youth. Around 1698, the governors of the London Workhouse established their institution partly with this very purpose in mind. They also proclaimed that the institution would control 'Vagrant orphans, known by the name of the *Black Guard* whose parents being dead, were reduc'd to the greatest Extremities: and being destitute of Relations, Friends, and all the Necessaries of Life, were become the Pest and Shame of the City, by Pilfering and begging about the Streets by Day, and lying therein almost naked in all the Seasons of the Year by night'.[3]

The Black Guard also contained youth who were not orphans. By choice or necessity, the children of the poor left home early; and some of these waifs joined the pathetic gangs that roamed the streets of London.

In a 1753 letter to the *London Chronicle*, Saunders Welch complained that poor families in manufacturing towns often allowed seven-year-old children to leave home without instructing them in the habits of industry. He stoutly maintained that the workhouse would actually prevent these youngsters from becoming 'a dreadful nuisance to society'.[4] This institution, however, seems to have had no effect: long after workhouses had been established, thousands of youth were still to be found clothed in rags, sleeping half naked in city streets, or living in cheap, filthy lodgings.

Consequently, whenever the causes of delinquency were in question, writers still emphasized personal destitution and parental supervision. The facts certainly spoke for themselves: in 1790, for instance, a boy was caught in the act of theft while his companions escaped. The young culprit did not live with his family but, a constable reported, he slept 'in a cellar in St. Giles, where fourteen or fifteen boys of different ages assemble, and pay two pence a night for their lodgings'. Upon examination, the constable found that 'the cellar where [the boys] all lay was filthy beyond description'.[5] The boy's theft, therefore, could certainly be accountable to his destitute condition and the simple lack of parental care.

Criminality among the young was also attributed to other relationships such as immoral upbringing and lenient authorities. Prison conditions were even considered as a causal factor. In 1776, for instance, reformers began to use the term 'juvenile delinquent' to emphasize the relative innocence and gullibility of young imprisoned offenders. Older criminals, the reformers said, corrupted the morals of juvenile delinquents in prison with innumerable tales of criminal adventures, strategems, and escapes. Exposure to hardened criminals in prison caused 'delinquents' to engage in even greater crimes.[6]

Thus, by the close of the early period of capitalist development, delinquency was being ascribed to a variety of causes. In 1816, in the first official survey of delinquency, a London Commission initially observed that thousands of boys and girls were daily committing crimes within the city. The Commission further reported that youths were organized into numerous gangs and 'resorted regularly to houses, where they planned their enterprises and afterwards divided the produce of their plunder'. After looking into these delinquent relationships, the commissioners took pains to enumerate the causes one by one. They stated that youth had become delinquent because of the lack of education, improper parental supervision, the want of employment, the association with thieves and prostitutes, the severity of the criminal code, the defective state of the police, and the inadequate system of prison discipline.[7]

In certain respects the Commission report seems to have been sophisticated for its time, because an unending flow of pertinent observations and causal analyses, written in a similar vein, has continued to appear to the present day. In actuality, however, the report merely reflected the myopic perspective which is always bound to founder, when delinquency is viewed as a chaotic jumble of causal factors, and apart from general capitalist conditions.

Interestingly, some general capitalist conditions were actually mentioned by very early bourgeois officials who, when they considered the origins of crime, may have had in mind the Wilde Rogues or the Black Guard. As early as 1516, for instance, the Sheriff of London, Thomas More, suggested that crime was increasing alarmingly because of impoverishment and the disintegration of parish life. These conditions, he said, were due in turn to the private appropriation of communal lands, the burgeoning unemployment among household retainers, and the growing avarice among clergymen, nobles, and gentlemen. His famous work *Utopia*, which was written at that time, attributed these factors to the increasing organization of societal relationships around cash payments rather than traditional obligations.[8] In fact, More was fully persuaded that social justice and individual happiness could never be attained for the greater part of humanity unless private property was utterly abolished.

Thomas More may have been wrong in some respects but history would show that he was certainly pointing in the right direction. Furthermore, the property relations that More condemned eventually evolved into a social order based on the accumulation of capital, transcending any plutocratic society that even he could have imagined. In addition to More's observations of changes in land ownership, historians have documented the gradual demise of the main forms of feudal servitude along with the evolution of the capitalist mode of production in the fourteenth and fifteenth centuries. By the turn of the sixteenth century, a great class of independent peasants had appeared alongside the independent artisans. But in the sixteenth and seventeenth centuries this type of petty property relation was subsequently transformed by the fusion of the domestic market with the world market, the rise of the great landowners, merchant-capitalists, and joint-stock companies, and by the imperialist plunder of overseas civilizations.[9]

Thomas More would also have been astounded at the changes in the seventeenth-century economic scene! Thousands of citizens at that time were investing in new trading ventures at home and abroad; the Merchant Adventurers alone numbered 7200 members. Tens of thousands of slaves were being shipped to the Caribbean Islands, and used in early capitalist plantation economies. By the end of the seventeenth century, over 100,000 slaves had been abducted from Africa by a single trading company and the proportion of wealth enjoyed by the joint-stock companies had increased a thousand-fold.[10] New class relationships had become clearly visible: the bourgeoisie had fully emerged in town and countryside and was being steadily expanded by the unprecedented growth of mercantile relationships. Simultaneously, part of the propertyless and part of the hitherto-property owning class were still being relentlessly transformed into able-bodied paupers and wage-earning proletarians.

Thomas More certainly perceived a few of the important connections between an alarming increase in early sixteenth-century crime and the forms of impoverishment that accompanied these changes in the class composition of English society. But he did not realize that the *state* would play an absolutely essential role in the endless reproduction of these relations. At first, the monarchy provided sporadic opposition to capitalist economic trends. Later, however, the crown and the parliament vigorously advanced economic policies that rode roughshod over the customary rights of aristocrats, petty guildsmen, yeomen, and ardent Catholics. Struggles against these policies occurred on all class levels and in all parts of English society. For instance, because of the imposition of oppressive fines, high rents and the forcible enclosures of communal lands, bloody rebellions against the wealthy landowners regularly took place among the farmers. Such rebellions were fought in 1549,

1550, and 1567; the largest of these, in 1549, led by Robert Ket, was brutally suppressed by an army of six thousand men! As a result, the disastrous effects of the commercialization of English rural life continued unabated.[11]

Thus, the early bourgeoisie relied on the state and its armed might to protect their claims to the ownership of the means of production. Equally important, however, was the role of the state in securing every conceivable species of labor power for their expanding enterprises. Depending upon the economic circumstances, the state enabled members of this social class to obtain and employ wage labor, bonded labor, convict labor, and slave labor for the accumulation of profit. By the end of the seventeenth century, government officials had utilized the sword, the musket, and the hangman's gibbet to enable the early bourgeoisie to appropriate the power of labor on an ever-increasing scale.

Because of these general capitalist conditions, countless numbers of people were placed between the jaws of a vise, which was largely fashioned on the one hand out of the annihilation of pre-existing modes of production and, on the other hand, out of a repressive, restricted, and unstable market for labor. People from many walks of life, such as the small landholders, artisans, monks, friars, military retainers, other servants, and wage laborers, were being cast off by the dissolution of the older modes of production.[12] They had become marginal members of the labor force; marginal because of unemployment, job instability and low compensation for their labor. Even when they did sell their labor power, they were barely able, or unable, to reproduce themselves and their families.

Because of the process of marginalization, entire families were denied consistent participation in self-sustaining economic relationships. The effects of this denial, which involved some children and adults in ordinary crime, were acutely recognized by the families hurled into the vortex of this agonizing social process. An anonymous tract, written in 1546, sadly exclaims:

> Many thousands of us which here before lived honestly upon our sore labor and travail, bringing up our children in the exercise of honest labor, are now constrained some to beg, some to borrow, and some to rob and steal. And that which is most like to grow to inconvenience, we are constrained to suffer our children to spend the flower of their youth in idleness, bringing them up to bear beggars' packs or else, if they be sturdy, to stuff prisons, and garnish gallow trees.[13]

Redundant youth

Eighteenth-century family members were pushed and pulled in all directions. Some attempted to escape economic hardships in rural areas by migrating to the cities. Others were driven like cattle to toil incessantly in the mines and the fields. Wherever capital secured a foothold in economic life, it sent agents to recruit men, women and children for the new industrial labor force.

Some families uprooted themselves completely from England and settled in the American colonies. Delinquency subsequently emerged in the new world, but the mere influx of marginals hardly represented the economic basis of this colonial emergence. Delinquency actually arose in the wake of economic and political conditions which were being established everywhere in nascent capitalist societies.

Consequently it is not surprising to find the lamentations of the sixteenth-century adult marginals being echoed by early nineteenth-century North Americans. In 1821, a Boston Commission noted that children were to be found everywhere 'begging in the streets, or haunting our wharves, market places, sometimes under pretence of employment, at others for the purpose of watching [for] occasions to pilfer small articles, and thus beginning a system of petty stealing; which terminates often in the gaol; often in the penitentiary; and not seldom, at the gallows'.[14] Citizens were also worried about the gangs of boys and girls in Philadelphia and Baltimore. Thereupon, reminiscent of the English workhouse, suggestions for the control of these youth were made throughout the following decades. In 1840, the inhabitants of Baltimore were confronted by a proposal for 'a manual labor school' that would only care for 'the class of boys [which forms] a distinct portion of the population of all large communities'. Understandably, this class of boys particularly included the half-fed, half-clothed, idle and delinquent children of the indigent.[15]

In the second half of the nineteenth century, marginalization had become consciously associated with indigent European immigrants, and their children, who at the crack of dawn sallied out from slum communities 'to do the petty work of the City, rag-picking, bone gathering, selling chips, peddling, by the thousands, radishes, strawberries, and fruit through every street'. A New York journalist stated in 1853 that these immigrants hung about 'the German boarding houses in Greenwich Street, losing their money, their children getting out of control, until they at last seek a refuge in

Ward's Island, or settled down in the Eleventh Ward, to add to the great mass of foreign poverty and misery there gathered'.[16]

The increasing density of the Eleventh Ward was as obvious as its poverty; in fact, Sanitary District A of this Ward eventually became the most densely populated area in the entire world. It contained 996.6 persons per acre for thirty-two acres. By comparison, 'The Josephstadt in Prague, the most slum-ridden area in Europe, had only 485.4 persons per acre, and even the most densely populated city in Asia – Bombay with 759.6 persons per acre – was less crowded'.[17]

The Eleventh Ward represented only one among the many inhuman expressions of the economic and political processes that produced concentrations of marginal populations. The Ward was located in Manhattan, a borough of New York City where, by the turn of the century, '14 per cent of the families . . . were evicted each year from their homes; 18 per cent of the population was continually on relief; and every year one person in ten who died was buried in potter's field'. With regard to the United States as a whole, 'even in prosperous years . . . four million Americans were public paupers [and] two million workers were unemployed from four to six months each year . . . '.[18]

On the other hand, regardless of whether their parents were marginals, propertyless children were an easily exploitable labor force, sought out for cheap employment. From the beginning of the nineteenth century, the expansion of the North American economy had incorporated large numbers of children who, along with their parents, had been previously employed in agriculture. But European farm children had not customarily been considered a distinct segment of the agrarian labor force. The notion of child labor eventually made this distinction when children became classified as one segment of the labor force within the factory system.[19]

The changing view of children as labor-force participants was illustrated by John Baxter, who sold textile machines when the industry was in its infancy in the United States. When selling equipment, he 'assured prospective customers that his new machines with six or twelve spindles respectively could be easily turned by "children of from five to ten years of age," while the twelve spindle machine would require "girls from twelve to twenty"'. Thus, the factory system measured the efficiency of child labor 'in terms of the necessary boy or girl power to produce a certain amount of yarn'.[20]

Children had therefore become clearly defined as a highly exploitable species of wage laborers. As distinct from feudal productive relations, these children did not exchange their labor power for their maintenance and instruction as apprentices. Instead, they received wages; and these wages were depressed, because in the factory a dual wage system was established, with one wage level for children and another for adults.

The manufactories integrated women as well as children into the new mode of production. Certain industries, in fact, employed women and children primarily. Take, for example, the labor force in the cotton mills of Rhode Island, southern Massachusetts, and eastern Connecticut between 1809 and 1816. At the beginning of this period, 4000 persons were employed in the mills but only 500 or 12.5 per cent of them were men. Seven years later, even though the mills employed 100,000 workers, 24,000 were boys under seventeen and 66,000 were women and girls. Women and children therefore still contributed 90 per cent this vastly expanded work force.[21]

Paradoxically, however, underemployment and unemployment among children as well as adults were eventually encouraged by the growth of industry itself. To compete successfully, industrialists invested in machine technology; hence, the same number of commodities could be produced with fewer hands. Wherever the expansion of capital was unrestricted, living labor was replaced by machines, and capital accumulation incessantly generated a redundant population of workers.

As indicated, the redundant workers included youth, who joined the ranks of the marginal population and sought further employment everywhere. The likelihood of finding stable employment, however, was subject to several interrelated conditions. It was dependent, in the first place, upon the expansion of the labor market. But this expansion itself was critically dependent upon capital's ability for self-accumulation by reconverting a portion of the profit into capital. (Thus, the reemployment of young technologically displaced workers was largely contingent upon the self-expansion of capitalist production and the subsequent expansion of job markets.) Furthermore, the self-expansion of capital was in turn dependent upon the realization of the values of commodities in circulation. (Capitalists must sell sufficient quantities of these commodities to make the profits that can be used for the expansion of capital investments.) Finally, the realization process was itself beset by the contradictions between the forces and relations of production. Periodically, these contradictions were manifested by the overproduction of commodities and capital, which satiated commodity markets, limited effective demand, and created widespread unemployment. Because of these interrelated economic conditions, job markets fluctuated in accordance with business cycles, with periods of growth and depression.

Stable employment for youth was also offset by long-term industrial trends. Though the rate of capitalist expansion surged sharply upwards after each economic crisis and gradually increased on the average throughout the nineteenth century, it was generally never high enough to absorb all the young workers in the labor market. As a result, the process of capital accumulation, which above all involved the production and overproduction of the means of production, continuously replenished the population of redundant youth.

The entire population of redundant workers was referred to as 'the relative surplus population' by Karl Marx. The population represented a relative surplus because it exceeded the labor force requirements that were sufficient for 'the average needs of the self-expansion of capital'.[22] Also called 'the industrial reserve army', these subemployed and unemployed workers were politically volatile. But, in the face of a weak labor movement, this army enabled the labor market to be regulated solely by supply and demand. Members of this army were used by capitalists to depress wage rates, break strikes, and ensure strict obedience to production norms.

The rise of the relative surplus population reflected historical changes in the process of marginalization. As indicated, whatever their ages, relative surplus workers are marginal members of the labor force; yet their genesis differs from that of other marginals. The discussion of marginalization heretofore concentrated on the dissolution of petty property relations and the remnants of pre-capitalist relations. However, with the growth of industry, capital affected the marginalization of its own industrial proletarians. Thus, while capitalism annihilated the older modes of production, it was simultaneously being afflicted with its own contradictions.

Contradictions, which are inherent to the capitalist mode of production, have in the twentieth century produced still further changes in the process of marginalization. In its most vigorous periods of development, capitalism accelerates the trend toward the replacement of living labor by machines. In its most advanced phase, however, another trend emerges: capitalism undergoes a long-term decline in the rate of accumulation of the means of production. Under advanced capitalist conditions, these forms of capital expand, but at a slower rate.

Taken together, the replacement of living labor by machines and the declining rate of accumulation of the means of production limit the rate of the expansion of the unskilled labor force in particular, as well as the rate of expansion of the entire labor force that is directly exploited for the production of surplus value.[23] Because they are generally employed in unskilled jobs, children and adolescents have particularly been affected by these developments. Child laborers were commonly employed by nineteenth-century industrial firms. In the twentieth century, children and adolescents were still employed, although they were being concentrated in the secondary labor market. Since the 1930s, however, their labor has become less profitable and youth have been gradually but not completely eliminated from the economy, first in basic industries and last agriculture.

Therefore, youth have not been excluded from labor markets because of child-labor laws, the decline of the 'family economy', or the emergence of the new occupational 'specializations' that require youth to abstain temporarily from employment to receive a high school or college degree. Youth have been excluded because the motive power of capitalist production is based on capital accumulation and the rate of profit rather than social needs.

These capitalist priorities also provide insight into 'the prolongation of the dependent status of youth'.[24] Today, youth are usually dependent upon parental support until later adolescence. (Some are even dependent through young adulthood.) Adolescents cannot maintain themselves in gainful employment and, because their educational activities do not produce immediate profits, their parents rather than capital have been forced to continue to bear the primary costs of their subsistence. As a result, millions of youth become subject to an extraordinary variety of social problems that accompany the statuses of dependent able-bodied persons in our society. As we shall see, certain kinds of delinquency among adolescents and young adults are due, in part, to prolonged dependency as well as to redundancy and dual labor markets.

On the other hand, one might argue that despite extremely high age-specific unemployment rates, many American youth today do manage to find work. But these youngsters often enter the most unstable and low-wage segments of the labor market, those called 'secondary labor markets' by dual labor market theorists.[25] According to these theorists, the development of dual labor markets is due to 'the historical processes whereby political–economic forces encourage the division of the labor market into separate submarkets, or segments, distinguished by different labor market characteristics and behavioral rules'.[26] The dual labor market in the nineteenth-century textile industry, for example, was segmented by age and sex. In modern times, however, the segmentation process has generated *primary* and *secondary* markets which are partly differentiated by a range of characteristics concerning job stability, wage levels, occupational mobility, etc. For instance, stable working habits are required by and developed within primary jobs. Wages are relatively high and opportunities for advancement exist. Secondary jobs, which are types of jobs generally available to youth, are quite different. Stable working habits are not generally required by secondary jobs; in fact, these jobs often discourage the development of these habits. Wages, furthermore, are relatively low and few opportunities for advancement exist.[27]

Turning back to primary jobs, we find that they are further segmented according to *subordinate* and *independent* primary jobs. Subordinate-primary jobs encourage routine behavior, dependability, discipline, responsiveness to rules and authority, and acceptance of a firm's goals. Independent-primary jobs, on the other hand, involve creative problem-solving and self-initiating characteristics and often have professional standards for work. In these jobs, individual motivation, creativity and achievement are highly rewarded.[28]

Minority workers and women workers are employed in all three labor market .segments: secondary, subordinate-primary, and independent-primary. Yet they are also segregated in distinct occupations within these submarkets. In addition, a great number of young Blacks, Chicanos, Puerto Ricans, and other third world people, are restricted to jobs that are 'race typed', that is, segregated by institutionalized racism. Many jobs are still dichotomized by sex and are organized around a discriminatory wage system. In these types of cases, labor market segmentation maintains social inequalities. It encourages racial, ethnic, and sexual chauvinism. It undermines working-class solidarity and the growth of class consciousness.[29]

Further discussion of labor market segmentation would describe the development of segmentation by type of firm, industry or economic sector. It would consider the role of unions in legitimizing and controlling the 'internal markets' within enterprises.[30] This discussion, however, would unnecessarily divert us from the general topic of marginalization and youth. To focus our attention once again on this topic, further observations should be made on the factors of segmentation and marginalization.

To begin with, the likelihood of marginalization itself can be seen to diminish as one progresses upwards from the situation of those who have been regularly unemployed, through workers in the secondary position, to the primary labor force, with its subordinate and independent segments. But members of the primary labor force can become marginals, because of the 'overproduction' of highly trained workers, technological displacement and economic stagnation. Marginalization, therefore, does occur within all segments of the labor market. In fact, job markets for highly trained workers may at times exhibit relatively greater instability because of particular economic conditions.

Furthermore, labor market segmentation blurs the boundary lines between the marginal members of the labor force and the other employed workers. Workers may be employed, yet remain marginal. When employed, marginals are generally confined to the secondary labor market and are the recipients of very low wages. For instance, the subemployed, who live at or below the poverty line, are employed marginals. In 1972, they numbered approximately two million workers.[31]

Finally, the factors of segmentation and marginalization are uniquely expressed within socialization agencies. In public and parochial schools, youth, while being prepared for labor market activity, are confronted by educational relationships that are synchronized with these economic factors. For instance, the 'tracking system', which segregates students according to their academic abilities, is synchronized with the segmentation processes that divide the labor force. In addition, the processes that produce academic failures as well as high achievers within the school are synchronized with the processes of marginalization within the labor market. These synchronic relationships will be described in the next section.

Greasers and intellectuals

Thus far we have seen that prior to the nineteenth century, marginals were originally produced and then 'chastized for their enforced transformation into vagabonds and paupers', *before* manufacturing establishments could absorb their labor power.[32] The process of marginalization subsequently annihilated urban artisanry and filled the debtors' prisons with artisans who were bankrupted by the rise of the pre-industrial manufactories and the domestic cottage industries. Afterwards, the expansion of industrialism marginalized the toilers who had worked within the cottage industries. Simultaneously, this expansion absorbed millions of other marginals while it was producing a relative surplus population. With the rise of monopoly capitalism, this population was generally restricted to the secondary labor market.

But long-term trends toward stagnation, which are characteristic of modern capitalist societies, inevitably occur and have only been overcome periodically. In colonial and semi-colonial capitalist societies, the effects of these trends on marginalization are particularly evident. Marginals in Venezuela, for instance, constitute almost one third of the population. The agrarian marginals live on subsistence payments or work without wages as such. On the edges of the cities, rural migrants and urban marginals, who are underemployed, intermittently employed, and just plain unemployed, live in rat-infested slums. Some of these persons are employed in part-time or otherwise unproductive jobs, largely concentrated in the inflated tertiary sector.[33] These persons are the menial 'service workers' or the 'penny capitalists', who desperately shift for themselves by scavenging, huckstering, working at odd jobs, and performing a variety of personal services for minimal payments.

The United States is also beset by long-term trends toward stagnation. The American economy no longer expands sufficiently to absorb most of its technologically displaced labor force – much less the new generation of workers. The rate of absorption has only surged for short periods during wartime or during a postwar boom. Generally, the younger, the older, and the most oppressed workers have been excluded from the labor market. Millions have become marginal! From an economic standpoint, these persons at any given time are either absolutely or relatively superfluous.[34]

We have also seen that advanced capitalism prolongs the dependent status of youth. This prolongation elevates the theoretical importance of certain factors in the socialization agencies, which include the family yet center on the modern school. These factors, as we shall see, uniquely recreate the process of marginalization *within* the socialization agencies themselves.

Analyses of the family and the school indicate that significant economic functions, which undoubtedly affect delinquent relations, are performed by these agencies. To grasp these functions abstractly, it should be recalled that capitalism matures with the generalization of commodity relations. This generalization involves the transformation of all the factors of production into commodities. In capitalism, therefore, workers, whose value-creating power is a factor of production, become commodity owners. They own their own creative power, that is, their labor power, which has been nurtured by the family and the school. In exchange for wages, workers sell to employers the right to dispose of their labor power in production.

To clarify this point, let us note that certain requirements must be met daily to *reproduce* the commodity, labor power. This power does not last: workers 'use up' their powers on the job. To renew their energies for each succeeding workday, they require, among other things, food, shelter, and clothing. For its own reproduction, labor power, therefore, requires the appropriation and consumption of 'the necessities of life'.

Finally, certain long-term relations are necessary for the *reproduction* of labor power. This power is a quality formed by the energetic acquisition of certain abilities, that is, certain kinds of knowledge, skills, experience, and discipline. Some of these abilities can be acquired on the job but, before or after employment begins, many basic skills, work attitudes, etc., can be partly learned within socialization agencies.

Most socialization agencies concentrate on youth who will generally become proletarians and who, therefore, require certain types of services for the production of their labor power. These services are largely provided by parents and by teachers, whose efforts, as indicated, are exerted in the family and in the school. With regard to the reproduction of labor power, both socialization agencies seem to operate separately while, in fact, they are quite interdependent.

Various kinds of interdependent relations characterize these agencies: obviously, a child's success in school is dependent upon his family relations. Empirical studies also indicate that the family is a stronger determinant of the child's eventual 'success' as a labor force participant. But *determination* of individual success cannot be equated with *domination* of the general standards which regulate successful striving. The family is forced to regulate its own productive relations according to the meritocratic and technical standards exerted by the school. With regard to the long-term reproduction of labor power, therefore, the school is the dominating agency.

The reproduction relations in the school are in turn largely dominated by industrial relations. Social scientists have clearly demonstrated that educational standards 'correspond' to the hier-archical and segmented organization of the labor force.[35] The standards used to reward and punish a student's behavior within the school, therefore, are synchronized with the standards that are used by managers to control workers.

The reproduction relations within the family are also dominated by industry, but this form of domination is partly mediated by the school. As indicated, the school, in spite of appearances, essentially organizes its production relations around industrially related stan-dards. By dominating production relations within the family, the school as well as industry imposes these standards on parents and children.

At least two general consequences flow from these serial relations of domination. First, the reproduction relations within socialization agencies are synchronized with the alienated social relations that generally characterize commodity production. These synchronized relations are not confined to the youngsters who are in the process of acquiring the power to labor. They include both the parents and the teachers, who are also involved in the long-term production of this commodity. Because of the essential nature of their reproductive relations, these adults, too, are alienated.

Second, these dominating relations are expressed in the same general laws of investment and profit maximization which culminate in the uneven development of various groups and nations.[36] Operatively, this means that investments in the development of the labor force are allocated unevenly. These investments concentrate on those groups of persons who are considered to have a greater potentiality for meeting the meritarian criteria which prevail in educational institutions. Conversely, the investments of private or public resources – which are calculable in terms of money, equip-ment, facilities, faculties, and even in the teacher's time, attention, and expectations – will be minimal for the development of those groups of persons who do not appear to meet these criteria.

Consequently, the allocation of educational resources favors those youth who have already been the recipients of superior resources. They are recipients because of the advantages that are passed on to the members of certain ethnic, racial, or occupational strata, or because of the compensatory time and energy expended on them by self-sacrificing parents. During the elementary school period, a mutually reinforcing relationship is set up between the activities of youth who show the productive signs of superior familial investments, and the patterns by which resources are selectively allocated within educational institutions. Throughout the child's formative period, educational capital continuously builds on the most favored students.

Simultaneously, the competitive position of the least favored students deteriorates and a process, which is analogous to marginalization within the economy, occurs in the context of the school and the family. This inherently contradictory trend becomes expressed in anarchic behavior patterns, created by youngsters who are not strongly motivated to achieve; who do not make any disciplined effort to achieve; and who actually do not achieve the cognitive and the non-cognitive traits that generally favor sustained labor force participation in the future. Although their chances for future employment are somewhat independent of their status in socialization agencies, these children manifest early in life the adaptive characteristics that evolve in capitalism among numerous owners of the least valuable forms of labor power.[37]

Thus, these relations that favor the uneven development of human capital early in life generate a youthful population of *prototypic* marginals, whose status is not actually determined directly by economic institutions. The members of this population are not usually counted among 'the employed' or 'the unemployed'. Instead, they are usually regarded as students and, during most of their adolescent years, workaday life is very far from their minds.

Within communities throughout the United States, adolescents speak about these prototypic marginals. Such names as Greaser, Vato, Dude, Honcho, Hodad, and Hood appear whenever they are mentioned in conversations. These metaphors refer to individual marginals and, among other social regularities in their personal behavior, to their conduct, carriage, attitudes, gestures, grooming, argot, clothing, and delinquent acts.

We shall discuss these names and their referents elsewhere. Those discussions, in addition, will assume that unless otherwise indicated, the term 'marginal' simply refers to 'prototypic' rather than labor force marginals. For now it should again be emphasized that the marginalization process under discussion is not directly determined by labor market relations. The effects of this process will therefore be reflected in family and school relationships, but they are not classified by any official economic category.

To avoid any misunderstanding it is taken for granted that certain types of family conflicts or 'breakdowns' will definitely enhance the possibilities of marginalization. But these possibilities are also mediated by parental resources. Wealthy families can employ such 'absorption mechanisms' as psychiatric counseling, boarding school, the tutorial trip abroad, etc., to cushion the effects of family disturbance on the child. If these mechanisms are unsuccessful, then their wealth further provides children who are becoming marginalized with a second chance later in life. Some of these children, in fact, never have to concern themselves with labor market activity: they can be sustained by inherited property.

By contrast, working-class families are exposed to greater hardships and difficulties. Absorption mechanisms are relatively unavailable and family problems directly influence the parent's and child's active contribution to the production of the child's labor power. They interact with the already disadvantaged competitive relations engendered by the school.

Consequently, traditional socioeconomic factors, such as the parent's income, education, and property, which represent the most widespread family characteristics, directly affect the likelihood of marginalization. Because of the long-term effects of the uneven development of capital, a greater proportion of marginal youth can be expected among lower status families. Alternatively, marginalization can certainly be expected among *higher* status families (or among 'middle class' families), but to a lesser degree.[38]

Let us now turn our attention to youth who, from the standpoint of the school, represent the most highly developed forms of labor power. Being high academic achievers, they strikingly epitomize the division of labor among mental and manual workers in capitalist societies. They are usually very articulate, and some have broad interests in political, cultural, and scientific relations. Others, who are noted for their narrow academic and technical interests, symbolize the degree to which young personalities have been influenced by the extreme labor force segmentation among mental workers. Their personal interests are 'overspecialized', and organized largely by experiences based on the appropriation and dispensation of technical knowledge.

In this work, the term 'prototypic intellectuals' will be used to characterize the youth who are mentioned above. The word 'intellectual' classifies the aggregate of persons who devote their occupational activities to the formulation of ideas, to the creation of artistic representations of ideas, or to the application of ideas, such as the application of scientific–technical knowledge to human affairs.

The development of modern intellectuals can be traced back to the early capitalist period. But this development has been accelerated enormously by expansion of monopoly capitalism and the modern state.[39] Today the category of intellectual includes writers, artists, librarians, social workers, city planners, teachers, and scientists.

The prototypic intellectual, on the other hand, refers to youth who manifest the personal interests and characteristics which have been generated among adults by the developments mentioned above. Historically, educational institutions have played a very important role in regulating the formation of this particular population. The schools have selected intellectuals from virtually every stratum in the population. Certain families, however, have contributed candidates disproportionately. Bourgeois families, including the small farmers as well as the independent professions, have supplied the greatest proportions. In recent years, the established families of such 'mental workers' as teachers, technicians, and scientists, are also contributing relatively higher numbers of prototypic intellectuals.

On the other hand, because of bourgeois educational policies and the intergenerational effects of uneven investment, young women, youth of both sexes who belong to racially oppressed groups, and children of unskilled workers become candidates to a lesser degree. It has been chiefly the white families of higher socio-economic status that have established a mutually dependent relation with the school. The children of families that *have* more *get* more, because the public educational system converts human beings into commodities and builds upon *that* human material which already has considerable investment.

In communities across the United States, one finds that the names for these types of youth also appear in peer conversations. Included among these names are Intellectual, Brain, Pencil-Neck, Egg-Head, Book-Worm, and Walking-Encyclopedia. We shall discuss these names and their referents in later work. For now, it should be noted that by contrast with many marginals, these youths are paragons of virtue. In fact, they are foremost members of the *least* delinquent population in a local society of youth.

Young gallants and apprentices

The previous sections discussed the objective conditions which lead to the development of prototypic marginals and intellectuals. The appearance of these conditions was synchronized with various phases in the development of capitalism. On the other hand, despite their different orgins, these conditions continue to operate today in certain respects throughout the world. The situation in advanced capitalist societies is no exception: for instance, marginal populations in these societies continue to emerge from decomposing self-earned property relations, from the relative surplus labor-force relations, from lower rates of capital accumulation, and from the commodification of social relations within the family and the school.

It has been noted previously that during early capitalism, pro-letarianization was accompanied by the rise of a bourgeoisie, who were the foremost representatives of the new order. Because this class emerged largely as a result of the commodification of agrarian production and the expansion of trade in agricultural goods, it was by no means populated solely by city burghers, independent craftsmen, merchants and guildmasters. It was also being populated with persons who were born in the countryside, including members of the nobility and other large landholders.

After noting the degree to which the economic changes in sixteenth-century England were based on a revolution in agrarian relations, R. H. Tawney, the eminent historian, called the bene-ficiaries of this revolution 'The Gentry'. Thus, gentlemen who belong to the gentry were usually landholders, though they were also distinguished at times by an aristocratic title, usually that of a lesser noble. Oftentimes there was no title at all, because they were simply prosperous 'clodhoppers'.

In the very beginning of the sixteenth century, the nascent development of this new social class began to yield a highly conspicuous pattern of personal consumption. To wit, in 1516, when Thomas More condemned the growth of avarice, he also pointed out that 'alongside of . . . wretched need and poverty you find ill-timed luxury. Not only the servants of noblemen but the craftsmen and almost the clod-hoppers themselves, in fact, all classes alike, are given to such ostentatious sumptuousness of dress . . .'[40] Ostentatious dress was also mentioned at Cambridge, whose officials complained that the attire of the student offspring of the gentry and the aristocracy had become 'disordered' and 'excessive', 'tending to the decay of learning, & other dissolute behavior'.[41]

Because of their opposition to traditional, austere consumption standards, the younger gentry were particularly vulnerable to social criticism. However, traditional restraint was also being swept aside by their socially active families. The seasonal tides of squires, gentlemen, ladies, and lesser nobility, in particular, rapidly transformed London into a notable center of conspicuous consumption.

The standards of the younger gentry were modeled after some older, more rakish members of their class. As their fortunes rose, these older members had adopted the leisurely patterns of the aristocracy. Some of them speculated furiously in the expanding money market, and indulged compulsively in luxuries that threatened them with personal ruin. For others, however, life in the city became a pleasant, lasting social occasion. They beguiled themselves on warm summer days 'with music and cup in barges upon the water'. Hours were spent riding in coaches about the city streets. Libraries were turned into gambling saloons, and the royal parks were used for dueling, commercial bowling, and quaffing wine leisurely under the trees.[42]

This parasitic existence and the ostentatious use of dress, jewels, and perfumes, were captured sarcastically by Ben Jonson: he advised propertied men to first discard their responsibilities in the country if they wanted to become accomplished gentlemen; and then, before traveling to London to live among the gallants, to exchange 'four or five acres of [their] best land into two or three trunks of apparel'.

London became the center of a sort of cultural revolution, organized and maintained by essentially bourgeois relations. True, some members of the gentry had aristocratic titles, but their conspicuous patterns of consumption represented early capitalist rather than feudal modes of production. Although diverse in origin, the gentry were largely early capitalist landowners;[43] and their emerging life styles represented but one aspect of 'the first complete bourgeois revolution'[44] in social, cultural, economic, and political affairs.

An expanding network of luxury trades and civil associations supported the lives of the London gentry. Hackney cabs appeared on the streets and the exclusive English club sprang into being, as gentlemen from similar parts of the country gathered together in their favorite taverns. The institution of the commercial theatre and new trends in architecture were sustained by their demand for commercial entertainment and housing.

This same bourgeois revolution produced the idle and mischievous companies of poor youth, who were castigated by Thomas Firmin. The scions of the landed gentry were even less identified with gainful employment and obedient conduct. Yet Firmin advanced no schemes for imprisoning them in a workhouse or for punishing their wrongdoings decisively. In fact, their misbehavior was rarely sanctioned by officials, even though they were, if anything, more malicious than the youngsters in the out-parts of the city.

Christopher Hibbert, for instance, describes the drunken escapades of the Bold Bucks, a group of young gallants, who committed rape frequently and with impunity. 'An expectation of inviolability', Hibbert notes, 'was indeed shared by many, if not most young men of [their] class'.[45] Crimes were committed without negative sanction by another gang of young gentlemen. In a letter to a friend, Jonathan Swift complained in 1711 that the streets were not safe, because he was terribly afraid of being beaten by 'a race of rakes' called the Mohocks. In another letter, he wrote, 'Lord Winchelsea told me to-day at Court that two of the Mohocks caught a maid of old Lady Winchelsea's at the door of their house in the park, where she was with a candle and had just lighted out somebody. They cut all her face, and beat her without provocation'. An additional report, this time by Lady Wentworth, indicated that the Mohocks 'put an old woman in a hogshead and rolled her down the hill'. They mutilated other persons, cutting off their noses, hands, etc., also without provocation.[46]

Allegedly, the Mohocks never took money from anyone; they were simply maliciously violent, yet always remained 'young gentlemen'. A member of the gang was a baronet's son, another, the youngest son of the Bishop of Salisbury. The Bishop's son was an ill-reputed young man about town, but he entered the profession of law eventually. He was appointed a judge in 1741 and knighted four years later.[47] Though earlier, his own violent acts had been committed with impunity, for all we know this knighted judge may have sentenced indigent youth to horrible mutilation or summary execution for similar crimes.

Bourgeois double standards were applied to a wide range of personal conduct, including sartorial preferences, and sexual activities and recreation. While the younger gentry were free to dress and live as they pleased, the styles of life among ordinary apprentices were regulated by stringent and detailed prescriptions. The guildsman and the authorities, of course, had always indicted and severely punished apprentices for being riotous and truculent, and for stealing from their masters.[48] From the sixteenth century onwards, however, apprentices were condemned for keeping mistresses, frequenting taverns and playhouses, and for displaying 'great excesses in clothes, Linen, periwigs, gold and silver watches, etc.'[49] The sexual behavior of apprentices in early capitalism was not unusual by contrast with the rest of society. About the fifteenth and sixteenth centuries Crane Brinton writes, 'as far as I know, [it] is the only period in the history of the West when the male wore very tight lower garments ("hose") with a conspicuous codpiece, which was often ornamented'.[50] Women also demonstrated a rough and ready equality in certain sexual matters. Their low-cut decolletage, provocatively flaunting the breasts, and the wild, hot pursuit of earthly pleasures by both sexes were among the factors that provoked the clergy to cry out against the changing standards of sexual morality.

The attempts to control apprentices reflected the standards restricting personal consumption within single occupational groups. Legal statutes were particularly applied to everyday attire because dress was associated with the wearer's servitude. The appropriate attire for apprentices traditionally included a flat round cap, coarse side coats, close hose, cloth stockings, and other such severe apparel.[51] As early as the sixteenth century, city ordinances specifically forbade the extravagant dress from being displayed by apprentices on the streets of London. In 1582, the Common Council proclaimed that from henceforth all apprentices must 'wear no Hat [other] than a Woolen Cap, without any Silk in or about the same . . . wear no Ruffles, Cuffs, loose Collar . . . wear no Doublets . . . enriched with any manner of Gold, Silver, or Silk . . . wear no Pumps, Slippers nor Shoes, but of English leather, without being pinked, edged or stitched, nor [garnished] Girdles nor Garters . . . wear no Sword, Dagger, or other Weapon, but a Knife; nor a Ring, Jewel of Gold, nor Silver, nor Silk in any Part of the Apparel'.[52]

Although punishment prescribed by the ordinance included public whipping and the addition of six months of service to the time specified by the indenture, these sanctions did not eliminate the errant behavior. It persisted for centuries. Eighteenth-century writers, like Sir William Maitland, continued to complain that apprentices as well as lawyers' clerks 'are under no Manner of Government; before their times are half out, they set up [like] Gentlemen, they dress, they drink, they game, they frequent the Playhouses and intrigue with the Women . . .' Even at the very end of the period of early capitalism, therefore, noted bourgeois citizens demanded more effective laws to curb the so-called 'destructive practices of our Modern Apprentices'.[53]

The ordinance of 1586 was part of a large number of legal codes that controlled the labor force. When applied to an apprenticeship, these codes required the employer to provide for an apprentice's training and subsistence needs. In exchange, by appropriating the full product of his labor, the master exploited the apprentice. In certain respects, therefore, the codes protected the apprentice, but they also buttressed the unequal terms of his exchange. It was recognized that apprentices, under these harsh conditions, would not be able to legally engage in any consumption which exceeded the necessities provided by the master. These necessities were generally limited to foodstuffs and other goods available within the master's household. Apprentices, however, did acquire money for greater consumption: they embezzled from their masters or covertly sold their services to other persons. Consequently, further ordinances were enacted to insulate them from the temptations, the personal discontent, and the unlawful conduct, which were being stimulated by the ostentatious and materialistic styles of life among the wealthier classes.

Beneath the surface of these ordinances lay the effects unleashed by money capital's increasing domination of everyday life. This domination, which consolidated the means of agrarian production in the hands of capitalist farmers, and the means of industrial production in the hands of merchant-capitalists and merchant guildsmen, intensified the lines of stratification in English society. The lines cut through this society in diverse directions. They obviously widened the chasm separating the great landowners from the landless. proletarians; but, in addition, class divisions were sharpened between the guildmasters, on one hand, and the journeymen and apprentices, on the other. Furthermore, status differentiation among poor and wealthy guilds deepened.

Simultaneously, however, exploited and exploiters alike were being influenced by the changing expectations which accompanied the competitive struggle for material advantage. In those sectors of mercantile and industrial production which were being vigorously propelled by capitalist developments, this struggle provided ample fuel for rising expectations and status usurpation. Although they were being generally subjected to harsher conditions, the apprentices' desires were stimulated by these developments. Apprentices, particularly from the wealthier guilds,[54] eagerly adopted the ostentatious styles set by the foremost fraction of the rising bourgeoisie, the landed gentry. Their conspicuous consumption was, however, grounded materially within the limits of the guild system. Because apprentices expected to join the ranks of the masters eventually, they generally aspired only to become members of the *petite bourgeoisie*. Some, however, aspired to acquire the greater powers of appropriation, which were being bestowed on the wealthier guildsmen. The development of trade and domestic industry placed these guildsmen among the *nouveaux riches* of their early capitalist society.

The apprentices, however, were not yet masters, and were subject to legal and economic forms of class domination. These same forms hardly applied to the younger gentry. Their mode of consumption opposed traditionally austere consumption standards, but they were not whipped in public for their transgressions. Young gentry were constrained to live within their means, but their disposable income was certainly not limited to that resulting from self-earned property. Though their social lives were determined by commodity relations, they were the beneficiaries of other people's labor.

Wherever possible, the gentry organized status relations in their own interests. To be conspicuous, their consumption certainly had to be invidious; it cultivated the sins and avarice, gluttony, and pride. Moreover, the malicious violence inflicted, particularly on social inferiors by young rakish gentlemen, was simply a quintessence of their class morals: of their own class arrogance and brutality.

In every class society, the morals of rising classes have been organized centrally around exploitative relationships. Although first expressed by transitional rhetorical forms, which imparted new meanings to traditional categories, such as avarice, sloth, and pride, the gentry's morals were moulded by their own struggle for the control of agrarian production. This struggle was quickly and completely rationalized by expedient bourgeois doctrines that defined all persons of lesser status essentially as natural social inferiors.[55] For example, the 'industrious poor' were denigrated by these doctrines, but the displaced marginals were considered the acme of inferiority. According to these new doctrines, the marginals got what they fully deserved, even if their 'just due' was akin to life in Thomas Hobbes's state of nature – namely, poor, nasty, brutish, and short.

By contrast, the younger gentry were accorded status by other classes, because their parents owned the land which was used by tenants and laborers to produce their revenue. But they were also set apart by the fine houses, the clothing, the food, and the personal services that were at their disposal due, once again, to their parents' vast economic power. This power was not to be denied. In fact, poorer aristocrats grudgingly intermarried with bourgeois families to acquire land deeds, stock certificates, and ready cash. The status of a lesser noble could moreover be purchased directly. Thus, the scion of the landed gentry acquired social honor, which was symbolized by the aristocratic title, the genealogist's chart, and the emblazoned family shield.

Although noted for their own ostentatious fads, the settled members of the aristocracy were generally contemptuous of the gentry's garish tastes, apish manners, and crass materialism. Some gentry in turn were sensitive to this hypocritical scorn, but their sense of humiliation was more than offset by the comforts of the money they possessed. It was further tempered by the obvious comparisons with the squalid realities, which they had imposed on others in acquiring and maintaining their wealth.

The gentry had learned the lessons of contemporary life accurately, even if Hobbes did not. They were not at all freed from the state of nature by a willing obedience to a common sovereign power. Their freedom was predicated squarely on the expansion of their own powers. In early capitalism, only the selfish use of power made their lives rich, pleasant, merciful, and long.

The socialites

English industrialists also indulged in the delights of conspicuous consumption. Some, however, had limited resources with which to launch themselves into the riptides of competition. Immediate profits supplied these self-made men with their revenues for personal consumption; but the profits also had to be divided into capital, into wages, etc., to ensure production on an ascending scale. Since expenditures for luxuries sharply diminished their capital, these 'men on the move' viewed conspicuous consumption with ambivalence.

By the eighteenth and nineteenth centuries, Protestant doctrines provided distinct moral standards for resolving this ambivalence. But the competitive market had little regard for personal anxieties or moral principles. If the self-made man was interested in the pursuit of money then he had to favor progressive accumulation. Until his fortunes rose, he was compelled to invest his profits and to abstain from a luxurious life.

Various 'theories of abstention' view the self-made man differently.[56] Some, for example, insist that his abstemious behavior was dictated by bourgeois piety. Rather than a mundane practicality and a greedy desire for personal gain, his religiosity, frugality, and asceticism created anxieties that drove him to accumulate incessantly. Because of these bourgeois virtues, it is said, the self-made man scorned the immediate joys of life. Anxiously sustained by the dictates of his calling, yet with little more in his hands than the sweat of his brow, the ascetic Protestant tightened his belt, bit the bullet, and accumulated an immense hoard of wealth.[57]

The 'theories of abstention' mystify the process of capitalist accumulation. The self-made man accumulated capital, but the essential mechanism involved was *exploitation*, not self-denial. If any population was truly forced to abstain from the joys of life, it was the population of slaves, indentured servants, convict laborers, and wage earners, that had to a large extent been forcibly created by capitalist developments. The infamous Manchester textile manufacturers, for instance, went through several phases before they expended their revenues on luxury goods. In the beginning they encouraged the lowly cottagers to pay a high premium for allowing their children to work as apprentices; but the children, who were starved and driven to exhaustion on the job, learned no trade. They merely tended machines. At the same time, since the average profits of these manufacturers were low, they had to be parsimonious and live like misers.[58] With regard to other types of early capitalists, temporary abstinence was generally dependent upon the circumstances. Some, who had been indulged with luxuries from birth, entered the market place with sizeable assets. They did not change their way of life.

The life styles of succeeding generations of manufacturers were adjusted to the changing circumstances. From 1770 onwards, the fortunes of the Manchester textile manufacturers soared. Concomitantly – as John Aiken observed in 1795 – their 'expense and luxury . . . made great progress, and [were] supported by a trade extended . . . throughout every part of Europe'.[59] With revenue and capital no longer severely restricted, these manufacturers abandoned plain living. Adopting the air of the capitalist who had been born wealthy, they conspicuously indulged themselves in luxuries.

According to Marx '[t]he progress of capitalist production not only creates a world of delights; it lays open, in speculation and the credit system, a thousand sources of sudden enrichment. When a certain stage of development has been reached, a conventional degree of prodigality, which is also an exhibition of wealth, and consequently a source of credit, becomes a business necessity. Luxury enters into capital's expenses of representation'.[60] Conspicuous consumption has, in all class societies, reinforced patterns of status, deference, and domination. The generalization of commodity production, however, adds new dimensions to this consumption that mitigate against petty bourgeois thrift and self-denial.

Luxury, as we have seen, also entered into the conspicuous styles of life adopted by the families of the wealthy bourgeoisie. Conspicuous consumption, in this context, also had additional meanings because capitalism makes individual worth equivalent to economic worth in social as well as economic relations. Whenever capital throws up a new stratum of wealthy bourgeoisie, the crass material foundations for bourgeois status relations are reaffirmed. In the last decades of the 19th century, the *nouveaux riches*, borne aloft by the expansion of monopoly capital, entered upper-class society in an orgy of conspicuous consumption. Families of finance capitalist led a luxurious and leisurely life, which was first centered on the eastern seaboard, where salons, circles, and inter-city communities, such as Newport and Saratoga Springs, served as congenial meeting-places and playgrounds. These families established a social world that became known as 'high society'.[61] In the 1890s, high society's leisure activities contrasted with its ruthless and exploitative business practices. The former were distinguished by a round of genteel parties, attendance at the opera, theatre, and participation in the arts. Sports of the land and sea, including tennis, polo, sailing, foxhunting, and gambling, were varied by the seasons or combined with the trip abroad. Like their English predecessors, the members of this society developed mannered and ritualized modes of flirtation, eating, drinking, speaking, and fashionable dress. They also developed snobbish exclusion standards to maintain the status distinctions between themselves and the new newly-rich of each succeeding generation.

Before the Civil War, upper-class status in the United States had been based on interrelations within relatively isolated, regional business and family networks. After the war, however, these institutional networks expanded. Certain institutions outside the family, such as the exclusive Eastern boarding school and the fashionable Eastern university, then became significant for the children of the very rich.

With regard to this development, Digby Baltzell states, 'In an age which marked the centralization of economic power under the control of finance capitalism, the gentleman bankers and lawyers of Wall Street, Walnut Street, State Street, and La Salle Street sent their sons to Groton, St. Paul's, or St. Mark's'. After receiving their secondary education at these boarding schools, the youth attended private universities such as Harvard, Yale, and Princeton, 'where they joined exclusive clubs such as *Porcellian, Fence, or Ivy*'. Marrying in the same circles, living in similar suburbs, commuting to the same places of business and attending the comparable clubs, these young men carried on and reproduced anew the contemporary patterns of upper-class life.[62]

Baltzell also mentions Exeter, an Eastern boarding school which caters to upper middle-class as well as upper-class families. Booth Tarkington, for example, attended Exeter although, according to one biographer, his father was 'a lawyer of modest means'. In varying degree, Tarkington's friends at Exeter seemed to have leavened their educational priorities with rowdyism, carousing, stylish clothing, and old-fashioned whoring. His school friends, who shared the same 'regular old fraud' of a landlady, 'raised more hell than any other six students in town', and the fashionable Eastern sartorial tastes acquired at school brought him ridicule when he returned during vacations to his midwestern home. During his senior high school year, he remarked to a friend that some of his classmates 'are handsome, some of them witty . . . but what a hot-bed of foulness and muck! Portsmouth houses [of prostitution] are full of them every night – Boston ones, every holiday.'[63]

Because he was born into a 'proper Philadelphian' (upper-class) family and attended Groton, George Biddle's autobiography is also instructive. It provides insight into upper-class attitudes toward education and high society. 'My mother', Biddle wrote, 'grew up in a large family . . . her upbringing was chaotic. There was no regular schooling, no disciplined routine. Uncle Moncure had unusual gifts but he suffered from weak eyes. Grandfather persuaded him to throw up his studies and gave him horses to keep out of mischief. *Before he was twenty* he was a gentleman jockey in the hardest drinking crowd in America'.[64]

By contrast, Biddle graduated from Groton and Havard: 'I had four happy years at Haverford School when it was decided, upon due consultation, that my education could be improved – intellectually, morally, physically, socially – by the benefits of a New England boarding-school at Groton, Massachusetts where my elder brother had already preceded me. Here I stayed for five years and another six at Harvard and the Harvard Law School.'[65] His experiences at Groton do not reflect a climate of strong commitment to academic studies. Although he describes the atmosphere at the high school as 'socially conservative rather than actually hostile to scholarship',[66] his accounts suggest a conservatism largely lacking in enthusiasm for the advancement of knowledge.

'To succeed at Groton, as later at Harvard', Biddle remarks, 'three paths lay open: athletics, social success and administrative ability.'[67] With regard to athletics, he complains 'we have to play football and baseball, no matter how thoroughly we disliked them and how indifferently we played, unless the doctor actually forbade it'.[68] Social success was accepted without qualification. It involved circles, rituals, clubs and parties. It even demanded at Groton a strict conformity to modified English 'fag and hazing traditions'. According to Biddle, these traditions simply imbued a 'mutuality of respect for the rights of the younger as well as the older'.[69] In actuality the traditions conditioned dominance–submissive relations. They fostered sentiments that dovetailed with hierarchical social arrangements. Social success was also important at Harvard.

At Harvard, then, the New England boarding-school boy went in for clubs – social success. If that were not one's line, one opted for major athletics – although even in the field of major athletics there were social overtones . . . From a social point of view one never went in for scholarship. One carried one's honors lightly, with just a note of depreciation. High honors did not actually leave one in bad odor, so much as under a cloud of suspicion.[70]

Administrative ability was the third path to success. The importance of this ability was largely taken for granted because many Groton students were certain to become financial and business leaders. The frank recognition of its importance at Groton was directed at maintaining the power of upper-class families on a hereditary basis.

Biddle was aware of the enormous resources that were made available for the development of the upper-class child. He stated,

Ninety-five percent of these [Groton] boys came from what they considered the aristocracy of America. Their fathers belonged to the Somerset, the Knickerbocker, the Philadelphia or the Baltimore Clubs. Among them was a goodly slice of the wealth of the nation, little Morgans, Whitneys, Webbs, McCormicks, Crockers, Stillmans. On the whole the equipment and the teaching were more admirable [at Groton] than at any other school in America.[71]

But Biddle complained that these educational resources were being wasted: 'Generally speaking, this aristocracy, this wealth, this admirable educational training was destined to flow into one channel: Wall Street or its equivalent. There were, of course, exceptions. Of the fifty-six of my two Groton forms the names of seven have even been listed in *Who's Who in America*. The greatest number, however, could in terms of manhood, be listed as absolute failures: parasites on the community, cheats, drunkards, lechers, panhandlers, suicides.'[72] Biddle asked whether the responsibility for these parasites, cheaters, alcoholics, etc. sprang from defects in the family or the school. His query is understandable: these agencies did not fulfil their goals without contradictions.

We have noted previously that, because of alienation and uneven development, 'socialization' (i.e., reproduction) relations, as they are embodied in working-class families and local schools, produce unproductive and parasitic behavior as well as unevenly developed pools of labor power. However, since they will generally become owners of capital, the socialization of upper-class youth does not center around the production of labor power. Instead, these youth will become commodity owners, but they will consume without producing. By appropriating the products of other people's labor, they will escape the alienating conditions which confront workers right at the point of production. They will also escape the training which seeks to ensure that workers will be docile under such conditions.

But capitalists as well as workers are alienated. The capitalist's power is derived from the thing called capital, which operates according to laws that are independent of his will. He is forced to meet the requirements of capital accumulation, and is dominated by the fetishized, impersonal market in which commodities are produced and exchanged.[73]

Furthermore, alienation deforms capitalists as well as workers. The capitalist's individualism, cruelty, arrogance, greed and hypocrisy are attributes of the exploitative relations that reproduce his existence; whatever his relations to his wife, children or friends, he is compelled by external coercive forces to relate to most of humanity as a predator.

These same external forces compel the capitalist to conform to the general laws of investment and profit maximization which favor most of all the capitalist and his family. His children are therefore also favored, and validated by the authorities of the exclusive boarding school because of the influence of their family resources. Some other types of students in these same schools, primarily those from middle-class families, are validated more indirectly. Through delegated authorities, the board of trustees implicitly sponsor the presence, hence the social mobility, of the middle-class youth, who have been so benevolently admitted to the upper-class institution.[74]

Within the exclusive private school, meritocratic educational canons still center on individual traits that are prerequisites for profit maximization. But the students are not educated to sell their own productive powers in a labor market. They are instead encouraged to develop traits that will enhance their personal influence and administrative powers. As a result there is no channeling of students into various educational tracks found in public schools, such as 'academic', 'commercial', and 'vocational' programs. Furthermore, the competitive academic standards are de-emphasized. Meanwhile, these standards are imposed inhumanly and incessantly on working-class youth in the larger society, but they are moderated within the private school by alternative reward mechanisms.

The moderation of conventional, competitive, academic standards is, at bottom, not merely based on administrative benevolence, vested student status, or the necessity to maintain family wealth. It is based squarely on the fact that the student body is being prepared to *rule* society. Conventional academic standards which have been applied in the public school, however, have been institutionalized primarily to train persons who will become *subordinated* to this rule.[75] As such, these standards cannot take precedence in upper-class schools over the formal and informal mechanisms which range from a classical liberal arts curriculum to the hazing tradition, and which ensure the hereditary continuity of a ruling class.

Thus, the relations of alienation and uneven development structure the lives of upper-class youth. These relations are generally supportive and augment personal manners and poise with a sense of power, confidence, and superiority.[76] On the other hand, these youth are not free from the forms of estrangement which are derived from alienation and which appear on the surface of their lives in competitive and hierarchical dominance relations. Although upper-class canons put competitive academic standards in their rightful place, other forms of competitive and dominance relations permeate their family, school, and social lives. Colossal snobbery and the canons of social success, competition among peers and the regimen of competitive athletics, interpersonal dominance relations and the socialization of administrative traits: all of these arrangements and conditions bear witness to the influence of alienated relationships and an ethos supported by exploitation and the concentration of wealth.

These relationships and this ethos stimulate parasitic and disintegrative forms of personal behavior that may survive into adult life. For those who are unable to sponge from their own families or prudently live on incomes from their own property, the consequences of this survival are less serious. But the consequences for others may be unmitigated disaster: in spite of supportive families, ruling classes in capitalist societies have produced their own share of downwardly mobile persons whose speed is accelerated by gambling debts or other effects of their irresponsible behavior.

The downward movement of the older rich is matched by the upward movement of the newly rich, who at first conspicuously reproduce upper-class styles of life. The production of millionaires has not ceased: immense fortunes have been garnished by exploitation, by denying workers the fruits of their labor. Wealthy families, furthermore, are no longer now concentrated in the older cities, such as Philadelphia, Baltimore, or Boston. In Dallas, Denver, Phoenix and Los Angeles, one can also find wealthy communities with their yearly 'coming out' debutante affairs, exclusive circles, and preferences for particular private schools. Here we also find in the metropolitan newspapers the 'women and society' section with the latest report on the charity ball, fashion show, night at the opera, and prominent socialites.

Although restricted by more limited revenues, similar alienated social relationships are generated among other bourgeois fractions. These fractions, who are subject to the same general laws of investment and profit maximization, include the lower levels of the managerial stratum, the independent professionals, the commissioned salesperson, and the smaller business men and women. Members of these fractions may derive their revenues for personal consumption from capital return. Others may base their spending for consumption on self-earned property relations and the sale of professional services. In fact, although they have no property of their own, some of these persons may pay for their style of life by managing another person's property.

The less affluent bourgeois parents may send their children to a private school, for instance a military school, where children are prepared for the military or for other bureaucratic institutions. On the other hand, these parents may prefer a private 'progressive school', where the children are socialized for the independent professions or the independent-primary labor market. Generally, however, the children are sent to an immense public high school, and are thereby provided with a variety of educational programs that also fixate student developments at uneven levels.

Within these public institutions, the children of the less affluent bourgeoisie become living contradictions. Because of their bourgeois backgrounds, they generate highly invidious and consumption-oriented styles of life. They are, furthermore, particularly sensitive to the unremitting 'sales efforts' as well as other monopoly-capitalist pressures, which are geared to increasing aggregate demand among consumers. However, in the advanced capitalist society, the metropolitan public school is increasingly unable to accommodate to the social needs of petty bourgeois youth. As a result, their styles of life and sensitivities create special 'tension management' problems in regard to public school activities. Relatively mediocre scholarship, absenteeism, and almost exclusive attention to extra-curricular activities, are some of the choices made in resolving these problems.

Caught in the flux of economic change, these youth who come from bourgeois families may not remain in the social class of their birth, but while in school they form various status groups. Although the instabilities of self-earned property, the separation from professional parents, and the attractions of independent primary occupations may eventually send them in other directions, for the short period of their adolescence these youth constitute their own prototypic forms of bourgeois life. Whenever they are concentrated, they sustain very complex, socially active status formations. These formations are characterized throughout adolescence by loosely knit, interlocking crowds and cliques. During high school, moreover, fraternity and sorority clubs frequently emerge within the crowd formations.

In communities across the United States, one finds that names for these types of youth appear in peer conversations. Included among these names are Socialites, White Shoes, Sedities, and the In-Crowd. It should be noted that by contrast with the young marginals, that is, the Greasers, these bourgeois prototypes are less likely to be involved in the most serious violent and economic forms of delinquency. However, we shall see in later work that with regard to vehicle violations, vandalism, gambling, petty theft, truancy, sexual promiscuity, cheating in school, and the other garden varieties of delinquent behavior, the Socialites are equivalent to the marginals, or not far behind.

Notes

1. For descriptions of early capitalist criminal types, see Frank Aydellotte, *Elizabethan Rogues and Vagabonds* (Oxford: Clarendon Press, 1913); Thomas Harmon, 'A Caveat or Warning for Common Cursitors, Vulgarly Called Vagabonds' in *Elizabethan Underworld*, ed. A. V. Judges (New York: E. P. Sutton, 1930); Jean Jusserand, *English Wayfaring Life* (New York: G. P. Putnam & Sons, 1931).

2. Thomas Firmin, *Some Proposals for the Imployment of the Poor*, 2nd ed. (London, 1681). Pages 1–4 and 37 of Firmin's Proposal are reprinted in *Juvenile Offenders for a Thousand Years*, ed. Wiley B. Sanders (Chapel Hill: University of North Carolina Press, 1970) 18–20.

3. Sir William Maitland, *The History of London, from its Foundation by the Romans to the Present Time . . . In Nine Books (London, 1739), Act. Parl. 14 Car. II (Brit. Mus.)*. The material in Maitland's work, which is relevant to the Black Guard, is reprinted in Sanders, 40–1.

4. Saunders Welch, *A Letter Upon the Subject of Robberies, Wrote in the Year 1753*; reprinted in Sanders, 51–2.

5. The report is reprinted under the title: 'Home Investigation of a Juvenile Delinquent by a Constable upon Order of a Magistrate, 1790', in Sanders, 91.

6. William Smith, *State of the Gaols in London, Westminster and Borough of Southwark* (London, 1776 [Brit. Mus.]). Material in Smith's work, which is relevant to delinquents, is reprinted in Sanders, 62–3.

7. *Report of the Committee for Investigating the Causes of the Alarming Increase of Juvenile Delinquency in the Metropolis* (London, 1816). Pages 5–10, 21–7, and 29 of this report are reprinted in Sanders, 102–6.

8. Thomas More, *Utopia*, ed., intro. and notes by Edward Surtz (New Haven: Yale University Press, 1964) 52–3.

9. Karl Marx, *Capital*, I (Moscow: Foreign Languages Publishing House, 1959) 713ff.

10. C. H. George, 'The Making of the English Bourgeoisie, 1500–1750', *Science and Society*, 35 (Winter, 1971) 396.

11. R. H. Tawney, *The Agrarian Problem in the Sixteenth Century* (New York: Burt Franklin, 1912).

12. Marx, 774. The destruction of pre-existing modes of production was also synchronized with the destruction of religious and political institutions.

13. Quoted in Ivy Pinchbeck and Margaret Hewitt, *Children in English Society*, I (London: Routledge and Kegan Paul, 1969) 93. Original source: *A Supplication of the Poore Commons, in Four Supplications 1529–1553*, ed. Furnival and Cowper (1871) 79.

14. *Report of the Committee on the Subject of Pauperism and a House of Industry in the Town of Boston* (Boston, 1821). Part of this document is reprinted in *Children and Youth in America, A Documentary History*, I,

ed. Robert H. Bremner (Cambridge, Massachusetts: Harvard University Press, 1970) 753.

15. *Niles Weekly Register* (15 December 1821) 256; John H. B. Latrobe, *Address on the Subject of a Manual Labor School* (Baltimore, 1840). Parts of both of these documents are also in Bremner, 753–4.

16. 'Walks among the New York poor: Emigrants and emigrants' children', *New York Daily Times* (28 June 1853). Reprinted in Bremner, 414–15.

17. Sigmund Diamond, *The Reputation of the American Businessman* (Cambridge, Massachusetts: Harvard University Press, 1955) 101.

18. Ibid.

19. Bremner, 145–9.

20. Ibid., 148.

21. Ibid., 146.

22. Marx, 628–40.

23. Martin Sklar, 'On the Proletarian Revolution and the End of Political Economic Society', *Radical America*, 3 (May–June) 9. Also, Robert B. Carson, 'Youthful Labor Surplus in Disaccumulationist Capitalism', *Socialist Revolution*, 2 (May–June 1972) 15–44.

24. The 'prolongation of the dependent status of youth' has been attributed to a variety of other relationships, e.g., the demise of the family 'economy', 'rapid social change', 'economic specialization', etc. See, for example, John Dollard, *Frustration and Aggression* (New Haven: Yale University Press, 1941). Also, James Coleman, *The Adolescent Society* (New York: The Free Press of Glencoe, 1961).

25. The concept of labor market segmentation is discussed in Michael Reich, David M. Gordon, and Richard C. Edwards, 'A Theory of Labor Market Segmentation', *American Economic Review*, 63 (May 1973) 359–65. Also, Thomas Vietorisz and Bennet Harrison, 'Labor Market Segmentation: Positive Feedback and Divergent Developments', *American Economic Review*, 63 (May 1973) 366–76.

26. Reich, Gordon and Edwards, 359.

27. Ibid., 359–60.

28. Ibid., 360.

29. Ibid., 361–2. Related to these conclusions is an interesting note on the history of the dual labor market. Dual labor markets existed in the early nineteenth century, for instance in the textile industry. Those dual labour markets were encouraged because early industrialism had also stimulated the progressive homogenization of the labor force. Craft skills had been eliminated, large numbers of semi-skilled jobs had been created, and job requirements had been standardized by the factory system with its mass production and mechanization. These developments, furthermore, had provided fertile conditions for the growth of working-class solidarity and class consciousness. Toward the end of the nineteenth century, militant workers engaged in nationwide strikes and other practices, such as 'soldiering' (e.g., slow-downs) and sabotage,

that undermined profitable rates of production. To secure greater control of the labor force, managers altered the division of labor within their corporations. The outcome, in the ensuing decades, was dual labor markets that incorporated various kinds of labor market segmentation. Segmentation, therefore, was certainly encouraged because it was profitable; it facilitated higher rates of exploitation. But it also enabled the employers 'to divide and conquer the labor force'.

30. Ibid., 361–4.

31. The Editors, 'Capitalism and Unemployment', *Monthly Review*, 27 (June 1975) 1–13.

32. Karl Marx, *Capital*, I (Moscow: Foreign Languages Publishing House, 1959) 731–44.

33. Wolfgang Hein and Konrad Stenzal, 'The Capitalist State and Underdevelopment in Latin America – The Case of Venezuela', *Kapitalistate*, 2 (1973) 31–48.

34. For the magnitude of this problem, see Robert B. Carson, 'Youthful Labor Surplus in Disaccumulationist Capitalism', *Socialist Revolution*, 2 (May–June 1972) 15–44.

35. The relation between the family, the school, and the hierarchical organization of labor is discussed in Samuel Bowles and Herbert Gintis, 'I.Q. in the U.S. Class Structure', *Social Policy*, 3 (January–February 1973) 65–96.

36. Barry Bluestone, 'Capitalism and Poverty in America: A Discussion', *Monthly Review*, 2 (June 1972) 64–71.

37. These owners are characterized by various subjective factors, including a false consciousness and an instrumental perspective.

38. This observation is important, because the literature on 'middle class' delinquency has glossed over the differences between marginal 'middle class' delinquents and other types of 'middle class' delinquents.

39. Herman Schwendinger and Julia R. Schwendinger, *The Sociologists of the Chair: A Radical Analysis of the Formative Years of North American Sociology (1883–1922)* (New York: Basic Books, 1974) 143–58, 360–1.

40. More, 27.

41. Charles Cooper, *Annals of Cambridge*, II (Cambridge: Warwick and Co., 1863) 613, 616.

42. F. J. Fisher, 'The Development of London as a Center of Conspicuous Consumption in the 16th and 17th Centuries', *Transactions of the Royal Historical Society*, 4th Series, XXX (1948).

43. Immanuel Wallerstein, *The Modern World System* (New York: Academic Press, 1974) 240–4.

44. Eric Hobsbawm, 'The Crises of the 17th Century–II', *Past and Present*, 6 (November 1954) 63.

45. Christopher Hibbert, *The Roots of Evil* (Boston: Little, Brown, 1963) 45.

46. Jonathan Swift, *The Journal to Stella*, ed., with intro. and notes by

George A. Aitken (London: Methuen, 1901) 419–21, 424–5, 430, 432.

47. Swift, 419–20 and n., 419.
48. Sir Walter Besant, *London in the Time of the Tudors* (London: Adam and Charles Black, 1904) 324–6.
49. Ibid.
50. Crane Brinton, *A History of Western Morals* (New York: Harcourt, Brace, 1959) 250–55.
51. Besant, 329.
52. Quoted in Besant, 324–5.
53. Besant, 325.
54. Pinchbeck and Hewitt, 232.
55. R. H. Tawney, *Religion and the Rise of Capitalism* (New York: New American Library, 1947).
56. For a discussion of these views, see Marx, 591–8.
57. This 'ascetic Protestant' is a justifiable caricature of Max Weber's *Protestant Ethic and the Spirit of Capitalism* (New York: Charles Scribner & Sons, 1958). Too much attention has been paid to Weber's own qualifications of what his theory is all about. Too little attention, on the other hand, has been paid to the psychologistic mechanisms that *actually* underlie the theory.
58. Marx, 594.
59. Quoted in Marx, 594–5.
60. Marx, 594.
61. Thorstein Veblen, *Theory of the Leisure Class* (New York: Mentor Books, 1953).
62. Digby Baltzell, *Philadelphia Gentlemen, The Making of a National Upper Class* (Glencoe. Illinois: The Free Press, 1958).
63. James Woodress. *Booth Tarkington* (Philadelphia: J. Lippincott & Co., 1955) 47–8.
64. George Biddle, *An American Artist's Story* (Boston: Little, Brown, 1939) 43, our emphasis.
65. Ibid., 32.
66. Ibid., 43.
67. Ibid., 45.
68. Ibid., 44.
69. Ibid., 46.
70. Ibid., 82.
71. Ibid., 66.
72. Ibid.
73. Bertell Ollman, *Alienation, Marx's Conception of Man in Capitalist Society* (London: Cambridge University Press, 1971).
74. For insight into 'sponsored mobility', see Ralph H. Turner, 'Acceptance of Irregular Mobility in Britain and the United States', *Sociometry*, (December 1966) 334–52.

75. Herbert Gintis, 'Education, Technology, and the Characteristics of Worker Productivity', *American Economic Review*, 61 (May 1971) 266–79.
76. See, for instance, the comments about 'the upper class mind' and the reference to Scott Fitzgerald's *The Rich Boy* in Baltzell, 333.

6
Any Woman's Blues

A Critical Overview of Women, Crime and the
Criminal Justice System

Dorie Klein and June Kress

Introduction

The changing nature of women's position in the workforce and in the
family has given rise to a new set of issues concerning women's
participation in crime. Among these are increasing rates of and
fluctuating patterns in women's offenses, and growing resistance
both through the emergence of political movements and through
rising militance in women's prisons. These developments, in turn,
have stimulated not only the portrayal of a new 'violent' woman by
the media, but also a flurry of speculation among criminologists.
However, the great majority of academic material has lacked serious
consideration of the economic and social position of women, and consequently has been limited by a narrow correctionalist perspective.

Therefore, this paper will present, in a more systematic and
politically viable fashion, several key elements critical to a radical
view of the phenomenon of female crime and experience with the
criminal justice system. First, we will briefly critique the traditional
criminological literature on women and describe how such scholarship has been utilized in the formulation of criminal justice planning;
and introduce the basic tenets of radical criminology and the
developing body of feminist literature that shape the parameters of
our analyses. Second, we will briefly sketch a picture of the position of
women in contemporary American society, a picture which we regard
as essential to any analysis of women and crime. We will then focus
on the criminal justice system itself as an instrument of control and
how it reflects and reinforces the particular position of women as well
as the ideology of sexism. This section of the paper will include an
outline of female offenses, and the responses of the police, courts, and
prisons, integrating an analysis of the factors that come into play in
the treatment afforded women by these institutions. Furthermore, we
will incorporate a critical discussion of what has been referred to as

chivalry and benevolence toward women offenders, and lay the groundwork for an alternative view of differential treatment of women with reference to their political and economic position. These ideas will be utilized to illustrate our main points about the exploitative character of American justice, and more importantly, to raise some of the relevant 'burning questions' for future investigation and practice.

The criminologists' study of women and crime

Traditional criminology: serving the state

In order to locate the theoretical underpinnings of our critical overview of women and crime, it is first essential to summarize and critique the role that traditional criminology has played in service to the state. Criminologists have almost unanimously accepted the legal definition of crime[1] and have centered primarily on the individual offender, who has been regarded as abnormal, in fact as inherently pathological. The conclusions drawn are that ill-adjusted individuals in conflict with society, in other words 'deviants', must be psychologically 'rehabilitated' by the criminal justice system.

This ahistorical, individualistic approach of academic criminologists has contributed to and has been reinforced by their close relationships with the criminal justice system in policy formulation. These mutually reinforcing tendencies are evidenced by the kinds of research grants they receive (for example from the Law Enforcement Assistance Administration), from the types of studies conducted in prisons at the invitation of the staff,[2] and by the rise of the number of criminal justice schools across the country that are training professional administrators.

As far as the subject of women and crime is concerned, its sparse body of literature has been written either by men or by women without feminist consciousness. Female criminality is viewed as the result of innate biological or psychological characteristics of women which are only marginally affected by social and economic factors. These writers have made universal, ahistorical assumptions about female nature in general, based on the reproductive role. Thus, sexuality becomes the key to understanding the deviance of a woman, since this is supposedly her primary social function.[3]

Specifically, women (and women offenders) have been characterized in the literature as devious, deceitful and emotional (Pollak,

1950), intellectually dull and passive (Thomas, 1907, 1923), atavistic (closer to animals in evolution) and immoral (Lombroso, 1920), lonely and dependent (Konopka, 1966), and anxious to serve and be loved (Herskovitz, in Pollak and Friedman, 1969). Moreover, the direct object of these studies, women offenders, are treated with condescension. The Gluecks (1934) called them a pathetic lot. Quite recently, female deviants were described as: 'Increasing numbers of broken gears and bits of flying debris . . .found leaping from bridges, wandering desolate city streets, and entering banks with pistols in their pockets' (Adler, 1975:24). Women criminals have rarely been accorded even the grudging respect shown male criminals, who at least are seen as a threatening force with which to be reckoned. Instead, women often have been the target of voyeuristic studies concerned only with their sexuality.[4] Further, delinquency is described as a symptom of homosexuality in girls (Cowie, Cowie and Slater, 1968), or unsatisfactory relationships with the opposite sex (Vedder and Somerville, 1970). One author argues that, for a delinquent girl, 'whatever her offence – whether shoplifting, truancy or running away from home – it is usually accompanied by some disturbance or unfavorable behavior in the sexual area' (Konopka, 1966:4).

Basing their work on the sexual theories of motivation, few traditional criminologists recognize sexist oppression itself as a causative factor or the need for its elimination. Their recommendations for rehabilitation impose standards of femininity which are in fact ruling class standards. One example of this is the imposition of certain conditions for parole, which we discuss later in the paper. Thus, social control, not social justice, is the underlying thread of unity in this literature. And, more importantly, any attempts at reform have neither changed the balance of power within the criminal justice system, nor have they fundamentally altered the class-biased nature of that system.

As previously mentioned, these writers have definitely had an influence on the control of women by the criminal justice system. Studies of 'violent' women prisoners and their menstrual cycles have been federally funded, with a suggestion being the chemical regulation of these women (see Austin and Ellis, 1971; West, 1973). That interest in the alleged new 'violent' woman is high is evidenced both by sensationalized media stories and by academics eagerly publishing confirmations (see *Newsweek*, 1975; Adler, 1975). Yet academics did *not* note the upswing of violence *against* women perpetrated, for example, by the state in Vietnam (see Bergman, 1974) or the continued, forced sterilization of women in this country (see Allen, 1974; Maclean, 1975). Consequently, one must look not to traditional criminology for an understanding of women and crime, but rather to the emerging movement of radical criminology and feminism.

Radical criminology: theory and practice

One of the outcomes of popular struggles waged during the 1960s by women, students, Third World people and various political organizations has been an ongoing transformation of the field of criminology. Taking its early direction from the ideas and writings of prisoners themselves, a radical analysis of crime and criminal justice was in fact created outside the academic community and adopted by students and a small number of faculty.

Theoretically, radical criminology utilizes a multi-disciplinary approach to examine the issues of crime and justice, emphasizing the study of political economy. Representing a sharp break from the traditional field, radical criminology has begun to challenge the dominant assumptions long held by academic practitioners and by workers within the criminal justice system. One such challenge is to the legal definition of crime. In contrast to the traditional definition, radicals see as a starting point the notion of human rights to self-determination, dignity, food and shelter, and freedom from exploitation. This perspective defines crime as a violation of these rights, whereby the focus is on specific systems of exploitation, or criminogenic systems, such as imperialism, racism, capitalism and sexism, because they promote inherently repressive relationships and social injury. In this orientation, the solution to crime is predicated on a total transformation of society and its inequitable political and economic system. Thus, in its broadest theoretical sense, radical criminology involves a move towards redefinition of crime and justice.

Coupled with this is an ongoing evaluation of the criminal justice system according to whether it meets people's needs. In challenging that system, we do not deny the existence of street crime such as rape or burglary, or consider that people who commit such crimes are totally victims of an unjust society. On the contrary, petty criminals do exploit working people, and street crime is a pressing problem that demands immediate attention. But a primary focus of our work is how the economic system *itself* promotes the conditions for typical criminal behavior (see Platt, 1974b). This requires an analysis of the material basis of criminality, the illegal marketplace of goods and services, e.g., drugs and prostitution,[5] and the connections between exploitative social relations and economic foundations.

In drawing its main attention away from individual offenders, radical criminology concentrates on the social structure through its recognition of the criminal justice system as a class phenomenon: that is, as an instrument of the ruling elite to maintain a social system that is class-biased, racist and sexist (see Balbus, 1973; Wolfe, 1973). Our work is guided by a perspective that views the state as serving certain segments of the population over others.[6] As one coercive arm of the state, the criminal justice system protects corporate and private property. While it brings full pressure to bear on petty property offenders from the poor sectors of the population, it virtually ignores major corporate crime and handles white-collar offenses through 'wrist-slapping' civil procedures.[7] Thus, the legal apparatus is in effect a dual system of justice for the rich and against the poor.

In making the study of women and crime a priority, radical and progressive criminologists have begun to confront the economic, social and political conditions that have a direct bearing on the incidence of crime. The historical and contemporary role of women in society is analyzed in order to account for the kinds of crimes that women commit. By attempting to break down oppressive sexual attitudes that surround women, radical criminologists incorporate a political view of justice. While our theoretical work emphasizes the need to eliminate sexism and ruling-class standards of femininity, our political practice concentrates on strategies of resistance to bring about fundamental change, for example anti-rape groups that are now growing on a national scale. This developing body of literature on women is characterized by a high degree of feminist consciousness. Moving well beyond mere critiques of traditional approaches, radicals and progressives have begun to develop their own political analyses of female criminality and the institutions of criminal justice that act as agents of control.

For example, the 'crime' of prostitution has been reinterpreted as a question of economic survival, as a crime *with* a victim – the prostitute herself – who is stigmatized by arrest, vulnerable to drugs and rip-offs, and faced with financial insecurity. Recent studies have concerned themselves with the class and racial hierarchy within prostitution (Sheehy, 1971), the creation of a whole class of prostitutes by U.S. imperialism in Vietnam in the 1960s (Bergman,

1974), and with convincing arguments that call for the decriminalization of prostitution (Roby and Kerr, 1972; Women Endorsing Decriminalization, 1973).

Another concern addressed by these more progressive writers has been the phenomenon of rape, which is a terrifying metaphor for sexist oppression shaped by class and race. Rape has been redefined as a crime against women, rather than its historical importance as a crime against *any* man whose property, i.e., his woman, had been violated by another man. Rape is now being analyzed as a form of terrorism that functions to keep woman in her place (Griffin, 1971; Brownmiller, 1975), and to drive an entire population into subservience (Bergman, 1974). Studies demystify long-held theoretical and legal assumptions about rape and rapists (J. Schwendinger and H. Schwendinger, 1974; Weis and Borges, 1973), trace racial stereotypes back to the Civil War period (Lerner, 1973; Davis, 1975), and explore particular problems faced by rape victims in obtaining justice from the criminal law (DeCrow, 1974).

Crimes against women which have not been legally sanctioned, particularly medical practices, have also become subjects of study: for instance, works on the politics of abortion reform (Humphries, 1973), the brutality of forced sterilization (Maclean, 1975; Allen, 1974), and the newly improved techniques of behavior modification that have been refined for use on women defined as 'deviant' (Klein, 1973a).

Turning their attention to the criminal justice system, feminist writers have examined the juvenile court's selective treatment of female delinqents (Rush, 1972; Chesney-Lind, 1973,1974). The issue of women in prison has also been a major undertaking, as evidenced by a growing body of feminist literature that exposes the deplorable conditions of incarceration and supports women in prison who are beginning to take control over their lives (Burkhart, 1973:Hansen, 1974; *Women, A Journal of Liberation*, 1972). Additionally, the subject of women and mental illness is seen as a priority, mainly because mental hospitalization is another form of incarceration and because of the large numbers of women undergoing psychiatric commitment (see Chesler, 1972; Roth and Lerner, 1975).

While many of these studies lack theory or explicit strategies for political change, all of them do illustrate a deep concern for women offenders and victims. No longer can traditional correctionalist perspectives be taken for granted. More importantly, today women are refusing to be the *objects* of class-biased and male-dominated social science and are increasingly speaking out for themselves. It is to this developing feminism as well as to the budding movement of radical criminology that this paper owes its existence.

The position of women

The family

An understanding of the relationship between women and criminal behaviour requires a brief examination of women's unique economic and social position in modern capitalist society, which is rooted in the sexual and maternal aspect of female life.

The economic position of women hinges on their location in the institution of personal survival, life-support, and emotional refuge known as the family. Within it, women have historically been treated as the laboring property of their individual men – fathers and husbands – who themselves have mostly had to sell their labor to other men. Thus, women have been, in the words used to describe the double oppression of black women, the 'slaves of slaves'. In the shift from pre-industrialism to contemporary advanced capitalism, the economic role of the family in the U.S. has changed from being a center of production, for exchange as well as use value, to being essentially a center of consumption, as the goods required for life-support, e.g., food, clothing, are increasingly mass-produced. Thus, women's work has changed, too (Rowbotham, 1973: 107–8). In that the family consumes the goods, reproduces the workers, keeps them alive, and helps to inculcate children and adults alike with the values required to maintain the legitimacy of present arrangements, women's work bolsters capitalism.

The structure of the family itself is legitimated by the ideology of sexism, which assures us that the roles filled by women are their 'natural' ones. Women are meant above all to be wives and mothers, either because of their physiology (not only do women bear children, they are soft and weak as well) or their psychology (women are passive, gentle, irrational, personal, expressive). Or, if one is a liberal sociologist who scorns such superstition, women are meant to be wives and mothers above all because they do it so well, and women's work is necessary work.

Women's work

Below we shall briefly outline the separate, though interrelated, elements of women's work, and note the sexist ideology that reinforces the ensuing web of oppression.[8] First, women are unpaid houseworkers in the family, doing the vital chores that allow their husbands, fathers, sons and daughters to leave home and do a full week's work at a job.[9] And although it might appear that technological advances and mass production would free women from much housework, it has been estimated that the average housewife spends 99.6 hours a week performing these tasks (Rowbotham, 1973). The tyranny of housework partly stems from the fact that a woman's self-esteem is tied into it: a woman is judged by the appearance of her house, and the ideal of the good housekeeper is promoted by the mass media to sell products.

Secondly, women are nurturing agents. They raise children, emotionally care for men, do unpaid charity work, and generally act as softening agents in a harsh and competitive society.[10] Sexist notions that women should be gentle and passive keep women nurturing others at their own expense.

Thirdly, women are the 'sexual backbone' of society. Particularly when they are young, their worth is measured by men as sexual objects. It is their function to uphold moral standards and preserve the monogamous marriage which ensures a stable society. Many young women must hustle to earn a living through their looks, as waitresses or secretaries; for unskilled women particularly, access to security depends on sexual attractiveness, whether as wives or prostitutes.[11] Further, hegemonic standards of feminine beauty keep women insecure about themselves, vulnerable to consumer exploitation, and competitive with one another for male approval.

The fourth role that women play in the political economy is that of a reserve labor force, which is bolstered by the unequal work and power structure within the family and the sexist ideology previously outlined. Women are used as part-time labor, as poorly paid and unorganized clerical workers in offices, as factory help in competitive industries with low capitalization and low wages, and as extra workers when the demand is high, for example during World War II.[12] Domestic workers, who are primarily Third World women, are among the most poorly paid workers and are lower in occupational status than anyone, performing traditional 'women's work' for other women.[13] For minority women in general, decent job opportunities have until recently been almost totally denied them, out of racial prejudice, inadequate education and sexual barriers.

It is in the area of labor force work where women are most sharply divided in their interests along class and racial lines. Female professors, for instance, do not have the same problems at work as female domestics. However, within each class, women find themselves in defined female roles with a sex-determined lack of opportunity and control. For most women, 'class privilege' is fundamentally a male prerogative that a woman marries for and loses if she loses the man. Thus, a feminist analysis must be integrated within a class analysis of women's position in order to understand women's oppression and their particular treatment within the different stages of criminal justice.

The criminal justice system: controlling women

Women and the law

The legal system mirrors and upholds the sexist ideology that legitimates women's position. Historically, women have been first the legal chattel of their fathers and later of their husbands. Only recently have women acquired independent rights in western countries, and these have been slow in coming.

The much-vaunted 'chivalry' of the law has afforded certain dubious privileges to women in return for curtailment of their rights and restrictions on their activities. Two examples are special protection on the job and the exemption of wives from prosecution for criminal conspiracy with their husbands. In the first case, the rationale of the protective legislation has been to protect women because they are mothers, and hence, in the words of the U.S. Supreme Court in the 1908 *Muller* v. *Oregon* decision, to protect the 'well being of the race'. This decision paved the way for separate job protective legislation. This same rationale was used to keep women off juries, out of state-supported colleges, and forbidden to vote. While often well-intentioned, this paternalism has been at a great cost to women, especially to poor and working women. They have been denied well-paying jobs because they are legally forbidden to work at night, to lift things, or to work overtime (see Murphy and Deller Ross, 1970). In the example of conspiracy exemption, the argument used to justify lenient treatment for wives has centered on women's legal irresponsibility. Like minors and slaves, wives have been not quite full persons in the eyes of the law. While they may not have been prosecuted for conspiracy, they may also then not possess marital property rights: the sword cuts two ways. They have not had control over their husbands' income and have been at their mercy for household money. After a divorce, despite long years of housework at a man's service, wives are dependent on alimony, which is awarded in only 2 per cent of the cases and even then it is usually defaulted on.[14]

Women have been 'protected' in the sense that they are valuable property. For example, rape has been mentioned as historically a crime against a man whose property has been violated. Rape laws attempted to regulate male ownership of women's sexual capacity and to preserve female fidelity in the nuclear family, ensuring patriarchal reproduction and inheritance. It is telling that a man cannot legally rape his own wife, and that it is extremely difficult to win a conviction of rape against a man who rapes a prostitute – she does not *belong* to another man. During the slavery era, it was an everyday occurrence for black women to experience sexual assault by their owners, white men, which also was not legally rape (see Davis, 1975).

Within the realm of female sexuality and marital responsibility, legal paternalism has been severe and restrictive. The function of the law in preserving premarital chastity and marital fidelity for women is evident in requirements that women furnish proof of freedom from venereal disease to marry, prohibition of intercourse for underage women, and the outlawing of prostitution and juvenile 'promiscuity'. Prostitution is both a challenge and an adjunct to the nuclear family, a Coney Island mirror of marriage itself, as previously mentioned.[15] Wifely submission has been controlled by the widespread ban on abortions and birth control, and by the legal definitions of a couple's domicile as the husband's and the handing over of property control to him. Women's rights over their children have been regulated and 'unfit' mothers lose custody and risk forced sterilization.[16]

The techniques of legal control over women take on broader significance when examining the class character of the law, as it becomes apparent that protection of women's rights is not a priority. From a radical viewpoint, the most critical thing to understand and to investigate is actually the *lack* of criminal law to deal with activities most harmful to a great number of women: production of unsafe birth control devices, profitable medical experimentation, industrial pollution, military violence, and economic injustice. Understanding these realities is crucial to understanding the following discussion of women who commit offenses and are processed through the criminal justice system at the stages of arrest, court sentencing, and prison.

Women arrested

The great majority of women arrested are petty offenders. Both in 1972 and in 1974, women and men were arrested in rank order for the offenses indicated in Table 6.1. For both years, the women's and men's lists are fairly similar. Women are apparently being arrested for proportionately fewer 'violent' offenses than men: 6.1 per cent in 1972 and 3.8 per cent in 1974 of female arrests (aggravated assault and other assaults) vs. 8.5 per cent and 7.1 per cent in 1974 of male arrests (aggravated assault, robbery, and other assaults). A relatively greater percentage of women are arrested for larceny and fraud (22.6 per cent in 1972 and 25.5 per cent in 1974), and of course women constitute almost all of the arrests for prostitution (which can be masked as 'disorderly conduct'). By and large, a good number of these women and men are not a dangerous lot. If certain 'victimless' offenses (prostitution, drug use, drunkenness, and juvenile running away) were decriminalized, the number of women arrested could drop considerably.

Women and men showed percentage increases for arrests in certain categories from 1960–73 and from 1973–4, as illustrated in Tables 6.2 and 6.3 (p.164). Along with rape, these seven offenses constitute the FBI index for which national data are collected.

Despite the increase in arrests for women, we must remember that they still comprise a small percentage of all arrests, although it is still growing. This is shown in Table 6.4 (p.165).

In studying the figures, it is obvious that arrests for women are going up, relatively and absolutely. However (see Tables 6.2, 6.3 and 6.4), over the last decade women's rate of increase for the so-called 'violent' crimes without obvious economic motive (murder, aggravated assault) has not been as great as men's or as great as their (women's) rate of increase for property and drug offenses. Over the past ten years, women's rate of increase *has* exceeded men's for robbery, burglary, auto theft and fraud, although it is still true that in these categories woman's actual number of arrests barely approaches that of men (see Table 6.4). Fraud has been one of the traditional 'women's offenses'. Women have also always been arrested for drug offenses. This stands in contrast to media reports and sociologists'

TABLE 6.1 Rank order of offenses and per cent arrested out of all female and male arrests, 1972 and 1974

		1972		
	Women		Men	
Rank	Offense	% female arrests	Offense	%male arrests
1	Larceny/theft	20.2	Drunkenness	22.9
2	Drunkenness	9.8	Drunken driving	9.0
3	Disorderly conduct	8.5	Disorderly conduct	8.5
4	Narcotic drug laws	6.0	Larceny/theft	8.2
5	Other assaults	4.1	Narcotic drug laws	5.8
6	Drunken driving	3.8	Burglary	4.7
7	Prostitution	3.4	Other assaults	4.5
8	Liquor laws	2.7	Liquor laws	2.9
9	Embezzlement/fraud	2.4	Aggravated assault	2.2
10	Aggravated assault	2.0	Robbery	1.8
11	All other offenses	37.1	All other offenses	29.5
	Total	100.0	Total	100.0

		1974		
	Women		Men	
Rank	Offense	% female arrests	Offense	% male arrests
1	Larceny/theft	22.5	Drunkenness	16.3
2	Disorderly conduct	11.2	Drunk driving	10.9
3	Juvenile runaways	8.8	Larceny/theft	9.8
4	Drunkenness	6.6	Disorderly conduct	8.3
5	Narcotic drug laws	6.5	Narcotic drug laws	7.5
6	Drunken driving	5.0	Burglary**	6.2
7	Prostitution	4.1	Other assaults	4.5
8	Other assaults	3.8	Liquor laws	3.1
9	Fraud*	3.0	Vandalism	2.6
10	Liquor laws	2.9	Aggravated assaults	2.6
11	All other offenses	25.6	All other offenses	28.2
	Total	100.0	Total	100.0

* Does not include embezzlement
** Includes breaking and entering.
SOURCES: Simon (1975:45), Federal Bureau of Investigation (1975:189).

T ABLE 6.2   Total arrests for men and women, 1960–73

| | Percentage increase | |
	Males	Females
Murder	141	103
Robbery	160	287
Aggravated assault	116	106
Burglary	76	193
Larceny	84	341
Auto theft	59	155
Fraud	50	281
Narcotic drug laws	995	1027

S OURCE: *Newsweek* (1975:35).

T ABLE 6.3   Total arrests for men and women, 1973–74

| | Percentage increase | |
	Males	Females
Murder*	5.6	1.2
Robbery	13.6	14.1
Aggravated assault	9.9	14.6
Burglary/breaking and entering	20.5	20.1
Larceny/theft**	25.6	23.0
Motor vehicle theft***	−2.9	3.8
Fraud	11.8	22.4
Narcotic drug laws	2.5	−.1

   * Includes non-negligent manslaughter.
  ** Includes larceny under $50.
 *** Includes all kinds of motor vehicles.
S OURCE: Federal Bureau of Investigation (1975:190).

warnings (see Adler, 1975) that a new 'violent' breed of female criminal is on the rise, and that women are becoming more aggressive. As Simon (1975: 46) states:

In sum, the arrest data tell us the following about women's participation in crime: the proportion of female arrests in 1972 was greater than the proportion arrested one or two decades earlier; the increase was greater for serious offenses than it was for all Type I and Type II offenses combined.[17] The increase in female arrest

TABLE 6.4 Percentages of females among all arrests, 1953–74

Year	All crimes	Serious crimes* Violent**	Property***
1953	10.8	11.9	8.5
1954	11.0	11.6	8.2
1955	11.0	12.0	8.4
1956	10.9	13.5	8.0
1957	10.6	13.1	8.5
1958	10.6	12.0	9.3
1959	10.7	12.7	10.1
1960	11.0	11.8	10.8
1961	11.2	11.6	11.4
1962	11.5	11.5	12.6
1963	11.7	11.6	12.9
1964	11.9	11.6	13.9
1965	12.1	11.4	15.0
1966	12.3	11.3	15.6
1967	12.7	10.8	16.0
1968	13.1	10.3	16.1
1969	13.8	10.6	18.0
1970	14.6	10.5	19.7
1971	15.1	10.9	20.1
1972	15.3	11.0	21.4
1973	15.6	10.0	21.1
1974	16.1	10.2	21.2

  * All those included in FBI Crime Index except rape.
 ** Homicide, robbery, aggravated assault.
*** Burglary, larceny, motor vehicle theft.
SOURCES: Adopted from Simon (1975:35, 38); 1973 and 1974 figures from Federal Bureau of Investigation (1975:190).

rates among the serious offenses was owing almost entirely to women's greater participation in property offenses, especially larceny. In 1953, roughly 1 out of 7 arrests for larceny involved a woman; in 1972, the proportion was approximately 1 out of 3. Contrary to impressions that might be gleaned from the mass media, the proportion of female arrests for violent crimes has changed hardly at all over the past two decades. Female arrest for homicide, for example, has been the most stable of all violent offenses.[18]

A rise or decline in arrest rates does not necessarily indicate a rise or decline in real illegal activity. It may reflect the political situation in or growth of law enforcement circles, different organization of the data, changes in arrest categories, and altered perceptions of women offenders by the police. (Not all offenders are equally vulnerable to capture. For example, rapists have often escaped being reported, and the high estimated rape rate is in contrast to the low arrest rate for charged rapists.) However, the arrest figures above do raise questions about women's participation in the illegal marketplace. As we have previously discussed, women are economically an underpaid group, and in a simplistic determinist view, we would expect very high rates of petty property offenses because of their economic situations. We do not agree with Pollak (1950) that women *do* commit as many offenses as men, but receive more lenient treatment and hence escape the law. There are other factors involved.

Due to women's historical position in the management of commodity production and distribution, including the competitive illegal marketplace of goods and services, e.g., drugs and prostitution, most women are not socially, psychologically or economically in a position at this time to steal aggressively, nor do those with male providers have such a need. Women are traditionally just as timid and just as limited by male constrictions on their roles and male leadership within the arena of crime as they are 'above ground'. They are no more big-time drug dealers than are they finance capitalists. They are, however, first, petty offenders in the area of 'consumerism', which reflects their position as houseworkers in 'straight' society. They shoplift, use illicit drugs purchased from men – especially the less-threatening barbiturates and amphetamines, often over-prescribed – and pass bad checks. Second, they may act as accomplices to men in offenses such as robbery. Third, just as most women must sell themselves, in a sense, in marriage, so prostitution affords other women the opportunity to earn a living through their sexuality. To understand why women become prostitutes, then, one must look, not only at their personal histories, but at women's general condition. As surrogate wives and lovers, prostitutes serve the same functions of sexual work and nurturance that other women do. Fourth, women 'on the streets' are harassed for vagrancy and drunkenness much as men in their situation are, chivalry notwithstanding. Fifth, juvenile females are apprehended for status offenses, such as running away. And finally, women commit 'crimes of passion' primarily against husbands and lovers, and strike out sometimes at children as well, which may reflect emotional frustration created by sexist roles.

Women's lack of participation in 'big time' crime highlights the marketplace. Also reproduced is the structure racism: for example, black streetwalkers are the worst-paid and worst-treated group of prostitutes, and young white call girls are most highly privileged. Of course, black prostitutes have disproportionately high arrest rates; in New York City in the late 1960s, blacks were arrested on that charge ten times more frequently than whites (Winick and Kinsie, 1971:43).

In the current economic crisis, with the likelihood that women – along with other non-favoured groups such as Third World people and the young – will be the first fired, one may expect that women may begin to commit more 'street offenses' as they are thrown out of work. Conversely, with the rise of job opportunities for certain classes of women, and the increased integration of women into the labor force partly due to the successes of the women's movement, women who *are* working may be more affluent and may also have more opportunities for the types of crimes once remote: white-collar offenses such as embezzlement. The change in the family structures and functions, such as women increasingly heading households, may also affect future patterns of illicit activity.

With these changes, does it mean that we will see a great change in women's crime rates? We do not have an answer to this question but we can pose some hypotheses. First, the incorporation of women into the labor force does not mean the end of sexism. Women continue to be trained for low paying 'women's work' in roles that require submissiveness and compliancy; and sexist ideology continues, of course, to be legitimated and reproduced by the mass media and educational and cultural institutions. This may mean, then, that we can expect an increase in or at least a maintenance of the rate of traditional women's crime (accomplices to men, check writing, etc.). On the other hand, if the women's movement develops a class analysis of women's oppression and a program around which working-class women can be organized, then we may witness a decrease in women's individualism, self-destructiveness, competitiveness and crime. Finally, what is the relationship between the deteriorating economic situation and women's crime rates? We can expect greater pressure on the wives and lovers of working-class men who are laid off from their jobs and perhaps an increase in crime-related activities such as welfare fraud and prostitution.

Whatever the outcome of this process, we are certain that the women's movement is not criminogenic. Freda Adler's book owes its popularity, no doubt, to the fact that it reinforces sexist stereotyping and is written by a woman. In contrast to her simplistic analysis of the roots of women's crime, we must look more deeply into the social relations under capitalism and to the systematic and special oppression that women suffer. Clearly, these relationships require further study.

Women and the judiciary

At the second stage of the criminal justice system, the judiciary, women appear to fare better than their male counterparts in obtaining leniency. Table 6.5 gives 1972 figures for California.

TABLE 6.5   Percentage of persons charged who pleaded guilty and who were convicted, 1972

	Women			Men		
	Number charged	Percentage pleading guilty	Percentage convicted	Number charged	Percentage pleading guilty	Percentage convicted
All crimes	6,394	69.2	83.2	49,567	72.1	87.6
Violent crimes	797	59.3	80.7	8,762	63.5	87.0
Property crimes	2,003	79.8	89.6	16,614	79.4	91.0

SOURCE: Simon (1975:64–5).

One might assume a relationship between the percentage of each sex pleading guilty and the percentage convicted; however, women are particularly prone to receiving acquittal for 'violent' crimes, especially murder, a crime for which almost the same proportion of women (42.2 per cent) as men (42.5 per cent) pleaded guilty, and for which only 77.6 per cent of those women were convicted (in contrast to 86.3 per cent of the men). And even those crimes for which women pleaded guilty more frequently than men (property crimes), the bias of leniency toward women holds. In the case of 'violence', part of the explanation for the clear-cut difference in the treatment afforded men and women may be due to the insignificant number of women charged with these offenses who come through court: in these rare cases, judges may tend toward leniency. Secondly, many women commit 'crimes of passion' against spouses or lovers, as opposed to the more frequent random shooting of strangers or casual acquaintances among men (see Wolfgang, 1958), and courts are traditionally forgiving in the former type of case. A factor that may operate across offense categories is that women charged are often accomplices in male-initiated crimes rather than themselves instigators, and hence are more likely to be acquitted.

In juvenile court, on the other hand, a different picture emerges. Girls have received *more* severe treatment than boys, in that they are referred to the juvenile courts more frequently for minor offenses. Table 6.6 gives 1964 figures for the Honolulu Juvenile Court.

TABLE 6.6 Delinquency referrals made to the Honolulu Juvenile Court, 1964: nature of alleged offense by sex of accused

	Male	Female
Part I (Type I) offenses	52.8	17.5
Part II (Type II) offenses	19.8	8.0
'Sex offenses'*	1.8	11.4
Juvenile offenses**	25.7	63.1
	100.0	100.0
	(2,191)	(537)

* Not including prostitution.
** Includes running away, curfew violations, incorrigibility.
SOURCE: Chesney-Lind (1973:60–1).

Unlike male delinquents, girls are by and large brought to the attention of the court for offenses that would not be criminal were they committed by adults. This is borne out by the findings of the 'Task Force Report: Juvenile Delinquency and Youth Crime' of the President's Commission on Law Enforcement and the Administration of Justice (1967), which found that over of half the girls, but one-fifth of the boys, were referred to court for juvenile (non-criminal) activities.

Girls are also detained longer in institutions than boys, despite the fact that their offenses are generally less serious. For example, in Honolulu in 1964, girls were detained an average of 19.3 days, compared with 8.9 days for the boys (Chesney-Lind, 1973:63).

Conversely, the frequency with which adult women are sentenced to imprisonment parallels their rate of conviction. Despite their proportional rise in arrests, women have barely risen as a percentage of prisoners. In California in 1952, women made up only 3.2 per cent of the prisoner population; twenty years later, they still accounted for only 3.9 per cent (Simon, 1975:75). Within each category of offense, women are more lightly sentenced, usually receiving a fine or probation. (They are also more frequently paroled once incarcerated.) Table 6.7 gives representative figures.

TABLE 6.7   California: percentage of convicted persons committed to prison by crime and sex, 1969

	Women	Men
Homicide	34.4	59.1
Robbery	28.0	42.1
Assault	6.0	11.3
Burglary	7.4	11.8
Theft	16.6	28.8
Forgery/checks	3.6	10.0
Narcotics	2.1	4.6
All above crimes	5.1	11.8
Violent crimes	14.3	27.3
Property crimes	6.2	14.0

SOURCE: Simon (1975:76).

However, there are differences in the leniency shown women for various offenses. They receive the relatively lightest sentences compared with men for traditional 'non-violent' female offenses: forgery and narcotics. Unlike the pattern of conviction, where 'violent' women are disproportionately acquitted (see Table 6.5), those convicted receive less benign treatment in sentencing.

Differential court treatment for women and girls, both economic and sexual offenders, has been dismissed as evidence of chivalry in the male-dominated criminal justice system. However, it is fundamental to view the system as an instrument of control over people, and in the case of women, reflecting and reinforcing the sexism in society at large. Its class bias explains the phenomenon that has previously been attributed to chivalry.[19]

The legal treatment of women offenders can only be understood in reference to the place of women in the economic and social structure. Because of their differences from men in production and reproduction, which we have outlined, women commit different sorts of offenses from men, as shown, and consequently are treated differently. That is, they are *de facto* penalized less harshly than men at this time at various stages of the criminal justice system—particularly with reference to Third World men—when they commit certain economic or 'violent' offenses. This has come about because, first, women comprise still a fraction of offenders in these categories; second, women are *seen* as economically marginal; and, in view of the previous factors and the stereotypes of female docility, women are not taken as serious threats to the social order. One may speculate that women's changing situation will create strains in the fabric of leniency.

In contrast to the benefit of the doubt shown women at the judicial level for certain offenses, they are penalized far *more* harshly than men for crimes defined as sexual, such as prostitution, juvenile promiscuity and incorrigibility. Again, this is comprehensible only in the context of women's central role in reproduction and the legal sanctions regarding their sexuality previously discussed. It is also the case that workers in the criminal justice system at various levels and stages tend to agree with the criminologists' tendency to view even female *property* offenders as sexually motivated deviants, due to sexist preconceptions. For example, scholars and psychiatrists see women shoplifters as women sublimating their sexuality (see Pollak, 1950). Prostitution, which is most often an economically motivated activity, is legally defined as a sexual deviation, like child molesting, and women entering this field are seen as promiscuous (see Davis, 1937). Consequently, prostitutes (and all female offenders) bear a social stigma connected to sexuality unshared by, say, thieves. (However, patronizing prostitutes and, to a lesser degree, pimping for them is not regarded as equally depraved or 'self-destructive', if one is a liberal.)

For example, girls brought to juvenile court for all sorts of offenses are routinely examined for virginity. Putting themselves *in loco parentis*, judges uphold standards of female chastity; in the name of sweet womanhood, girls are locked up for their own protection. Chesney-Lind (1973:54) notes:

> Since female adolescents have a much narrower range of acceptable behavior, even minor deviance may be seen as a substantial challenge to the authority of the family, the viability of the double standard, and to the maintenance of the present system of sexual inequality. It is the symbolic threat posed by female delinquency to these values that best explains (1) why the juvenile court system

selects out aspects of female deviance which violate sex role expectations rather than those that violate legal norms; and (2) why female delinquency, especially sexual delinquency, is viewed as more serious than male delinquency and is therefore more severely sanctioned.

In the case of adult women, on the other hand, it is contrary to the interests of society for large numbers of offenders to be incarcerated, given their nurturing and housekeeping functions. Women cannot care for children in prison; 38 per cent of mothers incarcerated lose custody of their children, and this creates a burden for the state (Hansen, 1974:2). As the superintendent of the California Institute for Women (CIW) states:

Almost all the women who come to prison have husbands and children. If a man goes to prison, the wife stays home, and he usually has his family to return to, and the household is there when he gets out. But women generally don't have family support from the outside. Very few men are going to sit around and take care of the children and be there when she gets back. So – to send a woman to prison means you are virtually going to disrupt her family (Simon, 1975:77).

Yet women *are* sentenced to prison. In the final analysis, chivalry is above all a classist and racist notion that has been extended primarily to affluent white women. For those outside the pale – Third World women, poor whites, political rebels – chivalry is less reliable. Documentation of police beatings, court severity and harsh imprisonment for female radicals throughout American history illustrate this (see Zinn, 1964). As Sojourner Truth, a black woman born into slavery, eloquently declared:

That man over there say that women needs to be helped into carriages, or over mud puddles, and to have the best place everywhere. Nobody ever help me into carriages or over ditches or gives me any best places . . . and ain't I a woman? Look at me! Look at my arm! I have plowed and planted and gathered into barns, and no man could head me – and ain't I a woman? I could work as much as a man (when I could get it) and bear the lash as well – and ain't I a woman? I have borne five children and I seen them most sold off into slavery and when I cried out with a mother's grief none but Jesus heard – ain't I a woman?

It is precisely women who are not 'ladies' by ruling-class standards who are likely to be sentenced to prison, and to commit offenses in the first place which make them vulnerable to arrest. The racism in the judiciary is illuminated by various statistical reports. In the Washington, D.C. correctional system, a study found 73 per cent of the 3000 women surveyed to be black, as opposed to 27 per cent white. Of the blacks, 14 per cent remained in jail over a month awaiting trial, as opposed to 8 per cent of the whites. More strikingly, 83 per cent of the blacks and only 17 per cent of the whites were returned to jail following arraignment (charges not dropped, disposed of; bail not granted or paid). The black conviction rate was 60 per cent, the white rate was 40 per cent (*Off Our Backs*, 1973).

It is not only that each level of the criminal justice system discriminates against blacks and the poor, not only out of judicial prejudice, but through procedures and standards which favor the affluent. Because of racism and poverty and white cultural hegemony,[20] blacks may in fact *have* higher rates of 'street crime'. The tragic forced 'emancipation' of black women into heading families and holding jobs has created a great economic burden for them; thus, the gap between black women and men in the commission of crimes of survival is narrower than that between white women and men.

Poor women of all races are disproportionately sent to prison. A study of the Federal Reformatory for Women at Alderson, West Virginia (where, in fact, one might expect a more affluent group than in state or local institutions) showed the prisoners to be poorly paid and poorly educated in their background. Of the 600-odd women, a third had been in service occupations. They were employed as laundry workers, hospital attendants, and beauticians; and more women did waitressing than any other occupation. About 10 per cent each were domestics, housewives, factory operatives and clericals. Only about 2 per cent owned or managed small businesses of their own. Half the population had only or less than a grammar school education, and only 28 women had gone to college (Giallombardo, 1966).

The hierarchy within the illegal marketplace also affects a woman's chances within the criminal justice system. Within prostitution, for example, young or attractive white call girls can easily evade arrest and earn considerable money, whereas older, black and working-class streetwalkers are most vulnerable. Gail Sheehy (1971:33–5) notes:

Probably no vocation operates with such a fierce system of social distinction as prostitution. The streetwalker has nothing but slurs for those 'lazy flatbackers,' meaning call girls. The call girl expresses contempt for the 'ignorant street hooker.' The madam wouldn't be caught dead with a 'diseased' street girl . . . The street hooker is at the bottom of the blue-collar end of the ladder. She far outnumbers anyone in the business.

Streetwalkers are financially victimized by 'revolving door' justice, the series of street cleanups that rarely result in lengthy imprisonment. The women are consequently at the mercy of pimps, corrupt police, lawyers, bail bondsmen, politicians and racketeers, who prey on them. Their treatment can hardly be described as chivalrous.

Women in prison

Within the third stage of the criminal justice system, the very insignificance of the volume of women prisoners, nationally 5600 women out of a total of 196,000 inmates in 1970 (Simon, 1975:69), adversely affects those women who *are* incarcerated. Firstly, only 15 states have separate women's prisons and only the largest cities have women's jails. Most go into makeshift quarters in men's facilities such as the one that housed Joan Little.[21] It is in city jails that prostitutes and drug offenders spend a good deal of their time, and there are few available resources for them. Secondly, in the women's prisons that do exist, few vocational or industrial programs comparable with men's (which are themselves inadequate) exist. While the average number of vocational programs in men's prison is 10, the average number for women is 2.7. Similarly, the choice of vocations that women can train for is extremely limited: compared with the 50-odd programs for men, women get cosmetology, food service, clerical skills, keypunching, and nurses' aide training (Simon, 1975:80–3).

A characteristic of the penal system for women is marked paternalism and false benevolence. Some prisons for women resemble school campuses, e.g., Alderson Federal Reformatory and the California Institute for Women. Inmates are treated in such a way as to reinforce their helplessness and dependence on authority. In other prisons, of course, such as the New York House of Detention, conditions are brutal and in no way campuslike.

In general, the rehabilitative ideal has fit nicely with the womanly ideal. Convicts are presented with the model of the lady, a hegemonic standard of conduct which speaks little to their own social and sexual needs. For example, 'ladylike' behavior may be required as a condition of parole.[22] The standards imposed are those of sexual virtue, namely monogamous heterosexuality confined to the nuclear family.

The ubiquitous psychological view held by treatment personnel, which sees offenders as individually responsible for their misdeeds, diverts attention away from social and economic inequalities such as sexism and inward toward the psyche. This underscores the way women are generally isolated, both physically in the nuclear family (unlike men, who work and socialize freely) and emotionally, tending toward a conservative personalization of the world. The rehabilitative ideal strengthens privatism and attempts to deaden movements of political or collective activity. The rehabilitative failure is evidenced by the deep and justified cynicism among treatment personnel, which reflects the reality that they are regulating and not reducing criminal activity.

The developing medical model of rehabilitation, that defines crime as illness and the prisoner as patient in traditional liberal form, again reinforces women's childlike helplessness. Women are commonly child/patients under the male domination of doctors and husbands (see Chesler, 1972; Roth and Lerner, 1975). Historically 'ideal' mental patients and medical guinea pigs, women convicted of 'crimes' now suffer the indignity of behavior modification and enforced therapies behind bars [23] Women have been the targets of extreme technologies of control; the 'father of psycho-surgery' in the U.S., Dr. Walter Freeman, contended that women made the best candidates for lobotomy, and cited one elderly housewife who 'was a master at bitching and really led her husband a dog's life' until surgery made her into a model housekeeper. A contemporary neurosurgeon has estimated that up to 80 per cent of his patients have been women (Klein, 1973a:7–8). Hospitalization and chemotherapy, less spectacularly, have been prime methods for controlling deviant women who might have been imprisoned for their conduct were they male. It is possible that high rates of mental hospitalization for women complement their low rates of imprisonment.

In sum, differential treatment of women in the criminal justice system has been based on an assumption that, treated paternalistically, women will not make trouble. They have not constituted a major problem so far, and the volume has been too small to trouble the state. Chivalrous treatment has been a double-edged sword, as our preceding arguments have made clear:

> Women are not oppressed in the same way as black people, for example: they are not at the bottom of many scales and at the top of none. There is a pedestal – they are respected and praised for many things, for greater sensitivity, for moral fortitude, for modesty . . . In some sense, then, one might say that the job of bringing up children has high status, but the status of a different kind than most. It is sex-specific, it is compulsory, and the price is too high (Quick, 1972:13).

Conclusion

In this paper we have critically reviewed the position of women with respect to the criminal justice system in the United States. We have indicated that the special oppression of women by that system is not isolated or arbitrary, but rather is rooted in systematic sexist practices and ideologies which can only be fully understood by analyzing the position of women in capitalist society. However, this is not to deny that there are changes occurring in the position and activities of women – changes in their participation in the labor force, in educational opportunities, political activity, and family roles. Consequently, all of this has had repercussions in the legal system: witness such upheavals as the inadequacy of rape laws that are currently being challenged, and the debate around the overcriminalization of prostitution.

The same conditions which are the root of the sexist oppression of women are also responsible for the rise in recent years of a revitalized women's movement, which has changed women's consciousness and has been organizing around the right to abortion, the decriminalization of prostitution, and the needs of prisoners. Although a full discussion is outside the scope of this paper, it is in this arena that we view the potential for struggles of resistance. For example, the emergence of a viable women's prisoners' movement in such places as New York, California, and Washington, D.C., has created concrete links between women inside and outside. This has encouraged organization around improving prison conditions and creating alternatives such as half-way houses and prison education programs with substantive content. Self-defense and self-help groups against rape have evolved into strong supportive mechanisms for victimized women. In cities across the country, these groups have exerted pressure on police and hospitals to treat women with respect instead of condemnation. Furthermore, the struggle for the decriminalization of prostitution has been carried out by prostitutes' unions (COYOTE in San Francisco, ASP in Seattle, PONY in New York) who, in the face of incredible social stigma, have fought creatively and successfully to educate people and win legitimacy.

These political activities, together with the increasingly active role played by women in militant organizations (see, for example, the number of women on the FBI's 'Ten Most Wanted' list), have brought women's groups under repressive fire from the government. Moreover, one can observe a trend towards the use of more blatant techniques of control in women's prisons previously reserved for men. The myth of the 'violent female criminal' has conveniently appeared in the popular media when women are asserting themselves. Repression does not only take the form of clubs and guns. Its ideological forms can be just as devastating in the long run. Clearly, women can no longer argue for special treatment, although activism has set in motion the dynamics of repression. We see these continued struggles against repression as the best way to work towards the creation of a more humane system of justice.

Notes

1. For a discussion of the legal definition of crime vs. radical alternatives, see Herman Schwendinger and Julia Schwendinger (1970).
2. For a discussion of 'agency-determined research', see Tony Platt (1974a); see also Herman Schwendinger and Julia Schwendinger (1974) for a lengthy treatment of the technocratic perspective in general.
3. See Dorie Klein (1973b) for a substantive discussion of the traditional criminological views on women.
4. An example of this is Ward and Kassebaum's study (1965) of the California Institute for Women which is primarily concerned with inmate lesbianism.
5. We are indebted to the Schwendingers for introducing us to this concept.
6. See Ralph Miliband (1969) for an analysis of the role of government in capitalist society and economic and state elites.
7. An excellent analysis of corporate crime may be found in David Gordon (1971).
8. For a fuller discussion of the elements of women's work, see Juliet Mitchell (1969), Margaret Benston (1969), and Paddy Quick (1972).
9. In discussing housework under capitalism, Paddy Quick (1972:67) notes:

'If it is admitted that the family is maintained at the expense of women, capitalism would have to devise some other way of getting the work done. Although this not inconceivable, the political and social consequences as well as the economic cost would be considerable. At present it would seem to be more profitable for the capitalist system to continue to "preserve the family".'

10. See Tony Platt (1969) for a historical analysis of women reformers.

11. It is still true that only marriage offers a woman any kind of economic security, as the following figures show. These are 1968 median earnings of full-time workers (Quick, 1972:6):

	Women	*Men*
Year-round workers	$4 818	$8 226
Unrelated individuals	2 239	4 986
Families headed by	4 477	096*

With wife working, $10,636; with just men working, $8215.

12. During that time, 4 million women joined the labor force while the men were overseas. Their occupations put the myths to rest about what women could do: 'Women became welders and shipbuilders; they built airplanes and produced ammunition: they made complicated electrical equipment and riveted the sides of tanks. By the end of the war, women were working in almost all areas of manufacturing' (Trey, 1972:44). Within a month after the war's end, however, 600,000 women were fired, and those women who did maintain jobs were often demoted to lower-paid 'women's jobs' within factories.

13. Nonwhite women suffer particularly within the labor force, as the following figures show. These are wages for 1967 (Beal, 1970:345):

White men	$6704
White women	3991
Nonwhite men	4277
Nonwhite women	2861

14. See Karen DeCrow (1974) for a fuller discussion of women and the law.

15. The law, by creating a 'bad' class of women, sanctifies only one form of sex-as-barter: marriage (see Goldman, 1970). Yet marriage and prostitution are inextricably linked. Simone de Beauvoir (1961: 523–4) has written: 'It has often been remarked that the necessity exists of sacrificing one part of the female sex in order to save the other and prevent worse troubles. One of the arguments in support of slavery advanced by the American supporters of the institution was that the Southern whites, being all freed from servile duties, could maintain the most democratic and refined relationships among themselves; in the same way, a caste of

"shameless women" allows the "honest woman" to be treated with the most chivalrous respect.' It is the irony of the legal system that it punishes individual prostitutes and in no way challenges the inevitability of prostitution in a society plagued by male sexual consumerism and female economic impoverishment. While prostitution may not be eradicated under capitalism, the well-being of women demands that it be decriminalized.

16. For example, 'in the U.S. over the last few years an estimated 100,000 to 150,000 low-income persons have been sterilized annually under federally funded programs' (Maclean, 1975:1). In Puerto Rico, by 1965 '34 per cent of the women of child-bearing age had been sterilized in so-called "family planning" programs paid for and controlled by the U.S. Department of Health, Education and Welfare' (Allen, 1974:6).

17. Type I offenses are the FBI Index Crimes. Type II offenses are, for example, non-aggravated assault, fraud, forgery, narcotics laws, and prostitution.

18. In 1953, women comprised 14.1 per cent of homicide arrests; by 1972, they were still only 15.6 per cent (Simon, 1975:40).

19. See Walter Reckless and Barbara Kay (1967) for a summary of this view.

20. Bias is shown, for example, in the prohibition of leisure activities widespread among minorities: gambling, use of certain drugs (see Helmer, 1975).

21. For a discussion of this case, see Angela Davis (1975).

22. At CIW, several hundred operations for plastic surgery were performed on prisoners in 1974. A good appearance was a condition for release (Angell, 1975).

23. 'The Management Cottage at CIW has about 40 women who were completely segregated from the rest . . . the behavior modification was inmates were trained to police each other 6 hours a day of group [therapy]. They wouldn't allow a person to come out . . . Put into this unit were always dissenters' (*Off Our Backs*, 1975).

References

Adler, Freda (1975) *Sisters in Crime: The Rise of the New Female Criminal* (New York: McGraw-Hill).

Allen, Barbara (1974) 'Stop Forced Sterilization', *Sister* – West Coast Feminist Newspaper (November).

American Friends Service Committee (1971) *Struggle for Justice* (New York: Hill and Wang).

Angell, Catherine (1975) 'Sex Role Stereotyping and Women in the Criminal Law System', paper presented at the 70th Annual Meeting of the American Sociological Association, San Francisco (August).

Austin, Penelope and Desmond Ellis (1971) 'Menstruation and Aggressive Behavior in a Correctional Center for Women', *Journal of Criminal Law,*

Criminology and Police Science, 6, 2, 3 (September).

Balbus, Issac D. (1973) *The Dialectics of Legal Repression* (New York: Russell Sage Foundation).

Beal, Frances (1970) 'Double Jeopardy: To Be Black and Female' in *Sisterhood Is Powerful*, edited by Robin Morgan (New York: Vintage).

Beauvoir, Simone de (1961) *The Second Sex* (New York: Bantam Books).

Benston, Margaret (1969) 'The Political Economy of Women's Liberation', *Monthly Review* (September).

Bergman, Arlene Eisen (1974) *Women of Viet Nam* (San Francisco: People's Press).

Boggs, Carl (1972) 'Gramsci's Prison Notebook', *Socialist Revolution*, 11 and 12 (September–October and November–December).

Brownmiller, Susan (1975) *Against Our Will: Men, Women and Rape* (New York: Simon and Schuster).

Burkhart, Katherine W. (1973) *Women in Prison* (New York: Doubleday).

Chesler, Phyllis (1972) *Women and Madness* (New York: Doubleday).

Chesney-Lind, Meda (1973) 'Judicial Enforcement of the Female Sex Role: The Family Court and the Female Delinquent', *Issues in Criminology*, 8, 2 (Fall).

—— (1974) 'Juvenile Delinquency: The Sexualization of Female Crime', *Psychology Today* (July).

Cleaver, Eldridge (1968) *Soul on Ice* (New York: McGraw-Hill).

Cowie, John, Valerie Cowie and Eliot Slater (1968) *Delinquency in Girls* (London: Heinemann).

Dalla Costa, Mariarosa (1972) *Women and the Subversion of the Community* (London: Falling Wall Press).

Davis, Angela (1971) *If They Come in the Morning* (New York: Signet Books).

—— (1974) *An Autobiography* (New York: Random House).

—— (1975) 'Joan Little – The Dialectics of Rape', *Ms. Magazine* (June).

Davis, Kingsley (1937) 'The Sociology of Prostitution', *American Sociological Review*, 2, 5 (October).

DeCrow, Karen (1974) *Sexist Justice* (New York: Random House).

Federal Bureau of Investigation (1975) *Uniform Crime Reports, 1974* (Washington, D.C.: U.S. Government Printing Office).

Firestone, Shulamith (1971) *The Dialectic of Sex* (New York: William Morrow).

Giallombardo, Rose (1966) *Society of Women: A Study of a Women's Prison* (New York: John Wiley).

Glassman, Carol (1970) 'Women and the Welfare System' in *Sisterhood Is Powerful*, edited by Robin Morgan (New York: Vintage).

Glueck, Eleanor and Sheldon (1934) *Four Hundred Delinquent Women* (New York: Alfred Knopf).

Goldman, Emma (1970) *The Traffic in Women and Other Essays on Feminism* (New York: Times Change Press).

Gordon, David (1971) 'Class and the Economics of Crime', *Review of Radical Political Economics,* 3, 3 (Summer).

Griffin, Susan (1971) 'Rape: The All-American Crime', *Ramparts* (September).

Guettel, Charnie (1974) *Marxism and Feminism* (Toronto: The Women's Press).

Hansen, Donna (1974) 'Mothers in Prison', *Sister*—West Coast Feminist Newspaper (November).

Helmer, John (1975) *Drugs and Minority Oppression* (New York: Seabury Press).

Humphries, Drew (1973) 'The Politics of Abortion: A Case Study of New York's Abortion Law', unpublished doctoral dissertation, School of Criminology, University of California, Berkeley.

Kittrie, Nicholas (1973) *The Right to Be Different* (Baltimore: Penguin Books).

Klein, Dorie (1973a) 'Notes on the Center for the Study and Reduction of Violence', *Pacific News Service* (August).

—— (1973b) 'The Etiology of Female Crime: A Review of the Literature', *Issues in Criminology* 8, 2 (Fall).

Konopka, Gisela (1966) *The Adolescent Girl in Conflict* (Englewood Cliffs: Prentice-Hall).

Lerner, Gerda (ed.) (1973) *Black Women in White America: A Documentary History* (New York: Vintage).

Liazos, Alex (1972) 'The Poverty of the Sociology of Deviance: Nuts, Sluts and perverts', *Social Problems* 20, 1 (Summer).

Lombroso, Cesare (1920) *The Female Offender* (translation) (New York: Appleton). Originally published in 1903.

Maclean, Pam (1975) 'Sterilization Hearings', *Plexus*, 2, 4 (June).

Marcuse, Herbert (1968) *One-Dimensional Man* (Boston: Beacon Press).

Miliband, Ralph (1969) *The State in Capitalist Society* (New York: Basic Books).

Mitchell, Juliet (1969) 'The Longest Revolution' in *Masculine – Feminine*, ed. by Betty and Theodore Roszak (New York: Harper and Row).

Murphy, Jean and Susan Deller Ross (1970) 'Liberating Women – Legally Speaking', in *With Justice for Some*, ed. by Bruce Wasserstein and Mark J. Green (Boston: Beacon Press).

New York Radical Feminists (1974) *Rape: The First Sourcebook for Women* (New York: New American Library).

Newsweek (1975) January 6.

Off Our Backs (1973) 'Prisons' (January).

—— (1975) 'Interview: Women Ex-Cons' (April–May).

Pearce, Frank (1972) 'Crime, Corporations and the American Social Order' in *Politics and Deviance*, ed. by Ian Taylor and Laurie Taylor (Harmondsworth: Penguin).

Platt, Tony (1969) *The Child Savers* (University of Chicago Press).

—— (1974a) 'Prospects for a Radical Criminology in the United States', *Crime and Social Justice*, I (Spring–Summer).

—— (1974b) 'Problems in the Development of Radical Criminology', paper presented at the 69th Annual Meeting of the American Sociological Association, Montreal (August).

Pollak, Otto (1950) *The Criminality of Women* (Philadelphia: University of Pennsylvania Press).

Pollak, Otto and Alfred Friedman (eds) (1969) *Family Dynamics and Female Sexual Delinquency* (Palo Alto: Science and Behavioral Books).

President's Commission on Law Enforcement and the Administration of Justice (1967) *Task Force Report: Juvenile Delinquency and Youth Crime* (Washington, D.C.: U.S. Government Printing Office).

Quick, Paddy (1972) 'Women's Work', *Review of Radical Political Economics*, 4, 3 (July).

Quinney, Richard (1974) *Critique of Legal Order: Crime Control in Capitalist Society* (Boston: Little, Brown).

Reckless, Walter and Barbara Kay (1967) 'The Female Offender', *Report to the President's Commission on Law Enforcement and the Administration of Justice* (Washington, D.C.: U.S. Government Printing Office).

Roby, Pamela and Virginia Kerr (1972) 'The Politics of Prostitution', *Nation* (10 April).

Roth, Bob and Judith Lerner (1975) 'Sex Based Discrimination in the Mental Institutionalization of Women', *California Law Review*, 62.

Rowbotham, Sheila (1973) *Woman's Consciousness, Man's World* Harmondsworth: Penguin Books).

Rush, Florence (1972) 'The Myth of Sexual Delinquency', *Women, A Journal of Liberation*, 3, 3.

Schwendinger, Herman and Julia Schwendinger (1970) 'Defenders of Order of Guardians of Human Rights?', *Issues in Criminology*, 5, 2.

—— (1973) 'A Report to the European Group at the Florence Conference', paper presented at the First Conference of the European Group for the Study of Deviance and Social Control, Impruneta, Italy (September).

—— (1974) *Sociologists of the Chair* (New York: Basic Books).

Schwendinger, Julia and Herman Schwendinger (1974) 'Rape Myths: In Legal, Theoretical and Everyday Practice', *Crime and Social Justice*, I (Spring–Summer).

Sheehy, Gail (1971) *Hustling* (New York: Dell Press).

Simon, Rita James (1975) *Women and Crime* (Lexington: D.C. Heath).

Taylor, Ian, Paul Walton and Jock Young (1974) *The New Criminology* (New York: Harper and Row).

Taylor, Ian, Paul Walton and Jock Young (eds) (1975) *Critical Criminology* (London: Routledge and Kegan Paul).

Thomas, W. I. (1907) *Sex and Society* (Boston: Little, Brown).

—— (1923) *The Unadjusted Girl* (New York: Harper and Row).

Trey, Joan Ellen (1972) 'Women in the War Economy – World War II',

Review of Radical Political Economics, 4, 3 (July).

Vedder, Clyde and Dora Somerville (1970) *The Delinquent Girl* (Springfield: Charles C. Thomas).

Ward, David and Gene Kassebaum (1965) *Women's Prison: Sex and Social Structure* (Chicago: Aldine).

Weis, Kurt and Sandra S. Borges (1973) 'Victimology and Rape: The Case of the Legitimate Victim', *Issues in Criminology*, 8, 2 (Fall).

Werkentin, Falco, Michael Hofferbert and Michael Baurmann (1974) 'Criminology as Police Science or: "How Old Is the New Criminology?"', *Crime and Social Justice*, II (Fall–Winter).

West, Louis J. (1973) *Proposal for the Center for the Study and Reduction of Violence* (Neuropsychiatric Institute, UCLA, April).

Winick, Charles and Paul Kinsie (1971) *The Lively Commerce: Prostitution in the U.S.* (New York: Signet Books).

Wolfe, Alan (1973) *The Seamy Side of Democracy* (New York: David McKay).

Wolfgang, Marvin E. (1958) *Patterns in Criminal Homicide* (Philadelphia: University of Pennsylvania Press).

Women, A Journal of Liberation (1972) Issue on Women in Prison, 3, 3.

Women Endorsing Decriminalization (1973) 'Prostitution: A Non-Victim Crime?', *Issues in Criminology*, 8, 2 (Fall).

Zinn, Howard (1964) *SNCC: The Student Non-Violent Coordinating Committee* (Boston: Beacon Press).

Part III
The State and Criminal Justice

7

The Penal Question in *Capital*

Dario Melossi

In the last few years, dissatisfaction has been felt in the ranks of what could be called the 'juridical left'. This has been due to the need to take a political position on situations of struggle or parliamentary confrontations, while moving from a solid theoretical base. This, in part, has been caused by insufficient elaboration of a Marxist vision of law and of the state, and in particular, of the penal question. There is a need for extensive research, with the principal objective of understanding the particular transitions that the social structure, and, therefore, the state structure, is going through in this moment. Although I do not believe that the exploration of Marxian thought can in any way take the place of such a historical and factual analysis, I do believe that there is a need to bring to light material found in Marx's work that is often overlooked. But above all, what we can derive from Marx is a lesson on method. This lesson lets us develop a truly Marxist analysis of phenomena such as crime and punishment which is still in touch with our own reality.

Marx dealt with crime and punishment neither as disconnected from the whole of the social structure, nor as severed objects of intellectual inquiry. He considered them to be expressions of man's condition under capitalist domination. Adopting this perspective makes it possible to study them in a scientific way. That is why I prefer here to focus on *Capital* more than others of Marx's writings, even though he deals more specifically with the problems of crime and punishment in other works. These include the articles in the *Rheinische Zeitung* or in later *New York Daily Tribune* pieces, some passages in the *Early Manuscripts*, and that little masterpiece of social, philosophical and literary critique, the eighth chapter of *The Holy Family*.

However, it is in *Capital* only that the social phenomenon of criminality is looked at in the context of the general Marxian scientific theory. This is where Marx investigates the problem of the origins of capitalist society, the 'primitive accumulation' that is shown to be the specific capitalist matrix of the penal question. By following Marx's analysis, in the historical context where primitive accumulation plays a central role, we can identify both the classic elements of the penal question in the nineteenth century as well as the fundamental and directing imperatives of bourgeois criminal policy. It is in the making of the proletariat that the relationship between the person as a criminal and the person as a worker is made clear. There, Marx's concept of a punishment-free society which appears in *The Holy Family* is connected to the scientific analysis of the repressive and training functions of the state's penal apparatus.

> The process, therefore, that clears the way for the capitalist system, can be none other than the process that takes away from the laborer the possession of his means of production; a process that transforms, on the one hand, the social means of subsistence and of production into capital, on the other, the immediate producers into wage-laborers. The so-called primitive accumulation, therefore, is nothing else than the historical process of divorcing the producer from the means of production. It appears as primitive, because it forms the pre-historic stage of capital and of the mode of production corresponding with it.[1]

Thus, Marx summarized the essence of the long gestation period of capitalist-dominated society. Part of the social and economic transition process which took place in the more advanced parts of Europe between the fifteenth and eighteenth centuries was the massive expulsion of farmers from the land and their transformation into workers. By this process, those farmers-turned-workers were denied access to the means of survival which had existed for them in earlier times. This certainly served to control them insofar as they found themselves in a situation created and controlled by the rising bourgeoisie, and without means of preventing the developments which were changing their very mode of existence. Throughout this period, the function of the state is shown to have been inextricably connected with economic *spontaneity*. That is, the priorities of the state were dictated by the priorities of primitive accumulation as they arose.

In *Capital*, Marx does not concern himself *ex-professo* with the penal question. However, his analysis provides us the means of understanding the intervention of the repressive, or preventive actions of the state. It is with this tool that we can analyze the historical and present problem of crime and punishment.

In one of his early writings, Marx shows how the unrestricted gathering of fallen wood in the forests was one of the last survivals of the medieval relations of property and of the collective use of common lands. He shows how bourgeois state power took on the task of legally prohibiting what had been a definite right of the 'poor masses'.[2] In *The Holy Family*, Marx shows that reduction of the person to something-other-than-himself is at the base of rebellion, of the desire for re-appropriation. This has its clearest expression in the introduction of a life-system based on capitalist social relationships, particularly in the workers' condition. All these points find clarification and their historical context in Marx's analysis of original accumulation.

The expulsion from the land was a concrete forerunner of Proudhon's famous motto: 'Property is theft'. Marx demonstrates that it was, in fact, theft, violence, and murder. The means by which 'original expropriation' was carried out are listed by Marx in the beginning of the 27th chapter of *Capital*. In part, the absolute monarchy provoked the process by the 'dissolution of bands of feudal retainers'. Additionally, the great landlords expelled farmers from the land entitled to the farmers and peasants under the feudal system of land tenure. They also usurped the common lands. Finally, the forced expropriation process was given new force during the Reformation when the bourgeoisie accomplished the 'colossal theft of ecclesiastical wealth'. With the widespread expropriation of the vast land and property holdings of the Catholic church, those who had lived and worked in the convents and other religious institutions were also thrown out to join the growing mass which became the proletariat. Thus, by 1601, during Elizabeth's reign, pauperism was already such an extensive reality that the complex charity system known as the Old Poor Law had to be introduced.[3] In the eighteenth century, the transformation was completed. Private owners had stolen all the land, or nearly so. The state, through the 'laws for fencing-off common lands', supported the appropriation of the farmer-masses' 'common property'. In reality, these were the infamous 'decrees of expropriation of the people'. Penal law shows itself here, assuring absolute immunity to the usurpers. This should come as no surprise, since the lawmakers and judges were among those 'acquiring' property in this manner. Thus, the new legal code became the negation of the legal legitimacy that had been represented by the customary rights of the oppressed classes. At the same time, as we shall see, the legal code provided negative sanction of those 'criminal' behaviors which were brought about by the same transformation.

What happens to these men, to these farmer-masses, transformed into labor-power, made 'free', that is, 'without anything' except the ability to labor?

> The proletariat created by the breaking up of the bands of feudal retainers and by the forceable expropriation of the people from the soil, this 'free' proletariat could not possibly be absorbed by the nascent manufactures as fast as it was thrown upon the world. On the other hand, these men, suddenly dragged from their wonted mode of life, could not as suddenly adapt themselves to the discipline of their new condition. They were turned *en masse* into beggars, robbers, vagabonds, partly from inclination, in most cases from stress of circumstances. Hence at the end of the 15th and during the whole of the 16th century, throughout Western Europe a bloody legislation against vagabondage. The fathers of the present working class were chastised for their forced transformation into vagabonds and paupers. Legislation treated them as 'voluntary' criminals, and assumed that it depended on their own good will to go on working under the old conditions that no longer existed.[4]

Thus the circle is closed. The emerging bourgeois society produced widespread vagrancy, and the bourgeois state proceeded to criminalize it. The notion of free will reveals itself here, not as a criterion for the determination of guilt, but rather as a metaphysical premise to justify the rightness of punishment. But what should the goal of punishment be? At that time, punishment consisted of the useless effort of making 'vagabonds' return to the land from which they had been expelled. Marx says clearly, in the above-cited passage, that punishment must consist of training in 'the discipline of their new condition'. Thus we return to *The Holy Family* and the *Manuscripts*; being a worker is seen as absolutely unnatural under such circumstances. It has become a state of emasculation and pain made historically concrete only by the violent process of expelling the farmer from the land and reducing his labor power to that of alienated labor typical of capitalistic society, and consequently, of the general social relationships characteristic of it.

The person of *The Holy Family* and the *Manuscripts* now becomes the 'free' worker of *Capital*. His suffering, which comes from his alienation, now becomes the historically determined suffering of a class which was forcibly expelled from the land. Instead, it has been transformed into the working class. Marx sees the person, no longer as a species-being, but as a single individual belonging to a class, now reduced and socialized to the worker's condition. In this history of his social existence, the individual enters into a relationship with the world of production and suffers his condition as a worker. The concept of human existence in the *Manuscripts* was already founded on materialism, on the necessity of existence. This is certainly not derived from metaphysical premises or vulgar materialism; even defining it as anthropological could be deceiving. Marx, already in the *Manuscripts*, puts the accent on the historicism of man – nature relationships, on the education to which the senses have been subjected, as well as on their distortion in a society built upon private property and exploitation.[5]

'The *human* being is a *social* being',[6] Marx states several times in the *Manuscripts*; and still more clearly in the *Sixth Thesis on Feuerbach*, ' . . . the human essence is not something abstract which is immanent in the single individual. In its reality, it is the set of social relationships'. Thus for Marx, it is not a question of any idealistic or materialistic *a priori*; he refers to the complex web of relationships which link person to person, and person to nature. The needs which develop historically are not, in any way, premises for the social being, but are created and become real within him. This understanding is to be found both in the *Manuscripts* and in *Capital*. What changes then? In what respect is *Capital* different, richer, than the *Manuscripts*? In *Capital*, Marx presents his analysis of our present concern, the state's use of violence and thus of penal law and punishment. Here Marx shows how these function to guarantee control over labor-power, and consequently guarantee surplus value, exploitation. Whereas in the *Manuscripts* and in *The Holy family*, repression was still connected to bourgeois society in a rather intuitive and analogical way, in *Capital* the *specific* mechanism and function of the process of containment and reduction of 'essential human forces' is described.

Coming from the ruins of feudalism, capital and 'free' workers come face to face and are materially united in manufacture. For the still-emerging proletariat, this embrace is neither voluntary nor in any way pleasant. They must adjust to seclusion, lack of light and air, loss of that relative independence of work in the fields, placing themselves under the unconditional authority of the capitalist, the ugliest and most tiring monotony and repetitiveness.[7] Not by chance are the historical origins of manufacture and prisons unified and interdependent. It is not necessary here to recall the poignancy of Marx's writings of manufacture. It is important, however, to note that in them is the transposition of certain themes that had appeared in the *Manuscripts*.

> Manufacture cripples the worker and makes a monster of him, cultivating, as in a greenhouse, his ability for details, by suppressing a whole world of impulses and productive tendencies, in the same way that in the states of La Plata an entire animal is slaughtered for its skin and fat.

With laws against vagrancy, laws that lengthen the working day, sanction the attempts at association, fix maximum salaries, etc., the bourgeoisie obliges the newborn working class to work on its terms. Here, as a matter of fact, penal law could boast great usefulness for capital. In the mercantile epoch, state violence was one of the easiest ways of bolstering the still-fragile onset of private initiative.

The 'way of the cross' walked for some time by the proletariat, 'punished' for a social transition that they did not initiate or understand and which they opposed with all their force, is, in a more developed moment, walked by the rebel, the criminal, by the ones Marx numbers among the 'lumpenproletariat.' 'Thus the rural population, expropriated by force, expelled from its land and made vagabond, was pushed by grotesque and terroristic laws to submit, by force of whip, branding, torture, to that discipline which was necessary to the wage-labor system.' Further:

> It is not enough for work conditions to be presented as capital at one end and men with nothing more to sell than their own labor-power at the other end. And neither is it enough to make these men sell themselves voluntarily. As capitalist production proceeds, a working class develops which, by education, tradition and habit, recognizes the needs of that mode of production as obvious natural laws. The organization of the developed capitalist production process breaks every resistance; constant production of a relative overpopulation keeps the law of supply-and-demand, and thus labor salaries, on a track which corresponds to the needs of capital accumulation. The silent compulsion of economical relations

affixes the seal to capitalist rule over the worker. *It is true that the immediate extra-economic force is still used, but only as an exception*[8] . . . Things go differently during the historical genesis of capitalist production. The bourgeoisie, at its birth, needs *State power*, and uses it, to *'regulate' salaries*, that is to restrict them within limits convenient to the extraction of surplus value, to lengthen the *working day* and to keep the worker himself at a *normal degree of dependence*. This is an essential moment of so-called *original accumulation*.[9]

Therefore, for both the worker-criminal of the sixteenth century and the *delinquent tout court* of a well-developed capitalist system, it is imperative to learn the discipline of the capitalist mode of production. But exactly what is that discipline? To answer this question, on which I believe the character of the structure of administering punishment in developed bourgeois society is based and depends, it is necessary to return to some of Marx's concepts as well as to the basic themes of penal history in Western society.

Marx says that after the enactment of England's Poor Law in 1601, various English landowners proposed 'a clever project for eliminating any confusion in executing the Act' and that was 'to construct a *prison* in the parish. Every poor person who does not want to be thrown into this prison will not be given assistance'.[10] Later, during the struggle of the English ruling classes to lengthen the working day, the anonymous author of 'An Essay on Trade and Commerce, Containing Observations on Taxation, etc.' which appeared in 1770, said the same thing as Marx, who observes:

To this end, as for 'rooting out laziness, corruption and romantic nonsense about freedom,' and 'for lessening the plight of the poor, furthering the spirit of industry and lowering the price of labor in industry,' our faithful capitalist Eckart proposes the tested system of closing those workers who become dependent on public welfare, in a word, the needy, into an 'ideal workhouse.' 'Such a house should be made a house of terror.' In this 'house of terror,' in such an 'ideal workhouse,' men should work for '14 hours a day including, however, periods necessary for meals, so that twelve full work-hours remain.' Twelve work-hours a day in the 'ideal workhouse,' in the house of terror of 1770! Sixty-three years later, in 1833, when the English parliament lessened the workday of 13 to 18-year-old adolescents to 12 full workhours in 4 groups of factories, it seemed as though the last judgement had come for the English! . . . The 'house of terror' for the needy, which was still a dream for capital's soul in 1770 rose very few years later as a gigantic 'workhouse' for the industrial worker: it is called the factory. And this time the ideal paled beside reality.[11]

Marx sees this link between the 'ideal' workhouse and the factory as particularly significant, especially since workhouses in 1770 were not at all ideal institutions. Rather, they were ideal in the sense of material productivity only. They furnished the model for the methodist system of cell-type prisons that has become the modern bourgeois form of punishment.[12] During the seventeenth and eighteenth centuries, in fact (that is, parallel to the rise and development of manufacture), 'workhouses' and 'houses of correction' opened in all the most developed countries of the Western world, while forms of corporal punishment progressively disappeared. These new forms were unknown in the preceding period. They were based on an ascetic and productive vision of life which was completely foreign to earlier places of confinement. It is the re-educative value of work, in fact, which was emphasized in this period and which determined both the ideological and practical novelty of these new institutions. The mystery of discipline thus becomes less and less obscure; this particular discipline that the lumpenproletariat (still, for the most part, future proletariat) must learn, is the discipline which rules the very heart of bourgeois society. But the heart of this society is capital, that is the extraction of surplus-value, which, as Marx says,

> is fulfilled outside the market, that is, in the sphere of circulation . . . The sphere of circulation, that is, the exchange of commodities, within the limits of which the buying and selling of the labor-power takes place, was in reality a true Eden of man's innate rights. There only Freedom, Equality, Property and Bentham rules.[13]

Thus there ruled law and the Hegelian theory of punishment. But if we go into the 'secret laboratory of production', equality and Enlightenment stop; there, at the very heart of capitalist development where lurks the essential condition for its existence (i.e., exploitation), the principles of hierarchy and subordination dominate. These principles appear in the discipline which the capitalist imposes upon the worker. This discipline is the basic condition for the extraction of surplus-value, and is thus the only real lesson that bourgeois society has to propose to the proletariat. If legal ideology rules outside production, within it reign servitude and inequality.[14] But the place of production is the factory. Thus, the institutional function of the workhouses and later of the prisons was to teach the proletariat factory discipline.

It is not surprising then that in the very developed mercantile capitalism of seventeenth-century Holland,[15] in the cradle of strictest protestantism, as in Quaker Pennsylvania, the next and decisive step could be taken, the transformation of 'welfare institutions' in the form of workhouses, into 'places for punishment', or prisons. Thus rose the 'methodist system of cell-type prisons' to which Marx refers in *The Holy Family*. The founder of an American state himself, William Penn, had foreseen this development, crystallized about a century later in the first modern penitentiary in Philadelphia (1970), when he said, in 1682, 'All prisons shall be workhouses for felons, vagrants and loose and idle persons'. But in the year that the first modern prison was inaugurated, the bourgeoisie in France, with inevitable historical force, was placing its heavy mortgage on the political management of society. It was a moment when, in the more advanced situations, the new class's economic and social hegemony was about to receive the mantle of state power. According to Marx's interpretation, this also meant that the new way of life was becoming habitualized for the working class. This, of course, was guaranteed by the force of economic relationships (generally expressed by the condition of the labor market) more than by the force of the state. The state by then seemed to have become a useless, inhuman and tyrannical instrument, unworthy of the new era, at least in English *laissez-faire* terms. But with its fierceness and its political servitude, the state of absolute monarchy had prepared the way for the fierceness and economic servitude engendered by the liberal state. The system of producing labor engendered by the whip of economic privation was by then useless. The workhouse was to become more and more an instrument for receiving the poor masses who could not find any other work. Rebellion, refusal, and *free will* found their most adept adversary in the institution of the modern prison. There, as Marx says in *The Holy Family*, morality dominated. The institution, made perfect by the Quakers, was a model of the life-style imposed by the religion of pious businessmen. The exploitation process, the axis of capitalist society, becomes the central axis of the prison reformatory process.[16] The Enlightenment battle for *sure punishment* provides the value created by the forced labor with an *exact measure, proportional to the value of the safeguarded wealth.*[17] After the factory had been recognized as an ideal workhouse, then prisons became ideal factories; punishment finally acquired the double characteristic of a tangible representation of the dominant social ideology. It was merely its extreme and radical expression, and simultaneously, it was the place for repression and re-education. Furthermore, it served as a clear and convincing lesson for those outside who refused to adapt or (and here it is the same thing) could not adapt.

If the mystery of modern prisons is discovered in the factory, and the criminal is condemned to the destiny of worker, then the way to redemption and freedom is the very same for both criminal and worker. Marx shows in his writing on the Paris Commune how in exceptional periods of revolutionary tension, when the noose of bourgeois relationships is loosened, the lumpenproletariat is able to participate in the common struggle, overcoming its individualism, and placing itself under the direction of the proletariat. But the factory, in the same way that it is the greatest representation of the workers' degradation and enslavement, is also the birthplace of solidarity, consciousness of common interests, planning and strug-gling for freedom. Similarly, the prison really becomes like the factory. TheHegelian ideal of consciousness-forming, even though a critical, negative, antagonistic consciousness, is nearly reached. A last suggestive contribution, strictly linked to Marx's analysis in *Capital,* is his critique of the vindication, in the Gotha program, of the German Social Democrat Party (1875) entitled, 'Regulation of Prison Labor'.Marx comments:

> A petty demand in a general workers' program. In any case, it should have been clearly stated that there is no intention from fear of competition to allow ordinary criminals to be treated like beasts, and especially that there is no desire to deprive them of their sole means of betterment, productive labor. This was surely the least one might expect from socialists.[18]

It is clear that productive work can be a real way of correcting criminals in the same dialectical way it is for the worker in general. It is necessary to negate and overcome alienated work and the society which corresponds to it.But first, it is 'corrective', in the sense that it transforms the lumpenproletariat into proletariat, removing it from the disturbed and irrational, individualistic conception of itself and leading it to unity, to association with other workers for a conscious, common program. This brings about a radical crisis of the institution. The prison as such has, in fact, its own specific features which make it different from the factory. As has been shown here, it tries to embody the bourgeois idea of punishment, to construct an institution of confinement as an abstract model of the factory-centered way of life. Paradoxically, it is this very effort which creates the difference between factory and prison. Prison life excludes the very things which workers struggle for outside of the deadening work they do during production.Cell isolation, subordination extended to every hour of the day instead of only working-time, imposed silence, complete sexual (or rather heterosexual) abstinence; in sum, a complete authoritative and hierarchical structure is what makes the prison an *extreme* model and what thus excludes those possibilities of consciousness and struggle offered by the factory. This is the reason why Marx wanted to put into a 'general workers' program' the compensation for prison work; to make it 'productive', so that, 'for fear of competition', prisoners would 'not be treated like animals'. That is, work conditions should be as much as possible like those of free workers.[19] Focusing on the struggle against forced work creates the conditions by which the entire prison becomes more and more a factory and less and less a place for punishment. We must look dialectically at the development of the institution along the lines that the bourgeoisie wanted. In so doing, we can see that in this case too, it becomes an integral part of the proletarian program. Inasmuch as the prison gets nearer to the factory, that real factory *imposed* by the workers' movement, not that 'ideal house of terror' imagined by the bourgeoisie, 'punishment' tends to disappear and the possibility of 'correction' appears. This comes about through a transition of the anarchic lumpenproletariat, subject to the individualist ruling ideology, into a worker who knows how to make the conditions for liberation from his own exploitation. From his own chains he forges the instrument for transforming not the prison within society, but society itself.

Very few elements have been added by Marxist thought to those described here. Recently, however, in connection with a crisis in the management of deviance in mature capitalist countries, a reconciliation of Marxism with what I defined as *the penal question* seems possible. The United States, England, and capitalist continental Europe, have been under the pressure of the illness which has afflicted the so-called 'total institutions' for decades, but which only in the last few years has become evident. The need for a critical analysis of deviance with a Marxist inspiration is becoming more and more imperative.[20] The analysis must be radical in the sense that, following Marx, it must 'grasp things at their roots'. But the roots of deviance are in the very essence of the society which produces it, in the particular forms which capitalist production relationships have assumed in this epoch of their development. Beyond the specifics of Marx's thoughts on the subject and beyond what I have tried to describe here, we must note how Marx's analysis gives us a lesson on method. The history of ideas or institutions, in itself, has no life; it does not exist. It can only be a particular display of more general processes which produce and form it.

In conclusion, I think it would be of some interest for us to recall the polemics arrayed against the Marxist, P. Hirst.[21] That occurred precisely because Hirst's argument is made on the grounds of method. Refusing the proposal of a 'Marxist theory of deviance', he argues that 'The objects of Marxist theory are specified by its own concepts'. And then he lists 'the means of production, class struggle, the State, ideology, etc.'[22] It is probably semantically correct to reject expressions such as 'Marxist theory of deviance', but the problem is restricted to the word 'theory' only. Instead we could say, for instance, a working-class (or a Marxist) point of view on deviance. I do not believe that the New Criminology theorists wanted to build a complete and definite theory. It is evident that our task is not to formulate an eclectic social theory made up of some Marxism mixed with some sociology. Rather, our task is to widen the hegemony of Marxism and its unique social scientific theory on the whole array of objects of the so-called 'social sciences'. In this way we tend to eliminate separate conceptions of sociology, law, psychology, economics, and so on. It is evident, too, that from a theoretical point of view, many of these 'objects' will be completely transformed.

If 'Historical Materialism is . . .a scientific general theory of modes of production', it is not only reductive but thoroughly anti-Marxist to conceive of this theory as dealing with its own fundamental object-concepts only.[23] The Marxian partiality for these concepts comes from a basic theoretical judgment that places them at the core of the whole social universe. If this were not true, Marxism would be a particular economic theory or a kind of sociology of labor and nothing else. Neither is it strange that bourgeois ideologists often try to show it in such a way. They know that the scientific hegemony of

Marxism proceeds together with the increasing social hegemony of the working class. On the other hand, they know that one of the weapons against the working class is to limit the general theoretical capacity of Marxism.

When Marxism takes possession of new fields of knowledge, such as criminology, it destroys criminology as such, while it enriches its own basic concepts; capital and labor, class struggle and so on. So the problem of criminality, or of 'deviance', in a given situation, becomes the problem of primitive accumulation; the problems of prisons becomes that of training proletarians to factory discipline, etc.

All this requires a continuous creative application of Marxism. Of course, from Luxemburg to Gramsci, from Lenin to Mao, all the greatest Marxist theorists have taught us this is true, both with respect to an incessantly moving social structure and to the new fields not yet covered by original Marxist doctrine. When we analyse the present situation of segregating institutions in the context of the social structure, we must recognize that deep changes have come about. Since the 'classic' situation of the first volume of *Capital*, both 'spheres', production and circulation, have been modified greatly. In the first sphere, labour-power rebelled against being a commodity and imposed bargaining for the consumption of its own use-value; this is truer and truer in the last few years. In the second sphere, capital suceeded in recovering what it lost inside the factory. It completely eradicated anarchy and the freedom-of-competition system. Consumption (and consensus), organization, and oligopoly agreement predetermine change on the broadest level. In this way, capital extended its authority from the productive sphere to the social one. If the crisis of a determined kind of authority principle is the grounds of the present malaise of criminal policies, as I think it is, then socialization of capital is the grounds on which the answer to the malaise will be built.[24]

A similar kind of consideration must be made about the other main point of the polemics between Taylor and Walton, the 'New Criminology theorists', and Hirst. That is the question of a so-called crime-free society.[25] By refusing to propose a Marxist point of view on the themes of crime and punishment, Hirst appears to come to a position subordinate to bourgeois ideology, or, more precisely, an old-bourgeois one. He speaks of the necessity of punishment, prisons, police and so on making use of the penal concepts of the last century, of *laissez-faire* capitalism in fact.[26] But a crime-free society, or rather, a punishment-free society, is already present when late capitalist society has replaced a certain kind of practice and theory of social control with a new one, where in the ideological content and the real phenomena of prisons, punishment, etc., become obsolete; where, on the other hand, in the society as a whole, preventive activity, extra-institutional social control, and treatment, are continuing to develop and appear ever more frequently. Even if this were not the *crime-free society* imagined by Taylor, Walton and Young, they probably referred to that declaration by Marx which marks his position more clearly than any other. In it, he rejects any coercion and expresses communism's program on criminality, punishment, kinds of punishment, and even criminologists – calling for their definitive disappearance:

> On the other hand, under *human* conditions punishment will really be nothing but the sentence passed by the culprit on himself. No one will want to convince him that violence from without, done to him by others, is violence which he had done to himself. On the contrary, he will see in other men his natural saviors from the punishment he has imposed on himself; in other words, the relation will be reversed.[27]

POSTSCRIPT

Quite a long spell of time has passed since, in 1975, this chapter was published as an article. Even if the core of the argument may still be judged valid and interesting – the way in which the 'penal question' is defined in Marx's *Capital* – some adjustments and precisionist comments are badly needed.

Beyond this core, in fact, made up of the research within *Capital*, the general theoretical context of this article has definitely gone. A context that for our generation (or at least for the part of it in which I found myself) was constituted by a certain Marxist dogmatism, belonging to a definite Marxist tradition. It was that 'left-wing Marxism', or 'western Marxism' between the two wars, shifting between Lukàcs and the Frankfurt School, where a political position critical of the 'real socialism' could go hand in hand with a 'left-Hegelican' idealism which appealed very much to our naivety, to our need of theoretical radicalism, of dogmatic truth and security.

This fundamental imprint could not be missing in approaching a question which in those years was felt as extremely urgent, the question of the State and, within it, the issue of the penal apparatuses, the penal and criminal questions, a whole sphere which had been barely touched upon by the various Marxist traditions.

As far as this article is concerned, this is particularly true of the last section, regarding the polemics between the 'new criminologists' and P. Q. Hirst. Here an argument which I believe is still valid lives on together with another one which is obsolete. I think there is no question about the need for a theoretical work aiming at a redefinition of certain social phenomena ('the criminal', prisons, punishment, etc.) in terms of Marxist conceptual categories. The problem is (theoretically) what to do with it. It's not 'to expound the truth' of the matter, to reach a 'super science', an Absolute, as it was more or less suggested in my article. Marxism is conceived of, here, as the truth, as that 'real thing' which comes after the philosophy which claimed to be the last one – Hegel's philosophy. The universe (and the theoretical discussion) stops there!

Unfortunately or, better, luckily, this was not what happened and the debate on sciences, both on so-called 'natural' sciences and on 'social' sciences, teaches us to be extremely cautious about epistemology. Today I would not say 'Marxism . . . destroys criminology' (even if 'criminology *as such*') but that some Marxist concepts help us in the process of destroying the criminology that we do not need (or want) and in building that set of notions (on 'the criminal', on punishment, prisons, etc.) that we need, now, here. This is all one can say. In using Marxian concepts from *Capital* to redefine some passages in the history of criminality or in the history of punishment I believe I have furnished our knowledge with a few useful tools against various old traditions which stand in the way and I will do it as long as I like, in spite of any Marxist or criminological sanctuary (and in this respect the polemics against Hirst is still wholly valid!). But I do not think I am building any general *Weltanschauung* in doing it . . . I might have liked to, but this is not the case!

At the same time the fine idea, also present in this article, of a 'real correction' of 'the criminal' residing in the process of 'transformation of prison into factory', is for sure very Hegelian but has not much to do with reality, at least with the prison system of this century. Here the problem was simply one of ignorance, a fact which brought me to superimpose nineteenth-century concepts on a twentieth-century situation. Especially in this latter period, the issue of the relation of prisons and prison movements to the social structure and social movements is extremely more complex. I have barely started to face it in some more recent essays, referred to in the notes.

Notes

1. Here we are considering Chapter XXVI of the first volume of *Capital*, first paragraph, 'The Mystery of Primitive Accumulation'. Also, regarding primitive accumulation, see M. Dobb's fundamental text, *Studies in the Development of Capitalism.*

2. That was in the articles, in *Rheinische Zeitung*, on the law against gathering of fallen wood in the forests. There, Marx held the legitimacy of customary rights of poor masses against the new bourgeois partial law.

3. The law of 1601 is nothing more than the last act in the construction of the normative complex of the Elizabethan Old Poor Law. Regarding this point, see the fundamental work by S. and B. Webb, *English Poor Law History*, Part I, *'The Old Poor Law'* (London: 1927); also F. M. Eden, *The State of the Poor* (London: 1928); and finally, the interesting volume, full of information and with a good bibliography, by J. D. Marshall, *The Old Poor Law (1795–1834)* (London, Melbourne, Toronto: 1968), which mainly talks about the crisis of the OPL. See also the writings of Engels about the conditions of the working class in England (1845).

4. See K. Marx, loc. cit., *Bloody legislation against the expropriated* . . . On the social character of the problems of vagabondage and brigandage and its repression, there is a very thorough bibliography. I shall refer here to several particular well-known and meaningful texts. The classic A. Vexliard, *Introduction à la sociologie du vagabondage* (1956) 42; E. J. Hobsbawm's analysis of what he calls *social banditism* in *Bandits* (London: 1969) and the chapter dedicated to this topic in the more general *Primitive Rebels* (Manchester: 1959); the first two chapters of G. Lefebvre, *La grande peur de 1789* (Paris: 1932); on France again, see C. Paultre, *De la répression de la mendicité et du vagabondage en France sous l'ancien régime* (Paris: 1906); about England see the works mentioned above in note 3 and overall, G. Rusche & O. Kirchheimer, *Punishment and Social Structure* (New York: 1968), the first two chapters; lastly the very well-known work by F. Molfese, on southern brigandage in post-unity times in Italy, *Storia del brigantaggio dopo l'Unità* (Milan: 1972).

5. See the third 1844 *Manuscript*, 'Private property and communism', in K. Marx, *Early Writings* (London: 1963) 145.

6. Ibid.

7. See K. Marx, *Capital*, First Book, Chapter XIV, 'The Division of Labor and Manufacture'.

8. The sphere of penal repression, that is, is the sphere of exceptions. The italics are mine.

9. See K. Marx, op. cit., Chapter XXVIII.

10. See K. Marx, op. cit., Chapter XXVIII. These proposals cited by Marx are only some of the many which were presented by authoritative representatives of the English bourgeoisie to eliminate completely

'outdoor relief', assistance for the able poor which did not include internment, in the two centuries of the life of the OPL. Finally, with the reform of 1834, this was the prevailing hypothesis.

11. See K. Marx, op. cit., Chapter X ('The working day'): 'The struggle for a normal working day', etc.

12. On this, and what follows about prisons, see G. Rusche and O. Kirchheimer, op. cit., Chapter III, 'Mercantilism and the Rise of Imprisonment', 24. M. Pavarini and D. Melossi have carried out research, in Bologna, on hypotheses of prison history.

13. See K. Marx, op. cit., Chapter VII, 'Buying and selling of labour-power'.

14. In the principal institutions of social control, schools, army, sanitary or criminal institutes of reclusion, alms-houses, and so forth, the link which unites these places to each other and above all to the factory is not casual. See D. Melossi, 'Hypotheses for a research about the historical role and the present development trends of segregating institutions in connection with the evolution of capitalist production process', paper presented to the second conference of the European Group for the Study of Deviance and Social Control (Essex, 1974).

15. This is not by chance, because to Dutch commercial greatness corresponds the fact – as Marx observes – the 'popular Dutch masses were already more worn out by work in 1648, more impoverished and more brutally oppressed than those of the whole of Europe'. On the subject of the workhouse in Amsterdam, the *Rasp-huis*, see the fine volume by T. Sellin, *Pioneering in Penology* (Philadelphia: 1944). In this constitution, which was to be the model for all the others on the Continent, for many years, the structures of seventeenth-century manufacture coincided with several phenomena that would be characteristic of nineteenth-century prisons.

16. Or, at least this is true of prison ideology, although we cannot here go into the question. In this sense, above all, prisons took workhouses as their model.

17. The knowledge that the principle of proportionality of punishment corresponds to a type of social relationship based on the exchange of equivalent values was clearly present in Enlightenment penal culture. See Beccaria's paragraph on theft (retributive principle shows itself evidently, here, as a form of compensation to society) and paragraphs 77 and 101 in Hegel's *Philosophy of Right*. The young radical-democrat Marx, in his work on the law against wood thefts, states: 'If the concept of crime requires that of punishment, the concrete crime requires a measure of punishment . . . The limits of its punishment must thus be the limits of its action. The actual content of the offense is also the limit of the actual crime, and thus the measure of the crime is given by the measure of this content. This measure of property is its value. . . . Value is the bourgeois way of property's existing, the logical term in which only it reaches the possibility of social comprehension and participation.'

This idea was to be expressed extremely clearly many years later, in 1924, by the Soviet author, E. B. Pashukanis, who, in the *General Theory of Law and Marxism*, states: 'Deprivation of freedom for a definite period indicated in advance in the sentence of the court is the specific form in which modern – that is to say, the bourgeois – capitalist criminal law effectuates the principle of equivalent requital. This method is closely (though unconsciously) associated with the idea of the abstract man and abstract human labour measured in terms of time. . . . A condition precedent to the appearance of the idea that accounts in respect of crime could be settled by a predetermined quantum of abstract freedom was the reduction of all the concrete forms of social wealth to the simplest and most abstract form of human toil measured in terms of time (*Soviet Legal Philosophy* [Cambridge, Mass.: 1951] 218).

18. In K. Marx, *Critique of the Gotha Programme* (New York: Little Marx Library, International Publishers, 1966).

19. The prison–factory relationship is quite a bit more complicated than what is presented here. In particular, as to the problem of prison labor, this historically depends quite a lot on the state of the labor-market in a given society. The worry that forced-labor could lower the wage level in some branches of production by the beastly exploitation of prisoners prevailed for a long time in the workers' movement. Here, Marx shows the right way in fighting not prison labor *tout court* but the way in which it is practised.

20. This effort is clearly presented in I. Taylor, P. Walton, J. Young, *The New Criminology* (London: 1973).

21. See P. Q. Hirst, 'Marx and Engels on law, crime and morality' in *Economy and Society*, 1, 1, 28; I. Taylor, P. Walton, 'Radical deviancy theory and Marxism, a reply to P. Q. Hirst: Marx and Engels on crime, law and morality' in *Economy and Society*, 1, 2, 229; P. Q. Hirst, 'A reply to Taylor and Walton' in *Economy and Society*,' 1, 3, 351; finally P. Hirst, 'The Marxism of the "New Criminology"' and I. Taylor, P. Walton, J. Young, 'Rejoinder to the Review' in *The British Journal of Criminology* (October 1973) 396 and 400.

22. P. Q. Hirst, 'Marx and Engels on law, crime and morality', op. cit., p. 29.

23. P. Q. Hirst, 'A reply to Taylor and Walton', op. cit., p. 354.

24. All this is developed in D. Melossi, 'Hypotheses for a research . . . ', op. cit.

25. See I. Taylor, P. Walton, J. Young, *The New Criminology*, op. cit., 212 and I. Taylor, P. Walton, 'Radical deviancy theory and Marxism, a reply . . . ', op.cit., 233.

26. See P. Q. Hirst, 'A reply to Taylor and Walton', op. cit., 353 and 'The Marxism of the "New Criminology"', op. cit., 397.

27. In *The Holy Family*, eighth chapter, section 3, 'Revelations of the Mysteries of Law'.

8

A Garrison State in 'Democratic' Society

Paul Takagi

This paper[1] reports on a study of police officers killed in the line of duty and civilians killed by the police. The study was originated in 1971 in reaction to news reporting on the several mass media outlets at the local and national levels which focused on FBI statistics indicating police officers were being 'assassinated' at an alarming rate. A police reporter for an educational television station alarmed viewers with a report that 125 law enforcement officers had been killed in 1971, an increase of almost two and one-half times over 1963 when only 55 police officers were killed in all of that year. Police killings of citizens, however, were reported as isolated events. Although the death of civilians at the hands of police occurred from time to time, no news analyst attempted to show this as a national phenomenon.

Sorel (1950) said people use words in selective ways to create alarm. When a police officer kills a citizen, the official language is 'deadly force', suggesting to the audience that the use of force was legitimate. But when a police officer is killed, it is characterized as 'violence', and therefore, illegitimate. In this way, news, reporting the killing of police officers in 1971, conjured the idea that the apparent increase in the killing of police officers was unprecedented. It was seen as an attack caused in part by the rising political militancy among revolutionary groups, and by the increasing race consciousness among people of color venting their frustrations by attacking a visible symbol of authority. This interpretation was entertained by officials at the highest levels. President Nixon, in April of 1971, called upon police officials; and as subsequent events revealed, other representatives from para-military organizations also met to deal with the 'problem'.

The approach by officials was to consider the problem one of defense, and to search for the best technical means and policies to protect their view of a 'democratic' society. It was viewed as a military problem, and the fortification of the police under increased LEAA funding and direction became a national policy (Goulden, 1970).

One hundred and twenty-five police officers died while on duty during 1971; the actual rate of death, however, did not increase because of the greater number of police officers who were on duty during the same year. Even if the number of police personnel has increased two and one-half times since 1963, the rate of death among police officers should not change. This is not said in an attempt to minimize the statistics that concern the officials. One could argue that the rate of police deaths should decrease. The point is to look at all the statistics, including previous studies that actually show the killing of police officers occurs at a relatively stable rate (Bristow, 1963; Robin, 1963; and Cardarelli, 1968).

The source of data is the FBI's own reports, which show an increase in the number of police officers killed, from 55 in 1963 to 125 in 1971, along with an increase of over 50 per cent in the numbers of full-time authorized police personnel. The data presented in Figure 8.1 show that the rate of such homicides, while fluctuating from year to year, does not result in a trend either up or down over the period. The rate did peak nationally in 1967 with 29.9 deaths per 100,000 law enforcement officers. This includes all ranks from patrolmen to higher officials and federal agents. Since patrolmen bear the greatest risk of being killed in the line of duty, they may feel that FBI reports should be more detailed to reflect accurately the hazards they face.

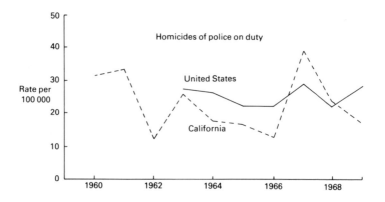

FIGURE 8.1

Reports to the FBI on the numbers of police officers on duty and the numbers killed may not give a complete picture, since the agency has been only gradually achieving uniform reporting. Indeed, the number of reporting agencies has increased since 1963. California, however, has had fairly complete and uniform reporting throughout the period, and the death rates among California police are available for the whole decade since 1960. They, too, show a peak in 1967, a year in which 12 officers were killed. That did not set a trend, however, as the rate decreased in the next two years.

For the 86 officers who were killed in California from 1960 through 1970, the police apprehended 117 suspects of whom 55 per cent were white, 25 per cent Black, and 19 per cent Mexican-American. (This is the same percentage distribution of ethnic/racial groups in California's prison population.) At the time of this writing, 65 of the 117 suspects were convicted of either murder or manslaughter, and 7 cases were still pending in court. W. H. Hutchins, Assistant Chief of the California Bureau of Criminal Statistics, noted in a paper delivered to the California Homicide Investigators' Conference on March 5, 1971 that the great majority of homicidal deaths among police officers occurred in situations where robberies were in progress or where robbers were fleeing arrest. But, noted Hutchins, 'the ambushing of officers, which has been relatively rare in the past, accounted for 25 per cent of peace officers killed in 1970' (Hutchins, 1971).

Mr. Hutchins is not entirely correct when he reports that the majority of police officers killed were in situations involving armed robberies. An earlier report by his Bureau of Criminal Statistics indicates: ' . . . 63 per cent of these officers died while conducting routine investigations, responding to disturbance calls and taking people into custody . . .' (Beattie, 1968:5). A special study on the deaths of 39 California police officers (1960 through 1966) shows 35 of the 39 died of gunshot wounds, in some instances by their own guns (Beattie, 1968: 11–14).

Klass, Richard J., 25-year-old patrolman, Daly City Police Department, killed May 6, 1966. Shot with his own gun by an escapee with whom he was struggling.

LeFebvre, Richard R., 23-year-old patrolman, Long Beach Police Department, killed August 15, 1965 at 8:00 PM. Died at the scene of a riot when a shotgun in the hands of a brother officer discharged during a struggle.

Ludlow, Donald E., a 26-year-old deputy sheriff, Los Angeles County, killed August 13, 1965 at 9:00 PM. Shot to death when brother officers' gun went off during struggle at riot scene.

Ross, Charles M., 31-year-old patrolman, Richmond Police Department, killed February 9, 1964 at 1:00 AM. Shot with his own gun while struggling with two drunks.

The four ca: es above were classified as homicides. To distinguish accidental death from homicide appears to require considerable judgment among those compiling crime statistics, and it is important to understand that these judgment classifications are included in the annual FBI reports on homicides of police officers.

It was noted earlier that the killing of police officers peaked in 1967 with 29.9 deaths per 100,000 law enforcement officers. Does this mean that law enforcement work is one of extreme peril? Robin (1963:230) argues otherwise:

. . . there is reason to maintain that the popular conception of the dangerous nature of police work has been exaggerated. Each occupation has its own hazards. The main difference between police work and other occupations is that in the former there is a calculated risk . . . while other occupational hazards are accidental and injuries usually self-inflicting.

Robin adjusts the death rate among police officers to include the accidental deaths (mostly from vehicular accidents), and compares the death rate among the major occupational groups (Table 8.1).

TABLE 8.1   Occupational fatalities per 100,000 employees, 1955

Occupation	Fatality rate per 100,000
Mining	93.58
Construction industry	75.81
Agriculture	54.97
Transportation	44.08
Law enforcement	32.76
Public utilities	14.98
Finance, gov., service	14.18
Manufacturing	12.08
Trade	10.25

SOURCE: Adapted from Robin (1963: Table 6).

It is apparent that the occupational risks in law enforcement are less dangerous than those in the several major industries. Mining, with 93.6 deaths per 100,000 employees, is almost three times riskier than law enforcement, while construction work is two and one-half times more dangerous, and agriculture and transportation show considerably higher rates of death than does law enforcement. Robin correctly concludes that the data do not support the general belief. that law enforcement work is a highly dangerous enterprise.

The other side of the coin is police homicides of citizens. This aspect of police–citizen interaction has received little attention except in the work of Robin (1963) and Knoohuizen *et al.* (1972). For example, the prestigious President's *Task Force Report* on the police (1967) devotes not one line to this issue.

What is generally not known by the public, and either unknown or certainly not publicized by the police and other officials, is the alarming increase in the rate of deaths of male citizens caused by, in the official terminology, 'legal intervention of police'. These are the cases recorded on the death certificates as 'justifiable homicide' by police intervention. After disappearing onto computer tapes, these reappear as statistics in the annually published official volumes of 'Vital Statistics in the United States'. Here they can be found under 'Cause of Death, Code Number 984', where they have attracted very little attention.

The deaths of male civilians aged ten years and over caused by police intervention gradually increased in rate, especially from 1962 to 1968, the latest year in which nationwide statistics were available at the time of this writing (see Figure 8.2). More dramatic is the trend in civilian deaths caused by California police, where the rate increased two and one-half times between 1962 and 1969. This increase cannot be attributed simply to an increase in the proportion of young adults in the population, among whom a larger share of these deaths occur, because each annual rate is age-adjusted to the age-profile of the population in 1960. There is an increase in the rate of homicides by police, regardless of the changes in that age profile.

Why should such a trend go unnoticed? The crime rate has, of course, increased at the same time, and this, it might be argued, indicates that more males put themselves in situations where they risk a police bullet. This is the argument that the victim alone is responsible. But that is too simple an explanation: an increase in such dangerous situations has not led to an increased jeopardy of police

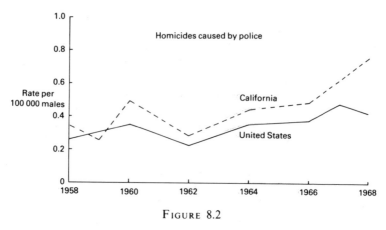

FIGURE 8.2

lives, for, as we have seen, their homicide rate did not increase over the same period.

The charts show police to be victims of homicides at an annual rate of about 25 per hundred thousand police, while citizens are victims of killing at the hands of police at a rate of 0.5 per 100,000 males aged ten and over, on the national level, and a rate of about 0.8 in California. This huge difference of 30 to 50-fold cannot be taken literally, because the civilian rate is based upon all males over age 9 even though most of them don't have the slightest chance of confronting a policeman in a desperate situation of anyone's making. There simply is no other population base to use in computing that rate. The point, however, is inescapable: the rate of death did not change for law enforcement officers during a period when it changed critically for male citizens.

Black men have been killed by police at a rate some nine to ten times higher than white men. From that same obscure, but published source in our nation's Capitol come the disheartening statistics. Between 1960 and 1968, police killed 1,188 Black males and 1,253 while males in a population in which about ten per cent are Black. The rates of homicides due to police intervention increased over the years for both whites and Blacks, but remained consistently at least nine times higher for Blacks for the past 18 years).

That proportionately more Blacks are killed by police will come as no surprise to most people, certainly to no police officials. The remarkably big difference should be surprising, however. After all, the Black crime rate, even if we rely upon measurement by the arrest rate, is higher for Blacks than for whites. But that does not explain the killing of Black men. In 1964, arrests of Black males were 28 per cent of total arrests, as reported by 3940 agencies to the FBI, while Black deaths were 51 per cent of the total number killed by police. In 1968 the statistics were essentially the same.

It might be argued that Blacks have a higher arrest rate for the seven major crimes: homicide, rape, robbery, aggravated assault, burglary, theft, and auto theft; and that arrests for these crimes will correlate better with deaths by legal intervention of police. In 1968, Black males accounted for 36 per cent of arrests for the major crimes; four years earlier, in 1964, Black arrests were less than 30 per cent during a year when they suffered 51 per cent of the deaths from police guns. Besides, it is not certain that the major crimes are a more accurate index of how frequently Blacks and whites commit crimes. Further, the threshold of suspicion is lower when a policeman encounters a Black man, thus the arrest rate is biased against Blacks. No matter how it is viewed, the death rate of Blacks is far out of proportion to the situations that might justify it.

Black people don't need these statistics to tell them what has been happening. The news gets around the neighborhood when someone is killed by the police. It is part of a history. But white people, especially policy-makers, don't live in those neighborhoods, and it is important that *they* explore the statistics further.

Take the age groups where 'desperate' criminals are much less likely to be found, the very young and the very old. Male homicides by police during 1964–8 were as shown in Table 8.2.

TABLE 8.2

| | Number of deaths | | Rate per million/yearly | |
	White	Black	White	Black
Ages 10–14	5	11	0.12	1.75
Ages 65 +	5	14	0.14	4.76

In proportion to population, Black youngsters and old men have been killed by police at a rate 15 to 30 times greater than that for whites of the same age. It is the actual experiences behind statistics like these that suggest that police have one trigger finger for whites and another for Blacks. The latest statistics, those for 1968, give no reason for altering that belief.

Whereas our analysis covered national data on police killings of private citizens, Robin (1963:229), utilizing the same data for the years 1950 through 1960, examined the rates of Black and white victims by selected cities (Table 8.3).

TABLE 8.3   Rates of Black and white decedents, by city

City	Black	White	Black/White ratio
	per 1 000 000		
Akron	16.1	2.7	5.8 to 1
Chicago	16.1	2.1	7.4 to 1
Kansas City, Mo.	17.0	2.2	7.5 to 1
Miami	24.4	2.7	8.8 to 1
Buffalo	7.1	.5	12.2 to 1
Philadelphia	5.4	.2	21.9 to 1
Boston	3.2	.1	25.2 to 1
Milwaukee	13.5	.4	29.5 to 1

In absolute numbers, Chicago police accounted for 54.6 per cent of the 350 police slayings of citizens in the eight cities; the mean annual rate, however, was highest for Miami, with Chicago second. The two cities with the lowest police 'justifiable homicide' rates, Boston and Milwaukee, killed Blacks in proportion to whites at a ratio of 25 to 29 times higher.

A more detailed analysis of police killing of private citizens was conducted by Robin for the city of Philadelphia. He reports:

> Thirty of the 32 cases (28 were Black victims) were disposed of by the medical examiner, who at the inquest exonerated the officers involved in the killings on the grounds that death was due to justifiable homicide. In the two remaining cases the officers were held for the grand jury, indicted, tried by a jury, and found not guilty (1963:226).

Black citizens have long argued that the police are committing genocide on Black people, and there is increasing evidence that these killings are indeed murder, and that real justice is rarely if ever carried out in this process. Knoohuizen *et al.* (1972) conducted a study of Chicago police killing of citizens, and provided further credence to the claim that police are murdering Black citizens. In their report,

Knoohuizen and associates examined the incidents as reported by the police, the reports of the coroner's office, and testimony or statements by credible eyewitnesses. In their Table 15 they summarized their findings from which we extracted three cases.

Case 1. The victim was Linda Anderson. Police action resulting in her death was ruled justifiable homicide because, according to police reports, she was killed accidentally during attempt to gain entrance to her apartment by shooting the lock off the door. The partner of the officer, and independent witnesses, corroborated the police officer's version. An independent investigation revealed that the officer used a shotgun standing four feet from the door, did not warn the occupant of impending shot, and missed the lock completely.

Case 2. The victim was Raymond Jones. Police action was ruled excusable because police officers did not strike the deceased and were only using the amount of force necessary to bring the suspect under arrest. Seven of 9 officers involved in the incident testified and confirmed each other's story. The report of the Coroner's pathologist, however, revealed that Mr. Jones was age 31 and in good health. He was also unarmed. The use of excessive force was implied when 9 police officers cannot subdue a suspect without causing his death.

Case 3. The victim was Charles Cox. The police report did not offer a justification or an excuse claiming the victim died from drug overdose rather than use of police force. Further reports from the police indicate blood analysis revealed some drugs in the victim's body. One of the arresting officers and one of the officers in charge of the lock-up both testified that the victim appeared all right when in their charge. A pathologist testified on the basis of his examination of the body that Cox died of blows to the head.

Knoohuizen *et al.* (1972:61) conclude from their analysis that in 28 of the 76 cases in which civilians were killed at the hands of the Chicago police, there was substantial evidence of police misconduct; and in 10 of the 76 cases, there was substantial evidence of criminal liability for manslaughter or murder.

Despite grand jury findings in those instances where police officers are held criminally liable, the courts have been reluctant to proceed with prosecution. All too often, such matters are thrown out of court or juries return the verdict of not guilty. For example, Superior Court

Judge Ross G. Tharp of San Diego County dismissed involuntary manslaughter charges against a California Highway patrolman indicted in the fatal shootings of an unarmed 16-year-old boy. According to police reports, Roland R. Thomas was shot by Officer Nelander following a high speed chase in an allegedly stolen car. The car ran off the road, and Thomas appeared to reach toward his pocket at which point the officer fired his gun. In dismissing the case, Judge Tharp observed: 'I think the officer deserves a commendation for doing his duty rather than standing trial.'

The only recent cases in which police officers were held accountable for killing civilians were shown on a recent TV program (Owen Marshall, ABC, Saturday, 2 March 1974), in addition to the highly publicized case in Texas where a 12-year-old Mexican-American youngster was shot while under custody in a police car. The circumstances in the latter case were so gross that a dismissal was out of the question. The court, however, sentenced the officer to a prison term of 5 years in a state where sentences of 1000 years for lesser crimes are not uncommon.

Authorities have been trying to combat what they view to be a rash of attacks on police, to the neglect of all the data that bear on the problem – a problem in which other lives are involved. The problem has existed all along; at least since 1950, and there is reason to believe for decades before that, Black people have been killed by the police at a tragically disproportionate rate, beyond the bounds of anything that would justify it.

Open warfare between the police and the citizenry might be one of the outcomes. Two recent attacks upon police station houses, one by a bomb and the other by shotgun wielding assailants resulting in the death of two police officers, are indicative. In the latter killing, the gunman thrust a shotgun through the speaking hole of a bullet proof glass shield separating the desk sergeant from the public. Portions of the police station house were protected by cyclone fencing. The wall of isolation surrounding the police is not only social and psychological, but physical, and the breaking down of these walls was considered by the National Crime Commission to be the single most important priority. Yet the federal government in appropriating billions of dollars for the Law Enforcement Assistance Administration program earmarked the funds primarily for the fortification of the police, thereby contributing to their isolation.

Currently, the concept of citizen participation is being stressed by the LEAA. The support the police get from some citizens' groups actually increases the isolation of police from minority communities. In Oakland, California, such a group, called Citizens for Law and Order, has a program of needling judges for their 'soft' handling of criminal cases, firing broadsides at the press, television and radio, and appearing before local governmental bodies to promote support for the police and more 'discipline' in schools. Programs like these are based on the belief that increasing the penalty for crime, increasing the powers of the police, and invoking police coercion of the citizenry will result in law and order.

Other citizens' groups have encouraged the introduction of reforms. People have worked on a variety of schemes such as Civilian Review Boards, psychological testing and screening of police candidates, human relations training, police community relations, racially integrated patrol units, and efforts to increase the hiring of Black and other minority officers. To the extent that they work to improve only the 'image' of police, they fail because the problems go much deeper. And to a major extent, they fail because policemen, most of them willingly and others unknowingly, are used as the front line to maintain the social injustices inherent in other institutions and branches of government.

Perhaps the only immediate solution at this time is to disarm the police. Observers have noted that provinces in Australia where the police are unarmed have a much lower rate of attacks upon the police, compared with neighboring provinces where the police are armed, and the corollary observation, a lower rate of police misconduct.

Disarming the police in the United States will doubtedly lower the rate of police killings of civilians; it does not, however, get at the causes of police misconduct, particularly toward black people. The findings that Blacks are killed by the police at a disproportionate ratio in cities like Milwaukee and Boston, and the attitudes of officials like San Diego County's Superior Court Judge Tharp, require a more fundamental understanding of the meaning of policing in contemporary America.

In distinguishing social justice from distributive justice, the former would not have been obtained, if, for example, Officer Lelander had been tried and convicted for the killing of a 16-year-old alleged auto thief, that would have been distributive justice, because it would have symbolized the fact that the police would not have received special treatment from the courts. Instead, the question that must be asked is why the police officer resorted to deadly force involving an alleged theft. To put it differently, why was the value of an automobile placed above the value of a human life? Judge Tharp's comments in dismissing the case provide a partial answer: 'For doing his duty', the duty being to enforce the laws having to do with the property rights of an automobile owner. The critical issue here is that the auto theft laws and for that matter most of the laws in American society essentially legitimize a productive system where human labor is systematically expropriated. Examine for a moment the social significance of an automobile: it involves an array of corporate systems that expropriate the labor of people that go into manufacturing its parts, the labor for its assembly, the labor involved in extricating and processing the fuel that propels it, the labor of constructing the roads on which it runs, etc.The fiction of ownership exacts further capital by banking institutions that mortgage the commodity, and automobile insurance required by laws that extorts additional capital. The built-in obsolescence, or more precisely, the depreciation of the commodity, occurs when the muscle, the sweat, and human potential have been completely capitalized. These are the elements embodied in an automobile. It is no longer merely a commodity value, but represents a social value.

The automobile is a commodity created by varied types of wage labor. And as noted by men with ideas as far apart as those of Adam Smith and Karl Marx, the wealth of nations originates in the efforts of labor. But Marx added that wealth based on production of these commodities is accrued through the expropriation of labor power; and thus, the concept of private property based on this form of wealth is in essence the theft of the value-creating power of labor. The criminal laws, the system of coercion and punishment, exist to promote and to protect the consequences of a system based on this form of property.

The rights of liberty, equality, and security are not elements to be exchanged for the right of property acquired by the exploitation of wage labor; nor should they be expressed in relative terms, that is, greater or less than property rights. One person's life and liberty is the same as the next person's. But in a society that equates private property with human rights, they become inevitably reduced to standards and consequences that value some lives less than others. The system of coercion and punishment is intimately connected with the inequitable distribution of wealth, and provides the legitimation under the perverted notion that 'ours is a government of laws' even to kill in order to maintain social priorities based on private property.

This is the meaning of policing in American society.

Why are Black people killed by the police at a rate nine to ten times higher than whites? We can describe the manifestations of racism but cannot adequately explain it. At one level, we agree with the observation that the existence of racism is highly profitable. The Black urban ghettos, created by America's industries, provided the cheap labor power for the accumulation of some of America's greatest industrial wealth at the turn of the 20th century, and again during World War II. These urbon ghettos still provide a highly exploited source of labor. In addition, the ghettos themselves have become a place for exploitation by slum landlords, merchants selling inferior quality goods at higher prices, a justification for higher premium rates on insurance, and the victimizing of people under the credit purchase system. To maintain this situation, the regulatory agencies, including the police, have ignored the codes governing housing, food, health, and usury conditions.

In cities across the country, the infamous ghettos are now deemed to be prime real estate, and the state under the powers of eminent domain claim for finance capitalism the areas for high rise buildings, condominiums, trade complexes, and entertainment centres ostensibly for the 'people'. Under what has been called urban redevelopment, the police are present to quiet individual and especially organized protest and dissent, and the full powers of the state are employed to evict, to dispossess, and to humiliate.

At another level, the concentration of capital has produced on the one hand, a demand for a *disciplined* labor force and, in order to rationalize its control, to rely increasingly upon administrative laws; on the other hand, it has created a *surplus* labor force that is increasingly controlled by our criminal laws. The use of punishment to control surplus labor is not new, having its roots in early 16th century Europe (Rusche and Kirchheimer, 1968).

Historically, people of color came to the United States not as free persons, but as slaves, indentured servants, and as contract laborers. They were initially welcomed under these conditions. As these particular systems of exploitation gradually disappeared and the people entered the competitive labor market, a variety of devices were employed to continue oppressing them, including imprisonment. In the present period described by some as the post-industrial era, increasing numbers of people, and especially Black people, find themselves in the ranks of the unemployed, which establishment economists, fixing upon the 5 per cent unemployment figure, dismiss as a regular feature of our political economy. Sweezy *et al.* (1971) disagree, arguing that the 'post-industrial' unemployment data are the same as that in the Great Depression when one includes defense and defense related employment data. When arrest and prison commitment data on Black people are viewed from this perspective, especially the sudden increase in prison commitments from a stable rate of 10 per cent up to and during the early period of World War II to almost double that after the war, there is some basis to suspect that the police killing of Black citizens is punishment to control a surplus labor population.

The labor surplus analysis, however, does not explain the sudden increase in police killing of civilians beginning around 1962. Did the Civil Rights movement in housing, education, and employment, and more specifically, the militancy of a Malcolm X, and the liberation movements in Third World nations around the world, re-define the rôle of the police? Did finance imperialism in the form of multi-national corporations beginning about this time create an unnoticed social dislocation? Why do the police kill civilians at a much higher rate in some cities compared with others, and why do they kill Blacks at a disproportionately higher ratio in cities like Boston and Milwaukee? Why do California police, presumed to be highly professional, kill civilians at a rate 60 per cent higher than the nation as a whole? We are not able to answer these questions.

We must, however, pause for a moment, and consider what is happening to us. We know that authorized police personnel in states like California has been increasing at the rate of 5 to 6 per cent compared with an annual population increase of less than two and one-half per cent. In 1960 there were 22,783 police officers; in 1972 there were 51,909. If the rate of increase continues, California will have at the turn of the 21st century an estimated 180,000 police officers, an equivalent of 10 military divisions. Is it not true that the growth in the instruments of coercion and punishment is the inevitable consequence of the wealth of a nation that is based upon theft?

America is moving more and more rapidly towards a garrison state, and soon we will not find solace by repeating to ourselves: 'Ours is a democratic society.'

Note

1. The ideas in this chapter are not original. They come from Fourier, Godwin, Proudhon, Marx, Kropotkin, and others.

References

Beattie, Ronald H. (1968) *California Peace Officers Killed 1960–66* (Bureau of Criminal Statistics, Department of Justice, State of California, September).

Bristow, Allen P. (1963) 'Police Officer Shootings: a Tactical Evaluation', *The Journal of Criminal Law, Criminology, and Police Science*, 54.

Cardarelli, Albert P. (1968) 'An Analysis of Police Killed by Criminal Action: 1961–1963', *The Journal of Criminal Law, Criminology, and Police Science*, 59.

Goulden, Joseph (1970) 'The Cops Hit the Jackpot', *The Nation* (November).

Hutchins, W. H. (1971) 'Criminal Homicides of California Peace Officers, 1960–1970', a report delivered before the California Homicide Investigators' Conference (Los Angeles, March) 5.

Knoohuizen, Ralph, Richard P. Fahey, and Deborah J. Palmer (1972) *The Police and Their Use of Fatal Force in Chicago* (Chicago Law Enforcement Study Group).

President's Commission on Law Enforcement and Administration of Justice (1967) *Task Force Report: The Police* (Washington, D.C.: U.S. Government Printing Office).

Robin, Gerald D. (1963) 'Justifiable Homicide by Police Officers', *The Journal of Criminal Law, Criminology, and Police Science*, 54.

Rusche, Georg and Otto Kirchheimer (1968) *Punishment and Social Structure* (New York: Russell and Russell).

Sorel, G. (1950) *Reflections on Violence* (Glencoe, Illinois: Free Press).

Sweezy, Paul M., Harry Magdoff and Leo Huberman (1971) 'Economic Stagnation and Stagnation of Economics', *Monthly Review*, 22 (April).

About the Authors

Dorie Klein has a Doctorate in Criminology and is currently a Research Fellow at the University of California, Berkeley.

June Kress has a Doctorate in Criminology, taught recently at Virginia Commonwealth University, and is currently a Research Fellow at the Institute for the Study of Labor and Economic Crisis, San Francisco.

Peter Linebaugh teaches history at the University of Rochester and is a member of the Editorial Collective of *Zerowork*.

Dario Melossi teaches on the Faculty of Penal Law, Bologna University, is co-editor of the Italian journal *La Questione Criminale*, and is currently doing research in the United States.

Tony Platt is a Research Director at the Institute for the Study of Labor and Economic Crisis, San Francisco, a co-editor of *Crime and Social Justice*, and an Associate Professor of Social Work at California State University, Sacramento.

Herman Schwendinger, a former editor of *Crime and Social Justice*, is an Associate Professor of Sociology, State University of New York, New Paltz.

Julia Schwendinger is an Adjunct Professor of Sociology, State University of New York, New Paltz.

Paul Takagi is a co-editor of *Crime and Social Justice* and Associate Professor of Education, University of California, Berkeley.

About *Crime and Social Justice*

Crime and Social Justice is published twice a year. Subscription prices are:$7 a year for individuals (US); $13 a year for institutions (US). Add $2 for mailing outside the United States or $5 for overseas airmail. (These are 1980 prices.)

Address correspondence to:

Crime and Social Justice, P.O. Box 4373, Berkeley, California 94704, USA.